3-9-77

Spain in the 1970s

edited by
William T. Salisbury
James D. Theberge

Published in cooperation
with the Institute of
International Studies,
University of South Carolina,
and the Center for Strategic
and International Studies,
Georgetown University.

The Praeger Special Studies program—
utilizing the most modern and efficient book
production techniques and a selective
worldwide distribution network—makes
available to the academic, government, and
business communities significant, timely
research in U.S. and international economic, social, and political development.

Spain in the 1970s
Economics, Social Structure, Foreign Policy

PRAEGER SPECIAL STUDIES IN INTERNATIONAL ECONOMICS AND DEVELOPMENT

Praeger Publishers   New York   Washington   London

Library of Congress Cataloging in Publication Data
Main entry under title:

Spain in the 1970s.

  (International relations series; no. 5) (Praeger special
studies in international economics and development)
  Papers presented at a conference held June 13-14, 1973,
at the Center for Strategic and International Studies.
  Includes bibliographical references and index.
  1. Spain—Economic conditions—1918-   —Congresses.
2. Spain—Social conditions—Congresses. 3. Spain—
Politics and government—1939-   —Congresses.
I. Salisbury, William Tallmadge, 1937-   II. Theberge,
James Daniel. III. Series: International relations series
(Columbia, S.C.); no. 5.
HC385.S664   330.9'46'082   75-19816
ISBN 0-275-55800-2

This volume is Number 5 of the International Relations
Series of the Institute of International Studies.

PRAEGER PUBLISHERS
111 Fourth Avenue, New York, N.Y. 10003, U.S.A.

Published in the United States of America in 1976
by Praeger Publishers, Inc.

Printed in the United States of America

ACKNOWLEDGMENTS

The present volume of essays is the outgrowth of the conference "Spain in the Seventies: Problems of Change and Transition" held in June of 1973 in Washington, D.C. The conference was made possible through the joint sponsorship of the Center for Strategic and International Studies, Georgetown University, and the Institute of International Studies of the University of South Carolina. The editors wish to express their appreciation to the directors of these respective institutions, Dr. David M. Abshire and Dr. Richard Walker, both for original support of the conference project and continued assistance during the editorial process.

1951281

The conference "Spain in the Seventies: Problems of Change and Transition" was held in Washington, D.C. on June 13-14, 1973. The Center for Strategic and International Studies of Georgetown University and the Institute of International Studies of the University of South Carolina jointly sponsored the meeting which was attended by over fifty persons with a professional interest in contemporary Spanish affairs. These individuals came from government and the private sector as well as the academic community.

The purpose of the conference was to examine major aspects of recent political, economic and social changes in Spain; to clarify the forces shaping Spanish society and politics in the seventies; and to review Spain's evolving relations with Europe and the Americas. Panel sessions examined the rapid transformation of the Spanish economy in the sixties and prospects for continued growth in the seventies; the changing urban and rural structure of Spanish society, including an examination of social institutions and forces such as the Church and regional nationalisms; and Spain's relations with Europe, Latin America, and the United States.

Except for the formal papers the conference discussions were on a non-attribution basis in order to encourage the frank and uninhibited expression of a wide range of viewpoints. The discussions were led by the panel members and discussants but were open to participation by all those attending. The present volume of essays has been collected and edited taking into account both the presentations by panelists and contributions made from the floor. In two areas, regime succession and church-state relations, the editors later commissioned additional papers and the essays by Vicente Pilapil and Tad Szulc have contributed to a more balanced treatment of these aspects of political and social life.

The conference sessions underlined the stunning changes which have occurred in Spain in recent years. The enormous growth and development of the Spanish economy over the past decade and a half have had an irreversible impact on the life of the average Spaniard. The once largely agricultural economy of Spain will be fully industrial by the middle of the 1980s. Presently only 27 percent of the labor force is in agriculture, down from 54 percent in 1940. The landless rural laborer has emigrated in response to opportunities available in the industrialized areas of Spain and Western Europe. If the existing migratory trends continue, three fourths of the Spanish population will be living in urban centers by 1980. The flight from the land will greatly increase the size of Spanish cities and by 1985, sixty percent of the total population will live in the five largest metropolitan areas of Madrid, Barcelona, Valencia, Bilboa and Seville. By then the population of Madrid will have doubled to six million.

Partly as a result of the pattern of urbanization described above, the quality of life of the average Spanish citizen has vastly improved. Since 1959, the year a new policy of economic liberalization was introduced, the Spanish economy has undergone a remarkable *volte face*. The average growth rate of per capita income from 1961 to 1970 was an extremely high 6.45 percent. Aggregate GNP has grown at an annual rate of 6.5 percent in the most recent decade, 1964-1974, a figure exceeded only by Japan and Greece among OECD countries. The average Spaniard is better housed, better fed and better educated than ever before in Spanish history. Living standards are approaching European levels and some studies project that Spain might even surpass countries such as England, Holland and Italy in per capita income by the mid 1980s.*

The political impact of the current wave of prosperity is difficult to assess. On the one hand many Spaniards who have gone heavily into debt to acquire consumer durables have a vested interest in economic and political stability and might be expected to respond in a conservative fashion during the period of transition after Franco's death. On the other hand industrialization and urbanization have made Spaniards less isolated from one another and more open to the new "liberal" ideas which are arriving from outside Spain either by way of the tourist influx, a massive wave of humans approximating each year the entire population of Spain, 35 million, or as a result of the Spanish workers returned from periods of residence in the industrial democracies of the north.

With Franco's death on November 20, 1975 and the assumption of the throne by Juan Carlos, Franco's chosen successor, Spain entered the long awaited, many times predicted, but oft postponed period of political transition. Significantly, by the time of Franco's death, most knowledgeable observers foresaw only non-status quo alternatives to the Franco system. These scenarios for the transition differ mainly as to the timing of political change, not the fact itself. They can be summarized as *apertura*, the historical rate of slow change under the Franco installed institutions, *cambio*, a several year transition leading to a much more liberal version of the Spanish regime, and *ruptura*, a total break with the Franco regime and its immediate substitution with a democratic system based on the traditional Western European parliamentary model.

The fact that the social and economic changes documented in the following essays will bring political change to Spain now seems beyond dispute. In addition, the current era of detente between East and West depreciates both the value of Spain as a military ally and depreciates as well the strength of those groups within Spain which have traded on their strong anticommunism. This will have the effect of increasing the effectiveness of pressures on Spain from the United States and other West European nations to bring the Spanish political system into closer harmony with other European democracies. Finally, the revolution in Portugal in May of 1974 has alerted Spanish officials to the dangers inherent in a policy of *imobilismo* in the political arena while the economy is changing at such a rapid rate.

---

*Ramon Tamames, "5 Reformas Para Cambiar Un Pais," *Actualidad Economica*, July 21, 1973, pp. 14-15.

Of the three alternative scenarios for change in the post Franco era, the data and judgements in the following essays tend to support either of the gradualist approaches to change, and stress the forces of continuity and strength within the present Spanish system. Though there may be manifestations of severe tension, bordering on regime instability, in the transition period, the average Spaniard appears to want peaceful change. Economic progress has been such that Spain has probably outgrown the need for a Marxist-style redistributive revolution. Violence may occasionally mar Spain's political life over the next decade. However, it will most probably be a sporadic, terrorist oriented type of civil disruption rather than the full scale struggle long since deemed passé by most close analysts of the current Spanish scene.

CONTENTS

LIST OF TABLES

THE ECONOMY
OF SPAIN
IN THE 1970s

SPAIN'S ECONOMIC
PROGRESS
SINCE 1960
Wolfgang Wipplinger

CHANGES IN THE POLICY FRAMEWORK SINCE 1960

The dramatic pace at which Spain, since the early 1960s, has been modernizing its economy and approaching the standards of living of other Western European countries has frequently been called the Spanish economic miracle, especially in contrast with the two decades of economic isolation and stagnation that preceded this takeoff. During the period from 1961 to 1972 there was a more rapid pace of economic development than in any period of comparable length in Spain's recent history, with the real gross national product (GNP) growing on average by 7.3 percent a year. The per capita GNP at factor cost rose, according to the official data, to about $1,130 in 1972; if the underestimation of Spain's national income is taken into account, the GNP per capita in 1972 exceeded $1,200. Also, substantial structural changes transformed Spain into an essentially industrial country, and by 1972 the balance-of-payments constraints on growth had ceased to exist, at least for the time being.

Spain's economic success was made possible by a drastic shift in the orientation of its economic policies, beginning in 1959, which led to progressive removal of the extensive controls that had earlier ruled over Spain's internal and

---

*Mr. Wipplinger is an economist with the International Bank for Reconstruction and Development (Latin American and Caribbean Region). The opinions expressed in this paper are those of the author and do not necessarily reflect those of the International Bank for Reconstruction and Development.

external economic relations. This policy shift was the direct result of the balance of payments crisis of 1958-59, which had brought Spain to the verge of economic collapse. With the financial and advisory assistance of the International Monetary Fund (IMF) and the Organization for European Economic Cooperation (OEEC), which was the predecessor of the Organization for Economic Cooperation and Development (OECD), Spain embarked in 1959 on a stabilization program, the success of which was the decisive precondition and motive power for further economic liberalization. Its success also established a basis for good relations with international organizations, including the World Bank, which issued the basic report, *The Economic Development of Spain,*[1] which became in many respects a guideline for later policy decisions.

It should be pointed out, however, that this economic reorientation of Spain was also indirectly influenced by the establishment of the European Economic Community (EEC) in 1957 and the introduction of external convertibility of the Western European currencies in 1958. A general acceleration of economic growth in Western Europe was expected from currency liberalization, and forward-looking Spanish politicians and economists saw a welcome chance for Spain to participate in this movement. Against this background, Spain applied in 1962 for an association agreement with the EEC.

Liberalization measures became oriented distinctly outward, mostly moving along with the introduction of extensive export promotion schemes, and were increasingly directed toward the long-term development of the economy, with growth becoming the key objective. Beginning in 1964, successive four-year development plans (1964-67, 1968-71, and 1972-75) set forth the general developmental guidelines, which included the public investment programs.

The integration of the Spanish economy into the world system was reflected in the following measures taken by the government.

Import Liberalization

One-third of total imports was freed from controls in 1959, and the share of free imports was brought to about 70 percent in 1967. In 1972 the list of free imports was expanded again; by this time the quantitative restrictions, which were the method most commonly used to curb imports before 1959, were being maintained for only about 7 percent of the total import value. The remaining imports had largely been liberalized, although some state trading schemes and bilateral trade agreements persisted. The Preferential Trade Agreement concluded with the EEC in 1970 provided for further liberalization steps and a reduction of the tariffs applied to imports from the EEC.

Export Promotion

Beginning in 1959, an ambitious export promotion program was introduced. Various export promotion measures were adopted, including the provision for export subsidies to offset domestic indirect taxes, for a rebate on import
duties on materials used for the production of export products, and for short-
and medium-term export credits to selling and buying firms at low interest rates.
Since 1963, export credits have frequently been provided at negative interest
rates in real terms. Some exporters have also benefited from special rediscount
facilities at the Bank of Spain that affect machinery, ships, and books.

Liberalization of Foreign Capital Imports

Foreign capital investment was freely permitted after 1960 in most
Spanish industries, in agriculture, in tourism, and in real estate. Also, the restrictions on the transfer of loan payments and on capital gains were abolished. As a
result, the net inflow of medium- and long-term capital rose from $126 million
in 1960 to an average of $573 million per year during 1967-70.* Direct invest-
ment, private loans to enterprises, and real estate purchases accounted for about
80 percent of this total. The liberalization of capital movements greatly helped
Spain's industrialization drive, and the capital inflow permitted many Spanish
firms to absorb new foreign technology and managerial know-how. Unfortunately, this process sometimes discouraged the emergence of indigenous
Spanish designs and techniques. There was little growth in expenditure on industrial research and development (R&D) in Spain during the 1960s.

The successful opening up of the Spanish economy should be viewed in
the context of three special circumstances that effectively facilitated this
process. First, Spain has benefited to an unexpected extent from the growth in
tourism. Foreign exchange earnings increased from $297 million in 1960 to
about $2.6 billion in 1972, when Spain was visited by approximately 31 million
tourists. Second, the impact of the liberalization of capital movements and of
the emerging favorable investment climate in Spain was enchanced by the
advantage of Spain's geographical location as a springboard to Europe, North
Africa, and the Middle East. The proximity of the large European markets also

---

*Long-term capital imports (net) decreased to $500 million in 1971, mainly because
of the slack economic climate in that year, but jumped to almost $950 million in 1972.

had built-in advantages, with respect to both industrial investment and real estate purchases. Third, Spain benefited considerably from the labor market situation in other European countries, particularly in France, Germany, and Switzerland. The emigration of workers during 1960-71 (about 730,000, or less than one percent of the average work force) facilitated structural adjustments in Spain and contributed, through the transfer of workers' remittances, to relieve the pressure on the balance of payments. These remittances rose from $55 million in 1960 to over $800 million in 1972.

It should be noted that the earnings from tourism, combined with the workers' remittances, amounted to over half of Spain's total import bill in 1972, a percentage only slightly higher than that of the early 1960s, in spite of the fact that exports had grown dramatically.

EFFECTS OF POLICY CHANGES ON GROWTH, FACTOR MOBILITY, AND RESOURCE MOBILIZATION

Economic growth during 1961-72 (7.3 percent per year) was to a large extent carried forward by the expansion of industry, which grew an average of 10 percent per year. Among the developing countries, the industrial growth of Spain was one of the most rapid, and Spain ranked second after Japan among the OECD countries. The share of industry in the gross domestic product (GDP), at constant 1964 factor cost, increased from 31 percent to about 40 percent, and the share of industry in the total labor force grew from 30 percent to about 36 percent, as manufacturing became the most important employer of labor in the Spanish economy. Agricultural output, on the other hand, expanded at an average rate of only 3 percent per annum. The agricultural sector's contribution to the GDP declined sharply, from about 25 percent in 1960 to less than 13 percent in 1972, with an even greater fall in the share of agriculture in the total labor force, from 42 percent in 1960 to about 27 percent in 1972. The service sector maintained its relative contribution to the GDP of about 44 percent, but absorbed an increasing share of labor.

The most important contributors to growth in industry were nontraditional and largely capital-intensive activities. National accounts data suggest that transport equipment, metal products and machinery, and chemical products together contributed about 45 percent to the absolute 1961-70 growth in manufacturing value added. Transport equipment contributed more to growth in manufacturing (17 percent) than any other industrial activity. An increasing part of industrial production went into export. While in 1961 Spanish manufacturers exported, on average, less than 5 percent of their output, the 1971 share was about 15 percent.

The regional distribution of income changed considerably over the last decade, resulting in a further concentration of income in Madrid, the Basque Region, and to a lesser extent in Catalonia. However, predominately agricultural areas along the Spanish-Portuguese border (the so-called "Inner Lusitania"), in parts of Galicia and Andalusia, and even in the Cuenca province near Madrid experienced a decline in income shares, a situation only partly mitigated by the transfer payments of workers now earning their livings in the cities and abroad. Problems related to the depopulation of the countryside began to emerge, with characteristics similar to those of the central and southern agricultural areas of France.

Since 1964-65 the Spanish government has been trying to offset the widening of regional inequalities in income and employment opportunities through the establishment of development poles and zones of preferential industrial location and other regional development schemes. Substantial financial and other benefits have been offered to investors who located in the less developed regions, with very unequal and in some cases disappointing results, particularly where the transportation and communication infrastructure remained inadequate and where administrative problems were too difficult to overcome. The overcentralization of administrative procedures in Madrid was a frequent source of frustration for both investors and local authorities. Spanish officials also have felt that past regional development schemes tended to neglect the linkages between the hinterlands and the development areas receiving official incentives. Consequently, current thinking now favors broader conceptions for future regional development efforts.

Economic development during 1961-72 was accompanied, and to a great extent facilitated, by the increasing movement of labor and capital, mainly toward emerging new industries, urban centers, and tourist resorts, and largely away from agriculture. From 1960 to 1971 the agricultural labor force declined, mainly through internal migrations, by almost 1,250,000 persons. The undercapitalization of agriculture, resulting partly from capital transfers into other sectors, became a critical issue. During these eleven years about 3.5 million people changed residence, most of them moving to large urban centers. By 1971 almost 60 percent of Spain's population lived in municipalities of over 20,000 inhabitants.

However, the labor market continues to exhibit certain imperfections. For example, labor legislation permits the discharge of unneeded workers only under exceptional circumstances, and the public sector applies inflexible and often outdated job descriptions to its job structures (*plantillas*), which often come close to "featherbedding." While these practices are designed to maintain a high level of employment, they frequently work in the opposite direction, since when they are combined with government-negotiated minimum wages they often bring the price of labor above the workers' opportunity costs. This encourages employers to economize on labor and to introduce capital-intensive methods of production.

The mobility of capital is partly restricted by government-established investment coefficients applies to banking institutions.* Along with other direct interventions in the financial markets, this procedure is responsible for major distortions in the flow and the allocation of domestic capital. Funds siphoned from the private banking system are lent at artificially low interest rates to private and public investors in line with the guidelines of the development plan, but frequently with no proper evaluation.

Compared to other countries, Spain has a surprisingly small public sector. Current expenditures, subsidies, and all other transfers of public administration, including Social Security, were only about 520 billion pesetas in 1971, corresponding to 20 percent of the GNP, while the fixed investment of the public administration amounted to 93 billion pesetas, or about 17 percent of the total fixed investment. Including public enterprises, the share of public investment in the total fixed investment was below 30 percent that year.

The relative size of the public sector changed little during 1961-72, although the rest of the economy changed dramatically. In particular, the overall tax ratio (23 percent of the GDP in 1970) has grown only marginally, although the sharply increased demand for social services and the growth in the economic infrastructure called for higher public expenditures. For example, the allocation of public funds for education has been increased significantly only since 1969, and other social services are in need of improvement. Public road construction projects (tollroads) have been assigned to private companies, which raised the funds needed to finance them in the domestic and international capital markets. In view of the low profile of the public sector, private resources mobilization and allocation has been of greater significance for economic development than in many other countries. The extraordinary performance of the Spanish economy during this decade was consequently largely the result of the dynamic expansion of the private sector in response to financial and other official incentives.

THE CHANGING PATTERN OF FOREIGN TRADE

This rapid pace of industrialization is reflected in the changing volume and composition of foreign trade. It was largely industry's heavy demand for investment goods, semimanufactures, and raw materials that caused total Spanish

---

*For example, in 1973 the investment coefficient for commercial banks was 22 percent of deposits.

imports to rise from $1.1 billion in 1961 to $6.6 billion in 1972. In that year almost 70 percent of the total commodity imports was direct imports to industry, with imports for the iron and steel industry, the metal processing industry, the electrical industry, and the chemical industry being predominant.

Commodity exports grew at an annual rate of 15 percent during 1962-70, rising to 23 percent in 1971 and 26 percent in 1972. Most of the export growth came from industrial exports, which increased at an annual rate of 26 percent during 1962-70, 40 percent in 1971, and 36 percent in 1972, thus accounting for 70 percent of the total export growth during this period. In 1972 the share of industrial exports in total exports reached 64 percent, compared to only 21 percent in 1961. Agricultural products, which weighed heavily in Spain's export list in 1961 (55 percent), accounted for less than 30 percent of total exports in the early 1970s.

The impressive growth of industrial exports was facilitated to a large extent by diversification and by specialization in products with a comparatively high labor content. It is significant that the predominance of small-scale enterprises in the shoe and leather industries and much of the equipment industry has been no major constraint on exporting, since Spanish manufacturers have been able to offer small individual runs and a high product flexibility, which most advanced industrial countries can no longer offer at competitive prices. In shipbuilding, which has become Spain's leading export industry, most of the dynamism has been provided by diversification mergers and the adoption of the most recent technologies. The advantages of an abundant labor supply and favorable climatic conditions have helped Spain to increase its ship exports from an insignificant volume in the early 1960s to approximately $200 million in 1972. Labor cost advantages and comparative freedom from labor unrest were important elements in Spain's export performance. Rough calculations suggest that about half of Spain's export growth since 1961 can be explained as increased competitiveness and half as the result of the expansion of world trade.

Over the 1962-72 period, Spain's exports increased most rapidly to the EEC (France, Italy, Federal Republic of Germany, Netherlands, Belgium, and Luxembourg), North America, and Latin America, with the EEC countries accounting for about 50 percent of total export growth toward the end of this period. The EEC countries taken as a group form the largest single export market, accounting in 1972 for about 36 percent of total exports. If the United Kingdom, Ireland, and Denmark are included, the EEC took about 48 percent of Spanish exports. As a supplier, the EEC (the Six) accounted for about one-third of total Spanish imports, but more than half of all Spanish imports of industrial goods.

An interesting feature of Spain's external trade relations is the relative importance of the developing countries, which absorbed one-quarter of total Spanish exports in recent years. The developing countries are Spain's most important customers abroad for machinery and transport equipment, with the

Latin American countries ranking first. In recent years, however, sales of machinery and transport equipment expanded most toward new markets, mainly in the Arab world. Spanish capital participation in production and assembly plants in Latin America and such mixed ventures as the proposed joint Spanish-Kuwaiti Finance Company should serve to consolidate and further strengthen Spain's foothold in the developing countries.

STRUCTURAL PROBLEMS IN THE 1970s

Spain's growth performance has not been without problems. Within the industrial sector, imbalances have developed between the basic and the processing industries, with the latter growing more rapidly and raising their productivity faster as a result of foreign investment and the import of technical know-how. Despite these structural improvements and the emergence of newer and more efficient manufacturing enterprises, many small family firms have continued as marginal producers, causing a critical fragmentation of production and distribution lines. Many of these enterprises cannot be expected to be competitive in a European context, and they will not be able to survive unless certain minimum economies of scale can be achieved. Mergers and other forms of association would greatly enhance their chances of survival.

In Spain's basic industries, still largely sheltered from foreign competition, change has been more difficult to achieve than in most branches of the processing industries. The National Institute of Industry (INI), the promoter of many key industries in the fields of iron and steel, chemicals, transport, and heavy equipment, has initiated major structural improvements in recent years, mainly through better balancing of production lines and reorganization. In time these measures should improve the competitive position of these industries.

Further industrialization in Spain will have to take into account factor proportions and prices. For example, as long as labor is plentiful and capital relatively scarce, industrial policy should encourage the use of more labor-intensive methods of production. A shift to a more labor-intensive industrial policy would not only mitigate the pressure of labor emigration and encourage domestic employment, but could also further improve the export competitiveness of Spanish industry.

There is a growing need for improvement in farm structure and land use to increase the ability of the agricultural sector to respond to the drastic demand changes that have resulted from higher incomes and increased urbanization. The shift in the consumption pattern away from food grains and toward more meat and other high-priced food products has opened new opportunities to raise farm incomes and improve income distribution. A major task of Spanish policy during the 1970s is helping Spanish farmers take advantage of these opportunities and to increase their output of products in heavy demand. Land consolidation, farm modernization, and selective price subsidies will be required to bring about the required adjustment of farm supply.

ECONOMIC PROSPECTS

The projections of the Spanish Planning Commission, which in 1973 became the Ministry for Development Planning, indicate that the Spanish economy will continue its strong growth performance, with the real GNP likely to grow at approximately 6.5 percent per year through the late 1970s. Spain still has considerable potential for manpower utilization and increased productivity, with labor costs that are still comparatively low by European standards. Maintaining and increasing Spain's international competitiveness will also require greater attention to the quality of output and to the development of new competitive products. Increases in the prices of imported fuels since 1972 may temporarily retard economic expansion, but over the long run this projected average growth should be attainable.

The manufacturing industry will continue to be the engine of Spain's economic development, growing at an annual rate of approximately 8 percent, and there will be a continuing trend towards heavy industries. Industrialization will strengthen the process of urbanization, and it is expected that over 75 percent of Spain's population will live in urban centers by 1980. The impact of this process on the physical infrastructure, on social services, and on the environment will be great, and avoiding the resulting urban and social crisis experienced by other countries will require much foresight on the part of Spanish urban planning authorities, including careful public sector budgeting.

NOTE

1. International Bank for Reconstruction and Development, *The Economic Development of Spain* (Baltimore: The Johns Hopkins Press, 1963).

2

SPANISH INDUSTRIAL DEVELOPMENT POLICY IN THE TWENTIETH CENTURY
James D. Theberge

THE EARLY PHASE OF INDUSTRIALIZATION

For reasons not adequately explained by historians, Spain's industrial revolution got off to a relatively late and slow start in the 19th century. A major brake on industrial development was undoubtedly the semifeudal, absolutist political structure, with heavily concentrated land ownership and commercial monopolies, which lasted until the end of the century.

Some historians point out that the domestic conditions for successful industrialization in Spain did not exist in the late 18th and early 19th centuries, in contrast to the situation elsewhere in Europe.[1] An entrepreneurial mentality was lacking; capital was scarce; technical know-how was in short supply; the domestic market was limited; and transport and communications were poor. However, this bare listing of the unpropitious conditions does not take us very far in explaining why they persisted longer in Spain than in France or Britain.

It is clear, however, that during the first two decades of the 19th century Spain's incipient industrial development suffered a serious setback that took a long time to repair. Spain's 1808-14 war against the French left much of the country's precapitalist economy in ruins. The destruction of factories by Napoleon's troops dealt a serious blow to Spain's incipient industry. At the same time, the 1808-22 wars of independence of the Spanish American colonies resulted in the loss of Spain's overseas markets and sources of cheap raw materials.

It was not, however, until the second half of the 19th century that Spain's traditional agriculture-based economy began to show indications of significant change and manufacturing industries began to assume some importance. During this period Spain began to manufacture food, paper, metal products, textiles, steel ships, construction materials, and steel. Nevertheless, when compared to the agriculture (cereals, fruits, vegetables, and oils) and mining (coal, copper, and iron ore) sectors, Spain's primitive manufacturing industry, dominated by handi-crafts and small-scale production, was still relatively insignificant. Spanish industry suffered from political turmoil, recurrent shifts in policy between free trade and protectionism, and the powerful opposition of vested agricultural and mining interests.[2]

Industrialization gradually came to be accepted as the objective of eco-nomic policy only after the defeat of the free-trade intelligentsia by protectionist-oriented groups and the loss of Spain's remaining major colonial markets (Cuba, Puerto Rico, and the Philippines) in 1898.[3] At the turn of the century, Spanish industrialization was facilitated by the inflow of foreign investment and the repatriation of capital that followed upon the loss of the colonies. It was not until 1907, however, that Spain adopted its first legislation for promoting local industry, by which the public sector was required to purchase manufactured goods produced by national industry.[4] During the next two decades additional legislation was introduced for the protection of specific national industries (such as shipbuilding) and for the fostering of national industry through a wide range of incentives, spurred on by the interruption of manufactured imports during World War I.*

Protective tariffs and other incentives made import-substitution industri-alization profitable. As a result, although industrial output stagnated from 1914 to 1922, it is estimated to have increased about 4.5 percent annually from 1923 to 1931. During the depth of the Great Depression industrial productivity declined, as Spain's traditional export markets collapsed.[5]

During the 1930s and 1940s, Spain's manufacturing industry was largely destroyed by the combination of world depression, the devastating civil war, and the shortages and dislocations of World War II. Manufacturing production stag-nated during the 1938-48 period, with industrial output increasing at an average annual rate of only .3 percent.[6] Spain's industrial growth performance began to improve in the late 1950s, and the most rapid industrial growth rate in modern Spanish history, about 9.5 percent annually, was achieved in the 1960s.

For Spain, the first half of the 20th century was a time of slow and irregu-lar industrial growth. In fact, Spain's overall growth performance was one of the poorest of those developing countries for which long-term gross domestic product (GDP) series are available.† From 1913 to 1950, Spain's GDP advanced

---

*The Law of 2 March 1917, for example, exempted new industries from import and export duties, reduced or postponed direct taxes in industry, and established preferential credit by official banks.

†Long-term statistical series for manufacturing output and gross domestic product should be treated with reservations, since they are subject to a considerable margin of error because of inaccurate data, index numbers, base years, and other problems.

at the exceptionally slow rate of 0.6 percent annually, lower even than those of Greece and India, two of the poorest performers during the period. Spain's average annual per capita income declined .3 percent over the same period.[7] As a consequence of the continued disruptive effects of the Civil War and World War II, per capita output in 1950 was estimated to be about 25 percent below prewar levels.[8]

Despite this generally slow and irregular progress of Spanish manufacturing from 1900 to 1940, by the outbreak of World War II Spanish industry still had advanced more than most of the developing countries. In 1940 manufacturing accounted for one-fifth of the GDP and employed about one-fifth of the labor force.[9] Production was concentrated in consumer goods (food, beverages, textiles, and footwear) and a few intermediate sectors (metal-working and chemicals), a pattern typical of a country in the early stage of industrialization.

INDUSTRIAL AUTARCHY AND STATISM, 1939-59

The industrial promotion measures adopted up to the Civil War emphasized industrial self-sufficiency. The high tariff barriers established during and after World War I made Spanish industry one of the most highly protected in the world. High customs duties remained a major instrument of import-substitution industrial development policy until 1939, when quantitative import restrictions (import licensing and exchange controls) were introduced.

From the end of the Civil War to the late 1950s, Spain followed a policy of industrial autarchy aimed at achieving industrial reconstruction, economic diversification and the strengthening of national defense. The objective of the new phase of government industrial policy that began in 1939 was to substitute national production for imports as much as possible, especially in defense and defense-related industries. State control of trade; the promotion of industry by tax, customs, and other incentives; and direct state participation in industry (through the National Institute of Industry or INI, which was created in 1941)[10] were the means employed during this autarchic and statist phase of Spanish industrial development policy.

During the 1940s the Spanish administration used import licensing to regulate the level and composition of imports and to protect manufacturing.* Domestic investors who benefited from official incentives were required to purchase raw materials, intermediate goods, and capital equipment in Spain whenever these goods were officially determined to be available locally. The Ministry of Industry was given the power to control the establishment,

_____

*Exports were also licensed.

expansion, and location of domestic manufacturing firms, as well as foreign participation in local industry.[11] It also controlled quotas for the importation of raw materials, the classification of products, and the fixing of prices for enterprises enjoying a monopoly or virtual monopoly in the domestic market.

State regulation of foreign trade was strengthened by the introduction of bilateral trade agreements (with country and product quotas) and a system of multiple exchange rates. The overvaluation of the official exchange rate at the end of the 1940s had the effect of stimulating imports and discouraging exports. To correct for the unfavorable impact that overvaluation had on the balance of payments, as well as on resource allocation between foreign trade goods (export and import substitutes) and domestic uses, the Spanish policy makers introduced special export incentives and import restrictions through the system of multiple exchange rates and foreign trade licensing. This "disequilibrium system of foreign trade," an overvalued exchange rate accompanied by special compensatory measures to offset the adverse balance of payments and resource allocation effects, lasted until the late 1950s and early 1960s, when it was progressively dismantled and replaced by a more liberalized system of trade and investment.

The policy instruments adopted by the government in the 1940s provided a high degree of protection and control of industrial investment. High protection made it more profitable to engage in import substitution to supply the domestic market than to produce for export. Export industries suffered because they had to bear the higher input costs that resulted from the protectionist policy. They also suffered from higher wage costs because the sheltered domestic industries earned high profits enabling them to pay wages in excess of the marginal productivity of labor.

Direct governmental regulation of private enterprise also aimed at influencing the sectoral and geographical allocation of manufacturing investment. The establishment, expansion, and relocation of industrial activities depended on permits that were authorized by the Ministry of Industry. These permits were granted arbitrarily and not according to any comprehensive scheme of governmental priorities. Larger enterprises, or those well connected to the government, were able to obtain permits, while more worthwhile investment proposals often were rejected. Bureaucratic control was inefficient, and investors often incurred unreasonable delays; this added unnecessarily to investment costs and sometimes inhibited investment. Moreover, foreign investment in Spanish industry was discouraged because of the insistence on majority national ownership and the strict limits placed on profit remittances.

The high protection afforded industry, the inefficiency of the bureaucratic administration of regulations, the privileged position of well-connected firms, and the rigid system of direct state control of industry suggest that industrial investment was substantially misallocated. These policies contributed to the poor organization, small scale of enterprises, low level of technical efficiency, and lagging export performance of Spanish industry at least until the late 1950s.

The deterioration of Spain's economic position in the late 1950s (reflected in acute inflationary pressures and declining international reserves) led to a drastic reorientation of economic policy and the abandonment of the policy of industrial self-sufficiency. Signs of political and economic reorientation could be observed as early as 1953, when the Spanish government reestablished diplomatic relations with most United Nations member states. A further indication of change occurred in 1958, when Spain became a member of the International Monetary Fund (IMF) and World Bank (IBRD). However, the decisive turning point came in 1959, at which time Spain became a member of the Organization for Economic Cooperation and Development (OECD) and adopted a sweeping economic stabilization program.

INDUSTRIAL LIBERALIZATION SINCE 1959

The new industrial policy orientation that took shape soon after 1959 was designed to replace the rigid bureaucratic regulation of national industry by a new set of more liberal laws and institutional arrangements. The Spanish authorities decided to accelerate the industrialization process, expand tourism and manufactured exports, and reduce regional income inequalities. Measures were taken to free foreign trade and investment, reduce state intervention, restructure individual industries to make them more competitive, and change the geographic distribution of industry in order to relieve industrial congestion and revitalize regions lacking an industrial base.

The new policy, which unfolded in the 1960s and has continued with some minor modifications into the 1970s, is composed of the following four major elements: (1) industrial pole (*polo*) and polygon (*poligono*) legislation, the purpose of which was to revitalize depressed areas and relieve the congestion of crowded industrial regions; (2) joint action (*accion concertada*) programs involving public-private cooperation, the purpose of which was to restructure, expand, and modernize individual industrial sectors in order to overcome structural weaknesses such as low productivity, suboptimal plant scale, and undercapitalization; (3) tariff and nontariff measures to protect national industry, including customs duties, border taxes, global import quotas, state trading arrangements, bilateral trade agreements, and "buy Spanish" legislation; and (4) export promotion measures, including export credit, export credit insurance, and tax and tariff rebates on imported raw materials and intermediates.

Regional Industrial Incentives

Spain's first development plan (1964-67) introduced a wide range of investment incentives—cash subsidies, official credit, and tax and tariff concessions—that aimed, among other things, at altering the regional location of manufacturing industry. As part of the general government policy of reducing regional disparities in population, employment, and income, relatively generous benefits were provided for establishing new industries and expanding existing ones in regions that were in urgent need of industrial development. By the adoption of these policies the Spanish government attempted to overcome the pull of resource endowment, locational advantages, and other factors that have led to the concentration of Spanish industry around Madrid, Barcelona, and Bilbao. These heavily industrialized regions enjoy relatively high per capita incomes, but they also suffer from serious industrial congestion and pollution. The low-income regions are highly dependent on agriculture and are characterized by a substantial out-migration of labor. The natural course of industrialization has created serious regional disparities in income, wealth, and population, which have become of increasing concern to local and national governments.

Industrial Poles

In 1964 the Spanish government authorized special benefits for eligible manufacturing firms that located within specific geographic areas or poles. Each *polo* encompassed an area of 100 to 200 square kilometers. The legislation established two categories of industrial poles: (1) industrial development poles (*polos de desarrollo*) for areas in which, in varying degrees, a manufacturing base already existed; and (2) industrial promotion poles (*polos de promocion*) for zones that had little or no industry and required exceptional promotional efforts.[12] It was assumed that the *polos* would act as catalysts to industrial activity in the surrounding areas and become self-sustaining focal points of industrialization. They were created in areas that appeared to have the necessary growth potential because of their locational advantages or resource base.

The government selected seven *polos,* or centers of industrialization, in 1964 to receive a wide range of industrial investment incentives. Two of them, Burgos and Huelva, were designated promotion poles, while the remaining five, La Coruña, Seville, Valladolid, Vigo, and Zaragoza, were declared development poles. Burgos and Zaragoza were to serve the additional purpose of reducing the congestion in Bilbao and Barcelona, respectively. By the end of 1971 the benefits under the five original development poles had been terminated, and in 1970-72 five new development poles, Granada, Cordoba, Oviedo, Logroño, and Villagarcia were created to replace those whose benefits had been canceled. Added to the two original industrial promotion poles, Huelva and Burgos, these new development poles maintain the total number of *polos* in operation at the legally required seven.[13] Thus a total of twelve *polos* had been created by 1972 to promote regional industrialization.

Eligible firms locating in the industrial poles are able to apply to the Ministry of Industry for a wide range of incentives, including subsidized official credit, cash grants of up to 20 percent of investment in a promotion pole and 10 percent in a development pole, and a reduction of up to 75 percent of the customs duties and border taxes on machinery and equipment acquired for the plant and officially certified as not being manufactured in Spain. Investors also are entitled to a reduction, normally 75 to 95 percent, of such taxes as the capital transfer tax, the turnover or sales tax, the levy on industrial activity (fiscal license), the real estate transfer tax, the urban property tax and certain other local taxes. Finally, local tax rebates, special land expropriation, five years' free depreciation, and other benefits are available to qualified investors under the law.

However, law and practice differ greatly in Spain. For example, the government rarely makes direct cash grants, and most investors do not bother to apply. Moreover, some of the benefits are more apparent than real. Free depreciation during the first five years is not a significant benefit to firms that realize little or no profits during the early years of the investment, which is not infrequently the case. There appears to be a rough uniformity in the maximum legal benefits available under the industrial poles legislation, but the actual treatment of investments in the different *polos* varies from project to project. Some attempt has been made to establish rough industry priorities to guide the allocation of incentives, but the vagueness and generality of the legislation leaves excessive discretion in the hands of government officials, with the foreseeable consequences: arbitrary decisions, resource misallocations, and abuses.

In order to qualify for the available benefits, a firm investing in the promotion poles must demonstrate that its activities "contribute directly to the economic and social development of the region"[14] by making a minimum required investment of 30 million pesetas and creating at least 50 additional jobs. Alternatively, to qualify in the development poles a minimum investment of 40 million pesetas and the creation of at least 100 new jobs is required. The government certificate approving each investment project specifies not only the authorized benefits but also the dates on which plant installation must commence and terminate. Furthermore, each development pole has a list in the pertinent government decree[15] of 20 to 25 specific industrial activities that qualify for incentives. However, a firm may obtain incentives for an industry not specified on the approval list for the development pole where it wishes to locate, providing a convincing case can be made to the authorities. In the promotion poles, all industries are eligible for benefits.

The value of the *polo* benefits to the individual firm appears to be substantial and may amount to as much as 10 to 15 percent or more of the total fixed investment during the early years. Some notion of the cost of the industrial pole benefits to the government in terms of cash grants and subsidized official credit can be gathered from the fact that over 7 billion pesteas in official credit and 2 billion pesetas in cash grants were made by the Spanish authorities in the seven years from 1964 to 1971.

On the available evidence, the industrial pole legislation introduced in 1964 to foster regional industrial growth appears to have been a mixed success. By early 1971 approximately 350 firms, with actual fixed investments of over 41 billion pesetas and responsible for the creation of some 41,000 new jobs, were in full operation, with another 237 under construction.[16] Vigo was the only *polo* that appeared well on its way to achieving the investment and job creation standards set by the firms and the government: actual investment had reached over 90 percent of planned investment, and about 85 percent of the planned new jobs had been created by the end of 1970. The investment performance of the other six original industrial poles fell far below target; actual investment varied from pole to pole within a relatively narrow range, from 46 to 58 percent of planned, with Valladolid and Burgos doing somewhat better, and Zaragoza and La Coruña somewhat worse, than average. Except in Valladolid, employment creation was also disappointing.

There is no doubt that implementation of the industrial pole strategy has been accompanied by an increase in manufacturing investment in all poles, but particularly in Huelva and Valladolid. In the absence of detailed studies, however, it is impossible to judge correctly the extent to which the investment was induced by the benefits provided by the *polo* legislation or by other factors such as preexisting locational advantages and the availability of economic infrastructure, skilled labor, and urban amenities.

The industrial pole legislation has been directly responsible for some net new investment. Some of the investment in each pole probably would have been undertaken in any event, within or outside the designated poles, but nevertheless the *polo* benefits appear to have accelerated investment in the manufacturing sector. The incentives, particularly customs exemptions on imported machinery and preferential access to official credit, make it possible for many firms to undertake larger investments at an earlier time than would otherwise have been possible. Investment performance was disappointing in poles with inadequate transport and communications and poor access to skilled or unskilled labor and sluggish markets. In some instances the government failed to provide the promised incentives, such as preferential credit or cash grants, or granted them only after costly economic delays that adversely affected industrial investment. It is alleged that in other instances nonviable projects were approved, which were unable to prosper even with the incentives.

The government has been somewhat disappointed with the industrial pole strategy as a means of revitalizing backward regions, and no new industrial development poles or preferential location zones were included in the Third Development Plan (1972-75). Benefits under existing poles or zones are to be terminated at the expiration of the maximum ten-year period. During the 1970-72 period, five new industrial development poles were established in Logroño, Cordoba, Villagarcia, and Oviedo, but the poles in Valladolid, Seville, La Coruña, Zaragoza, and Vigo were discontinued. The government did not want to prolong the benefits to new investments, since the incentives were to act as a "pump priming" device to stimulate self-sustaining industrial growth within the poles. It was also felt that the proliferation of industrial development poles was undesirable, since the *polo* strategy would lose its selective character and increase the possibility of wasting scarce resources. Since 1972 government policy has aimed at consolidating and strengthening the limited number of existing development poles through infrastructure investments.

Zones of Preferential Industrial Location

Another device aimed at altering the geographical allocation of industrial investment is the "zone of preferential industrial location." Whenever it is deemed appropriate, the Ministry of Industry may designate an area a preference zone, and the area thereby becomes eligible for incentives.* Normally a decree is issued that sets forth the benefits available to investors locating in a specified area and the conditions they must meet in order to qualify for the incentives.

In 1966 the Gibraltar area was declared a "zone of preferential industrial location," and a list of industries was announced that qualified for benefits, including foodstuffs, textiles, chemicals, metals and metalworking, construction, and various light industries, following the practice of the development poles.[17] In 1968 the two coal mining towns in northern Spain, Mieres and Langreo, were declared preference zones in order to encourage investment in capital goods, metal-mechanical, textile, and other labor-intensive industries that would absorb the surplus of semiskilled and unskilled labor created by the structural contraction of the coal mining industry.[18] The depressed province of Caceres and the Valle de Cinca were also designated preferential zones in 1968, with the Canary Islands following in 1969.[19] On the whole the Ministry of Industry has seldom employed this approach to regional industrial development, preferring to rely on the industrial poles formula. The results of the preferential zones seem to have been disappointing, and the incentives offered to industry, which are similar to those provided under the industrial pole legislation, have not been sufficient to overcome the natural disadvantages of the areas singled out for special treatment.

Industrial and Decongestion Polygons

The Spanish government has also created industrial polygons, or geographic areas in which investors are granted most of the same incentives enjoyed

---

*The Ministry of Agriculture may also declare preference zones for industries related to agriculture. In fact, in September 1964 the Badajoz and Jaén regions were designated preference zones for the location of industries devoted to the elaboration, conservation, or utilization of local farm production.

by firms in the *polos,* with the exception of cash subsidies. An area is declared an industrial polygon when the government is convinced that it can support reasonably efficient industrial growth. Polygons are sometimes located within *polos,* and in such cases firms may receive the most favorable treatment granted under either category. The advantage of locating in a polygon is that the investors can obtain land much more cheaply than outside the area, since the authorities establish favorable maximum prices for industrial property. Firms in a polygon are eligible for reductions or waivers on urban property taxes and local property surtaxes on land purchases. By the early 1970s, over thirty industrial polygons had been established. Incentives are also provided to encourage decentralization of industry and to relieve the pressure on such major industrial centers as Madrid and Barcelona, which have been designated "decongestion polygons." The benefits offered to investors who locate in decongestion polygons are similar to those provided under the industrial pole legislation.

Structural Incentives

Joint Action Programs

A unique program of industrial incentives called *accion concertada* was created by the First Development Plan (1964-67). The term refers to a joint action program established by the government and several enterprises in the same industry sector that aims at: (1) expanding production; (2) raising productivity; (3) sector reorganization through the merger of firms, provision of common services, and creation of larger-scale production units; (4) plant modernization; (5) improvement of product quality; and (6) better wages and working conditions, including professional training.

The Ministry of Industry created *accion concertada* in order to overcome structural weaknesses, such as low productivity, sub-optimum plant scale, and inadequate capitalization for modernization and expansion in those industrial sectors that require special assistance to reach the national planning goals. This joint action program, adapted from the French system of "quasi contracts" between private firms and the government, is a novel and flexible incentive instrument. Private firms obtain a series of special credit, tax, tariff, and other benefits in return for voluntary acceptance of certain contractual obligations, such as merging with other firms and achieving the production targets set by the Ministry of Industry. The joint action program steers a middle way between compulsory and indicative planning, permitting the expansion and modernization of an industrial sector in accordance with development plan objectives.

Joint action programs have been established in the following industries: iron and steel; shipbuilding; leather and footwear; fruit and vegetable canning;

pulp and paper; flour milling; coal mining; iron ore mining; beef cattle production; and freezing. From 1964, when the first joint action programs were introduced, until 1972, about 200 firms, with realized investments exceeding 60
billion pesetas, had adhered to the basic agreement in the following sectors:
iron and steel, coal, leather, canning, pulp and paper, iron ore mining, and shipbuilding. These enterprises were responsible for 90 percent of the total production of certain sectors, such as coal and shipbuilding. In other sectors, such as
leather, canning, and pulp and paper, the firms subscribing produced one-third
or less of the total sector output. The subsidized official credit authorized under
the joint action agreements financed between 25 and 50 percent of the investment requirements of each sector.

The basic agreement establishing a joint action program is negotiated
between the interested firms, on the one hand, and the Ministry of Industry (or
Agriculture) and Ministry of Finance, on the other, in consultation with the
Planning Commission and the *sindicato* that represents the enterprises concerned.
The agreements, which must be approved by the cabinet, specify in detail the
contractual obligations of the subscribing firms: production targets, employment
creation, percentage of output to be exported, labor policies (worker training,
social services, and remuneration), and the reorganization of production of the
adhering firms in accordance with the industry sector plan. Uneconomical plants
may be closed down and small firms required to merge. The joint action is
limited to the period necessary to strengthen the industry, which normally varies
from four to eight years. The Ministry of Industry establishes termination dates
for the joint action programs, except for those industrial sectors whose objectives have not yet been met. These sectors will receive special assistance to reach
the agreed objectives.

On the available evidence, the success of the joint action programs in
achieving the various objectives set forth in the basic agreement varies considerably from sector to sector. A few industrial sectors, such as leather, canning, and
shipbuilding, generally have achieved, or come close to meeting, most of the
agreed standards. The performance of other sectors, notably coal, pulp and
paper, and iron ore mining, has been unsatisfactory. The most striking success
has been the shipbuilding industry (steel ship construction), which has been
successfully restructured and merged. In less than a decade, it has been dramatically transformed from a fragmented, inefficient industry into one of the largest
and most competitive shipbuilding industries in the world.

As an instrument for industrial reorganization, Spain's joint action
program has met with partial success. Efforts to encourage mergers in sectors
where economies of scale are important (such as pulp and paper and canning)
have encountered considerable resistance. The official incentives and technical
assistance were not enough to induce small and medium-size firms to merge. In
the case of the shipbuilding industry, it was the heavy ship construction sector
that was successfully merged and modernized, leaving untouched the hundreds

of undercapitalized builders of small boats. Finally, few firms in any of the industrial sectors covered by joint action legislation have signed the basic agreement with the Spanish government. Apart from the steel, shipbuilding, and coal-mining sectors, large numbers of small- and medium-size enterprises, accounting for over half of the output of their respective sectors, have remained outside the joint action program.

Tariff Protection

Nominal Protection

As part of its economic liberalization policy, the Spanish government introduced a far-reaching tariff reform in 1960, under which the Brussels nomenclature was adopted, specific duties were replaced by ad valorem duties, and an import tax (*tarifa fiscal*) was introduced. The tariff reform was responsible for the establishment of some initial simplification of the tariff structure and the lowering of ad valorem duties on imports. General tariff cuts of 5 percent were made in 1963 and 1964, and a number of tariff reductions covering special customs categories were introduced in various other years.

During the 1960s, Spain's customs duties, whether measured by a simple, unweighted arithmetic average of ad valorem duties or weighted by imports, declined gradually. (See Table 2.1.) The average level of customs duties on all imports declined from 12.7 percent in 1961 to 7.3 percent in 1970, or by 74 percent. The combined duties plus border tax on imports declined less, from 18.7 percent in 1961 to 15.5 percent in 1970, or by 21 percent. The border tax on imports ranged from 6 to 9.4 percent during the 1960s and had shifted slightly upwards by the end of the decade. The special tariff concessions granted to industrial investments under the joint action program and the industrial pole and polygon schemes lowered the effective average duties on imports of machinery and equipment. Furthermore, other legislation promoting tourism and modernization of the railroads provided tariff concessions for certain categories of imports, further lowering average tariffs on manufactures and complicating the problem of establishing a rational, development-oriented tariff policy.

The decline in the nominal protection of Spanish manufacturing industry between 1962 and 1966 was negligible, from 32.1 percent to 30.5 percent.* The

---

*The nominal rate of protection of a commodity is the percentage by which the domestic price exceeds the world price as a result of protective measures. Nominal protection is defined here as being equal to the ad valorem customs duties, plus border taxes, both expressed as a percentage of the import value of manufactures.

TABLE 2.1

Nominal Tariffs and Customs Duties, 1961-70

Year	Customs Duties[a]	Nominal Tariffs[b]
1961	12.7	18.7
1962	11.9	17.1
1963	11.8	17.7
1964	11.6	18.9
1965	8.8	17.9
1966	10.0	19.3
1967	9.6	18.4
1968	8.0	15.2
1969	7.8	16.2
1970	7.3	15.5

[a]Average annual customs duties weighted by domestic imports for Spanish peninsula and Balearic Islands.

[b]Customs duties plus border tax. This specification of nominal tariffs differs from estimates of nominal protection based on direct price measurements.

Note: The purpose of the fiscal tariff is to insure that imported goods are burdened with a tax equal to the indirect taxes on domestically produced goods of the same kind. The fiscal tariff was subsequently replaced by the border tax.

Source: Luis Gamires, "El proteccionism o avancelario en España actual," *Información comercial española* 463 (March 1972): 54, 57.

reduction of nominal protection has proceeded slowly since the mid-1960s. Spain's nominal protection is high compared to that of the industrial countries for which estimates are available. For example, in 1966 Spain's nominal tariff (customs duties plus border tax) was 30.5 percent, while at approximately the same time it was 3.8 percent for Sweden, 6.5 percent for the European Common Market countries, 9.1 percent for the United Kingdom, and 9.4 percent for Japan. On the other hand, the degree of protection afforded Spain's manufacturing industry is lower than that of most developing countries for which data are available. (See Table 2.2.)

Effective Protection

The effective rate of protection is the protection accorded to value added in the manufacturing process, which can be measured in different ways. It is defined as the percentage by which domestic value added exceeds foreign or world value added resulting from the imposition of tariffs or other protective devices on the product and its inputs. The encouragement given to a particular activity or process is better measured by effective protection than by nominal protection, since it takes into account the amount by which the prices of the output are raised. It enables us to measure more accurately the force which protection exerts in attracting productive factors into the protected activity.

In general, the rate of effective protection of manufacturing industry declined from 77.2 in 1962 to 51.1 in 1966. Whereas in 1962 most textile

TABLE 2.2

**Average Tariff Levels for Manufactures,
Selected Developing Countries**

Country	Year	Nominal Tariff (in percent)
Argentina	1958	141
Brazil	1966	99
Chile	1962	134
Colombia	1962	106
Mexico	1960	22
Pakistan	1963/64	93
Peru	1962	35
Philippines	1961	46
Spain	1966	31*
Taiwan	1966	30

*Customs duties plus border tax.

Source: For Chile, Colombia, and Peru, Harry H. Bell, *Tariff Profits in Latin America* (New York: Praeger Publishers, 1971), p. 65; for the remaining countries (except Spain), Ian Little et al., *Industry and Trade in Some Developing Countries* (London: Oxford University Press, 1970), p. 163.

sectors, shoes, paper and cardboard, plastic articles and synthetic materials, automobiles, and motorcycles and bicycles, had effective rates in excess of 100, by 1966 only cloth, motorcycles and bicycles fell into that category. However, the general decline of effective protection is the result of a sharp fall in relatively few sectors (textiles, shoes, paper and cardboard, plastic articles, synthetic materials, chemicals, and agricultural machinery) not completely offset by the moderate rise in effective rates observed for over half of the 29 industrial sectors. In the heavy-industry sectors, effective protection increased for shipbuilding, iron and steel, nonferrous metals, metal casting, railway vehicles, and aircraft.

Nominal and effective rates of protection in Spain are, as one would expect, highest in the nonimport competing manufacturing industries, which include textiles and durable consumer goods (plastic articles, bicycles, and motorcycles). High nominal rates effectively discourage imports, thereby limiting import competition. In general, these industries are characterized by relatively simple technical processes and small-scale production. They have developed behind high protective barriers, are relatively inefficient, and may enjoy high profits. It is, of course, not possible in the absence of detailed studies to know how much of the high rate of protection reflects excessive profits or inefficient use of resources.

Estimates of effective rates of protection by industry group indicate that rates are highest for durable consumer goods, followed by intermediate goods at higher levels of fabrication, transport equipment, intermediate goods at lower levels of fabrication, processed foods, nondurable consumer goods, machinery, and construction materials, in that order.

A number of broad conclusions emerge from a brief examination of Spain's tariff policy and its impact on Spain's manufacturing sector. First, Spain's tariff structure is characterized by a wide diversity of rates of both nominal and effective protection, although the diversity is greater for effective rates than for nominal rates, implying the need for more equal protection of value added than is the case at present.

Second, there appears to be relatively less discrimination against manufactured exports than there is in some developing countries. In large part this is the result of a generally lower protective structure and substantial tariff reductions, rebates, and exemptions under various industrial and export promotion schemes. Spain's effective rates seem to be on the high side for the limited number of export industries for which effective protection has been measured.

Third, effective protection for manufacturing appears to be on the average lower than in such developing countries as Argentina, Brazil, India, Pakistan, and the Philippines, for which comparable effective rates have been calculated. However, Spain's effective rates are considerably higher than the average rates on manufacturing for the EEC countries. From the standpoint of Spanish manufactured exports to the EEC countries, this is not as favorable as it appears. The

TABLE 2.3

Nominal and Effective Protection of Export, Import-competing, and Non-Import-competing Manufacturing Industries by Selected Countries in Selected Years
(in percent)

Country	Year	Export Industries		Import-competing Industries		Non-Import-competing Industries		Total Manufacturing	
		Nominal	Effective	Nominal	Effective	Nominal	Effective	Nominal	Effective
Chile	1961	1	– 6	69	68	130	288	98[a]	125[a]
Mexico	1960	43	88	27	43	33	52	33	63
Malaya	1965	– 4[b]	–20[b]	7	12	22	17	13	– 4
Philippines	1965	– 8[c]	–19[c]	30	59	26	83	24	48
Norway	1954	0	– 4	13	18	—	—	11	12
Spain	1966	18[d]	41	14[d]	37	21[d]	72	17[d]	51

[a]Excluding export industries.
[b]Excluding rubber products.
[c]Excluding sugar.
[d]Customs duties only.

Note: Export industries are those in which more than 10 percent of production is exported; import-competing industries are those in which imports provide more than 10 percent of domestic supply; and non-import-competing industries are those in which international trade does not exceed 10 percent in either direction. Effective protection is calculated by the Corden formula. See W. M. Corden, "The Structure of a Tariff System and the Effective Protection Rate," *Journal of Political Economy* (June 1966).

Source: For all countries except Spain, Bela Belassa, *The Structure of Protection in the Industrial Countries and Its Effects on the Exports of Processed Goods from Developing Countries*, IBRD (International Bank for Reconstruction and Development) report No. EC-152a, February 28, 1968, Country Tables; for Spain, L. Gamires, "Evolucion del Proteccionismo nominal entre 1960-1970," unpublished manuscript, 1971.

graduation of the tariffs in the industrial countries from lower to higher stages of fabrication discriminates against the manufactured exports of developing countries such as Spain.[20]

Nontariff Protection

Like other countries, Spain protects her manufacturing sector from import competition by various nontariff restrictions on imports. Direct state regulation of foreign trade (state trading, bilateral arrangements, and quotas) formerly was the main method of restriction. The remaining import restrictions under the old trading system, which has been progressively dismantled since 1959, now affect only a small share of total imports, most of which enter free of quantitative or other restrictions.[21] In 1970, some 84 percent, or 3,108, of the commodities listed in the Spanish Customs schedule, were free imports, and currently about 70 percent of the total value of Spanish imports entered under the free import regime. Included in the free list are many foodstuffs (not under the state trading regime); most raw materials, machinery and equipment; and some consumer goods. The principal nontariff restrictions on Spanish imports in the early 1970s were the global quotas, the state trading regime, the system of bilateral trade or individual licensing, and the "buy Spanish" legislation.

It is important, however, not to exaggerate the role that tariff and non-tariff protectionist policies have played in the structural transformation of Spanish industry during the past decade. Other factors, which tend to be neglected, have also had a strong influence on industrial and export performance. Among these should be noted, increases in the size of the effective domestic market; increasingly qualified and relatively cheap labor; improvements in the economic infrastructure; official credits favoring industry and supporting exports; foreign exchange income from tourism and emigrants' remittances; and the existence of political stability institutional arrangements generally favorable to private foreign and domestic investment. The two most valuable official incentives from the viewpoint of an investor are the reduction in customs duties and border taxes on imported machinery, and the preferential interest rates of official credits.

CONCLUSION

Growth Performance

Spain's liberal and outward-looking industrial promotion and trade policies clearly were a major factor in the extraordinary growth performance and structural transformation of Spanish industry in the 1960s. This improved growth performance was facilitated by the easing of the external constraint on growth resulting from the rapid rise in foreign exchange earnings from tourism and remittances from emigrant workers. Also, industrial development benefited from the more liberal treatment of foreign investment, which provided impetus to the transfer of foreign technical know-how and management skills to Spanish industry.

Manufacturing industry grew at the rate of 10 percent annually during the 1960-70 period, with the industrial product rising from 178.3 billion pesetas in 1960 to 461.6 billion pesetas in 1970, measured in constant 1964 prices. During this period, Spain's industrial growth was among the highest of the developing countries and second only to Japan among the OECD countries.

Two growth periods can be observed for Spain's manufacturing industry in the 1960s. From 1961 to 1966 manufacturing production expanded very rapidly, on the average 11.7 percent per annum. Industrial growth slowed down between 1967 and 1971, averaging only 5.7 percent per year. The slower advance of industrial production during the later 1960s was caused by restrictive government policies that were dictated largely by balance of payments considerations.

As a result of this rapid growth, industry's share of the total labor force increased from 29.9 percent in 1960 to 36.1 percent in 1970, and industry's share of the GNP (at constant 1964 factor prices) rose from 31.1 percent to 39.5 percent over the same ten-year period, indicating the very rapid pace of structural change in the Spanish economy.

Within the manufacturing sector, chemicals, basic metal products, machinery, and transport equipment (especially cars and ships) had the highest growth rates. While these modern sectors expanded rapidly, the more traditional sectors, such as food products, wood manufactures, and textiles, lagged behind.

Industrial investment increased sharply, from 23 percent of total fixed investment in 1960 to 32 percent in 1969, with notable gains made during the 1961-66 period, when government investment restrictions were relaxed and liberalized. This led to a large increase in domestic investment in manufacturing, and foreign capital responded favorably to the improved investment climate and expanding domestic market.

Exports of manufactures increased a dramatic sevenfold during the 1961-70 period (about 22 percent per annum), rising from $163 million, or 22.9 percent of total exports, in 1961 to $1,184 million or 49.6 percent of total exports, in 1970. Exports of industrial goods (such as ships, shoes, machine tools, electrical equipment, and automotive parts) have been growing rapidly since 1964. The highest rates of growth were achieved after 1968, when lagging domestic demand and the November 1967 peseta devaluation strongly encouraged manufacturers to increase sales abroad. Industrial exports made a major contribution (about 70 percent) to Spain's total export growth in the 1960s. Skillful economic management, heavy investment in capital equipment

TABLE 2.4

**Economic and Demographic Growth Projections
for Spain, 1970-80**

	1970	1980	Average Annual Growth Rate (in percent)
GNP at market prices (in billions of 1970 pesetas)			
III Plan estimate, low	2,412	4,528	6.5
III Plan estimate, high	2,412	4,745	7.0
Population (in millions)	33.9	37.4	1.0
Per capita income (in U.S. dollars)			
Low	818	2,000	
High	818	2,100	
Labor force (in millions)	12.7	15.0	1.7
Industrial value added (in billions of 1970 pesetas)			
III Plan estimate, low	866.4	1,842.3	7.8
III Plan estimate, high	866.4	1,930.3	8.3

Source: Official Planning Ministry figures and estimates.

TABLE 2.5

GNP Growth Projections for Spain, the OECD, EEC, and EFTA, 1970-80

	Average Annual Growth Rate (in percent)
Organization for Economic Cooperation and Development (OECD)	5.3
Total European members of OECD	4.8
European Economic Community (EEC)	5.2
European Free Trade Area (EFTA)	3.6
Spain	6.5 to 7.0

Source: Official Planning Ministry figures and estimates.

and new technologies, labor cost advantages and relative freedom from labor unrest enabled Spain to take full advantage of the rapid expansion of world demand for manufactures and to achieve its remarkable export performance.

Shipbuilding became Spain's most important export industry in less than a decade, assisted by government incentives, successful mergers of major ship-yards, and the aggressive adoption of the latest technologies. By 1970 Spain was exporting about $125 million in ships, whereas exports had been negligible in the early 1960s. Spain has become the world's fifth exporter of ships (sixth as a producer), competing successfully with the advanced industrial countries of Japan, Sweden, Germany, and the United Kingdom. Shoe exports, mainly to the United States, constitute the second largest export item, with sales over $100 million in 1970. In addition to ships and shoes, Spain is now exporting a wide range of investment and consumer goods.

Growth Prospects

Spanish industrial policy faces a far more complex domestic and inter-national environment in the 1970s than it did in the 1960s. The 1972-73 indus-trial recovery in Spain was cut short by the balance-of-payments and inflationary impact of the price increases of the OPEC (Organization of Petroleum Export-ing Countries) and the resulting massive shift in income from oil-importing to oil-exporting states. The energy crisis was a major factor in the world recession of 1974-75, which sharply reduced Spain's industrial growth, to only 5.6 percent in 1974. The massive redistribution of world income due to the energy crisis has shaken the world economy, imposed new limits on the growth prospects of the Western economies, and presented policy makers with severe problems of internal and external adjustment.

Spain's industrial growth prospects for the remainder of the 1970s are still relatively good, but Spanish industry faces a number of problems. Structural weaknesses remain, particularly in the large number of small-scale, inefficient firms found in most of Spain's industrial sectors and in the excessive industrial concentration in the north and northeast. In heavy industry (such as steel and engineering), few Spanish firms are capable of competing with their European Economic Community (EEC) rivals. A major effort will have to be made to improve the cost competitiveness of Spanish industry in order to meet the severe competition from the more highly developed Common Market industries that can be expected in the late 1970s and the 1980s.

Assuming there is no prolonged world recession, Spain's manufacturing industry should be able to expand at the 8 percent per year rate that is projected by the Spanish Planning Commission, with assumed annual GNP growth rates of between 6.5 and 7.0 percent, for the 1971-80 period. Such industrial-sector growth rates imply further structural changes in Spain's manufacturing industries, with chemicals, basic metals, machinery, and transport equipment increasing their relative shares in industrial value added and food, textiles, apparel, and footwear continuing to decline in relative importance.

An industrial growth rate of 8 percent year year for the 1970s is well within Spain's capabilities and would transform Spain from a semiindustrial to an industrial society, with the industry share of GNP rising from about 39 percent in 1970 to nearly 45 percent in 1980. These industry growth rates appear entirely feasible, since Spain's present industrial capacity is not fully utilized and there is considerable room for raising labor productivity and shifting labor from agriculture to industry. Spain's GNP and industrial growth performance should exceed those of the OECD and the enlarged European Economic Community.

During the 1960s manufacturing industry received a growing share of total investment resources compared to other sectors of the economy. The expansion of the domestic market and the strong investment incentives provided to industry by the government created the conditions for rapid expansion of industrial investment and output. By 1980 this situation may change considerably, since the government is committed to allocating a larger share of investment funds to the neglected social sectors, education, health, housing, and urbanization. In turn this could lead to a decline in public investment in industry and more restrictive and selective application of fiscal, credit, and other incentives to private-sector industrial investors.

The sharp worldwide rise in oil prices in 1973-74 that resulted from the OPEC cartel pricing policy contributed to the Western economic recession of 1974-75 and a worsening of Spain's balance of payments. Spain's trade balance deteriorated and the tourist income declined, as did the emigrant workers' remittances from Europe. The upward trend of wage, fuel, and other costs in the manufacturing sector may induce the Spanish authorities to pursue more restrictive monetary and fiscal policies in order to dampen inflationary pressures, protect the balance of payments, and insure that Spain's industrial costs and prices do not deteriorate relative to its European competitors. Balance-of-payments pressures could pose a serious threat to Spain's industrial growth in the latter half of the 1970s and early 1980s, unless the export performance is improved and the import content of domestic investment is substantially reduced.

Political factors may also have an adverse impact on Spain's industrial growth over the remainder of the 1970s. Spain has entered a period of transition to a still undefined post-Franco political system that is likely to permit organized political parties and much more free expression of political views. The nature of this transitional phase, that is, whether it is peaceful and orderly or marked by political instability and violence, will influence Spain's economic growth performance. Despite these political and economic uncertainties, it seems probable that Spain will reach its goal of becoming one of the first ten industrial powers in the world by 1980, with a pattern of industrial development similar to that of other Western European countries. Spain's per capita income, which reached $2,000 in the mid-1970s, should exceed $2,500 by 1980 without difficulty. The standard of living of the Spanish people is increasing rapidly, and the income gap between the Spanish and the peoples of the European Economic Community is being steadily narrowed. As long as political stability and cohesion is maintained, Spain seems destined to increase its importance in the world economy and exert a growing influence in international affairs.

NOTES

1. See Ramon Tamames, *Estructura Economica de España* (Madrid: Guardiana de Publicaciones, 1969), pp. 224-25.

2. J. B. Donges, "From an Autarchic towards a Cautiously Outward-looking Industrialization Policy: The Case of Spain," *Weltwirtschaftliches Archiv* 107, no. 1 (1971): 34-35.

3. Ibid.

4. Law of 14 February 1907.

5. According to the *Consejo de Economia Nacional,* cited by Tamames, op. cit., p. 230.

6. Donges, op. cit., p. 43.

7. Angus Maddison, *Economic Progress and Policy in the Developing Countries* (London: George Allen and Unwin, 1970), pp. 29-30.

8. Ibid., p. 32.

9. Guillermo Ibáñez's *Anuario financiero que comprende el historial de valores públicos y de sociedades anónimas de España, 1943,* vol. 27, has a higher estimate, between 25 and 28 percent, of the industrial share in the national income in 1940-42.

10. The key laws that were introduced in 1939 to protect and regulate industry were Law of 14 October 1939 (industrial protection and promotion) and Law of 24 November 1939 (regulation and defense of national industry). INI was established in 1941 under Law of 25 September.

11. Law of 2 November 1939 (Ordenación y Defensa de la Industria).

12. See Law 194/1963. This law approved the *Plan of Economic and Social Development, 1964-67,* Spain's first comprehensive development plan.

13. Art. 7, Law 194/December 1963.

14. Article 1, decree of 24 September 1968.

15. Ibid.

16. Ministerio de Industria, *La industria española en 1970* (Madrid: Servicio de Publicacións, 1971), p. 87.

17. Decree 1, 325/28 May 1966.

18. Decree 1, 107/1 June 1968.

19. Decree 1, 882/27 June 1968; Decree 2, 225/14 September 1968; Decree 484/27 March 1969.

20. Bela Belassa, *The Structure of Protection in the Industrial Countries and Its Effects on the Exports of Processed Goods from Developing Countries,* International Bank for Reconstruction and Development, Washington, D.C., Report No. EC-152a, February 28, 1968, p. 3.

21. Trade liberalization was initiated by Decreto-Ley de Ordenacion Económica de julio de 1959 (Decree-Law of Economic Reorganization of July 1959) and expanded by subsequent orders until 1966, since which time no additional commodities have been added to the free list.

3

SPAIN AND EUROPE:
THE ECONOMIC
REALITIES
William T. Salisbury

In any study of Spain's relations abroad, two points emerge clearly and consistently. In the first place, one recognizes that Spain occupies a position of great strategic and geopolitical importance in the global arena. In the second place, it is apparent that, historically, Spanish foreign-policy makers have been unable to exploit this position of strategic preeminence effectively. This failure has sometimes been attributed to the continued desire of Spanish officialdom to pursue policy in all geographic directions at once, a holdover, no doubt, from Spain's days of global empire

It is the thesis of this chapter that in foreign policy Spain has opted for the European alternative, in the idiom used by those who have given this new direction to policy, "España a jugado la carta europea." The fond hope of basing Spanish foreign policy on the leadership of the Latin American republics, in a revived version of the *hispanidad* of the 1930s and 1940s, has been discarded. In recent years Spain has practiced her own version of *Ostpolitik,* the *apertura al este,* but this alternative, for all its publicity value, remains devoid of substantial economic content and thus is largely a public relations operation designed to demonstrate to her Western European neighbors and the United States that Spain is up to date. Finally, Spain has chosen to de-emphasize the special relationship developed with the United States by utilization of joint military bases on Spanish soil, and though U.S. and Spanish ties remain cordial and close, the relationship has become a residual rather than a dominating factor in the minds of Spanish policy makers. This shift in the focus of Spanish foreign policy has been gradual but definitive. Beginning in the late 1950s, partly through a series of domestic reforms that increased her foreign policy capabilities, but more importantly through a fundamental realignment of her priorities abroad, Spain embarked on a new and forceful policy course, placing her European interests first.

SPAIN AND EUROPE

The motive force for this foreign policy realignment came essentially from the natural and growing tendency of the Spanish economy to interconnect with the economies of the European Economic Community (EEC) member countries. This growing together of the two regions was particularly marked in the economic areas, foreign trade and foreign investment, and in the human movements, tourism and emigration. In the 1960s the foreign exchange flows generated in these four crucial areas assured the pace and direction of Spanish economic growth. The progressive interlacing of the Spanish and Common Market economies also served to alert Spanish officials to the need for developing institutional ties with the Common Market that would place these economic flows on a preferential and hence a more stable basis. Both within and outside Spain, however, powerful voices were raised protesting any Common Market link with Spain of a preferential nature. It became the task of Spanish officials to soften this criticism while advancing acceptable arguments supporting Spanish association with the Six, France, Italy, Federal Republic of Germany, Netherlands, Belgium, and Luxembourg.

In Spain, data on mass and interest group opinion toward the proposed association with the Common Market are difficult to acquire because of the limitations placed on Spanish political life. What data are available seem to indicate that mass opinion about European integration and the Common Market has remained highly favorable since the late 1950s. At the elite level, however, the views of both businessmen and opposition political figures seem to have shifted from early support of Spain's European aspirations in the late 1950s and early 1960s, to various degrees of fear and suspicion, beginning approximately in 1962, when Spain made formal application for Common Market membership. Many businessmen fear a Common Market link for obvious economic reasons, while the political opposition believes that the present regime will be reinforced as a result of its successful conclusion of a Common Market accord and thus will be in a position to continue to deny certain political freedoms.[1]

Outside Spain, opposition to the Spanish association with the EEC centered in Brussels, where the secret negotiations were being held. For eight years, from 1962 until 1970, various interest groups accredited to the Common Market, the labor unions, and European political party secretariats, notably the Socialists, made attempts to block the Spanish bid. This opposition was effectively neutralized by astute Spanish diplomacy with a judicious accent on the economic benefits that would accrue to the Six in any such agreement and the occasional use of economic threats designed to underscore the fact that Spain was not necessarily negotiating from a position of weakness.

In March 1970 the Common Market and Spain were finally able to reach agreement concerning the contents of a preferential commercial trade pact. The agreement had two parts, with the first stage of six years to include a series of reciprocal tariff reductions on industrial products, with Spain the commercially weaker country receiving the larger reductions, 60 to 70 percent compared to 25 to 30 percent on the part of the Common Market. The agricultural section of the agreement bound Spain to certain levels of purchases from the EEC in return for trade concessions on oranges, olive oil, some other fruits and vegetables, and registered wines. The contents of the second six-year stage were not elaborated but presumably were to include a gradual harmonization of economic and social policies as well as the final movement into a customs union. Achievement of these aims would have resulted in Spain's effective inclusion in the Common Market.

Unfortunately, Spanish aspirations for Common Market membership suffered a severe blow as the pace of the European integration movement quickened after the Hague summit in December 1969. The lifting of the French veto to British membership resulted in the successful conclusion of negotiations for the enlargement of the EEC, with expansion beginning January 1, 1973. In the late 1970s the expanded grouping will feel the presence of states with long traditions of parliamentary rule, states that are already on record as seeking the "democratization" of EEC decision making and institutions. Thus Common Market enlargement has complicated the task facing the Spanish diplomats in Brussels, who in the past had been extolling Spain's economic virtues while de-emphasizing its lack of progress in instituting domestic political reforms.

A further complication for the Spanish occurred as a result of the merger in July 1972 of the former EFTA (European Free Trade Association) members with the EEC in a Europe-wide zone of industrial free trade. In this vitally important European grouping, Spain is the odd man out. The impact of this exclusion should not be considered as simply another in a long series of rebuffs to Spain's European overtures. The sixteen-nation industrial free trade area comprised a market of over 300 million people, the largest of its kind in the world. Further, it included Spain's neighbor Portugal, a nation at that time not normally considered among the ranks of states possessing democratic traditions and institutions. Spain's continued exclusion from the latest stage in the European unity movement was thus a painful political as well as economic blow.

In the longer run, however, the economic pull of Western Europe will no doubt exert an irresistible attraction for the Spanish. Spain must ultimately be included in any unified European economic bloc because her economy has become so closely geared to those of her northern neighbors. This coupling of Spain's economy with that of the rest of Western Europe has been accompanied by a remarkable leap in the pace of Spanish economic development. In fact, in terms of sheer rate of increase in gross national product (GNP), Spain was exceeded in the decade of the 1960s only by Japan. Economically, Spain has no choice but to affiliate herself with a wider Europe if she is to maintain the developmental momemtum built up in the 1960s.

The Spanish economic advance has been uneven, however. In consumer durables, enormous progress has been achieved in the last ten years. Government statistics for 1970 revealed that 16 families out of 100 owned a car, 43 out of 100 a TV set, and 42 out of 100 a washing machine and a refrigerator. In more basic human comforts, however, progress, at least by U.S. standards, was not so rapid. Only about 2 out of 3 Spanish homes had running water, with this figure falling to 1 out of 5 in some rural areas. On a national average, only 1 out of 5 Spanish homes had a telephone.

Despite notable improvements in recent years, public services are also deficient, particularly in education. In the late 1960s the Spanish were devoting only 2 percent of their GNP to education, compared with an average of more than 5 percent for the other Western European countries. One serious result of this lack of attention was a rate of illiteracy that was abnormally high for a continental country. In the middle of the 1960s, Spain's years of most rapid development, as much as 13 percent of the Spanish population was still considered functionally illiterate.[2] Such deficiencies will no doubt be alleviated and eventually overcome in the years ahead as Spain continues to draw closer to her European neighbors, both in economic interdependence and in terms of levels of economic development. The extent of the "special relationship" Spain enjoys with the EEC is now examined with special emphasis on trade and foreign investment flows and the movement of people, both workers and tourists.

SPAIN AND EUROPE: ECONOMIC REALITIES

Foreign Trade

From the point of view of foreign trade, the typical image of Spain is of a country that through accident and design has been more or less closed off from world commerce, at least since its golden age. This image has certainly been justified by events. A League of Nations study published in 1927 cited Spain as the country with the highest average tariff barrier in Europe. High tariff barriers meant a high degree of autarchy, as Spanish manufacturers tooled up for the protected domestic market. They were unable to export, however, since their costs were substantially above world levels. Aside from exports of agricultural products, particularly citrus fruits, the Spanish economy remained in relative isolation from the rest of the world until Spanish officials embarked on the trade liberalization policy of 1959. The result of this earlier policy of autarchy was that Spanish agricultural exports were used to pay for the raw materials necessary for the industries producing for the protected home market.

As Spain has moved from agricultural to industrial production, foreign commerce has become more important relative to national income. Imports and exports as a percentage of national income increased from 11 percent in 1961 to 19.8 percent in 1967.[3] In the same period, manufactured products moved from 31 percent of total exports to 50 percent. In 1972, agricultural exports represented only 12 percent of the Spanish total, although they were still the largest single export category.[4]

In regard to foreign trade, several disturbing trends coalesced in the early 1960s, causing Spanish policy makers to reevaluate their conception of Spain's role in the European integration movement. On the one hand, foreign commerce was clearly becoming more important in the overall functioning of the Spanish economy, and key agricultural exports were threatened with new administrative barriers thrown up by the Brussels bureaucrats. On the other hand, the locus of Spanish trade was shifting slowly on a worldwide basis. In 1960 roughly 70 percent of Spain's exports went to Europe, 39 percent of them to the Common Market countries. Of her imports, 46 percent originated in Europe, with only 25 percent coming from the EEC.[5] A decade later only 57 percent of Spanish exports were going to Europe, with the Common Market countries taking only 31 percent of the total. Imports by value from Europe were 52 percent, with the Six providing 35 percent.[6] Although the Common Market was becoming more important as a source for Spanish imports, especially capital goods and consumer durables, Spain was becoming an increasingly smaller factor as a supplier for the EEC. Faced with this changing pattern of trade, Spain has felt obliged to follow a conscious policy of augmenting her exports to the Common Market countries.

It was true that in the 1960s Spain tended to import by value about twice what she exported. The deficit in merchandise was balanced by invisibles such as receipts from the tourist industry and remittances by Spanish nationals working abroad, principally in European countries, and of course in the capital account by the flow of long-term investment funds. These three sources of foreign exchange were considered by Spanish officials to be less stable than export earnings; tourism and workers' remittances were felt to be particularly vulnerable to a European recession. Therefore, in the long negotiations over Spain's relationship with the Common Market, Spanish policy makers took great pains to emphasize the imbalance in trade and to plead for favorable access for Spanish goods into the EEC.

Foreign Investment

In terms of foreign investment, Spain seems to have followed a less autarchic policy over the last years than she did for trade, and in the early years of the 20th century there was extensive foreign investment in the Spanish economy, much of it European. The Belgians invested in the chemical industry, while the Dutch and Germans moved into electrical equipment manufacture and the Swiss into the food industry. One study quotes figures that show that in the years preceding World War I, the amount of foreign capital was often superior to the amount of Spanish capital in newly created enterprises.[7] In 1918 roughly 40 percent of the foreign investment in Spain came from the countries that would eventually be the original members of the Common Market.[8]

The Civil War and World War II completely closed Spain off to foreign sources of finance, however, and in the postwar period there seemed to be little interest in investing in a country that was sealed off diplomatically from the rest of the world, with tight exchange controls and legislation forbidding foreign participation in Spanish enterprises beyond 25 percent of their total capital. In 1959 the Spanish legislation regarding foreign investment was considerably liberalized. Under the new law, no limitation was placed on direct investment in a Spanish enterprise if the investment represented less than 50 percent of its capital. For more than 50 percent participation, foreign investors needed the prior authorization of the Spanish authorities.

If one examines the current statistics relating to foreign investment in Spain, one is again surprised at the underlying movement of Spain toward the EEC or, more exactly in this case, the movement of the EEC toward Spain. Utilizing comparable statistics from the Banco Exterior de España for the decade of the 1960s,* the following picture emerges regarding the flow of investment capital into Spain. In this ten-year period, the United States supplied 34 percent of foreign investment, the Common Market followed with 25 percent, and Switzerland was third with 21 percent. During this period, however, there existed a shift away from U.S. sources of capital and toward Common Market investors. In 1968 the EEC furnished 41 percent of Spain's foreign investment, while the United States supplied only 26 percent; in 1969 the EEC still furnished 31 percent of Spanish foreign investment, while the United States supplied 32 percent. These figures must be compared with the average of

---

*The figures that follow are not representative of the total foreign investment during this period, since much direct investment did not reach the 50 percent mark and therefore did not require official authorization. These data are not usually published in the official sources. Such is the case for the petroleum industry, in which foreign control never reaches 40 percent.[9]

1961-62, when the United States accounted for roughly 45 percent of foreign investment in Spain while the EEC furnished only 20 percent.[10]

Although the U.S. presence is as dominant in terms of foreign investment as it is in most other European countries, there is clearly a movement toward European sources of capital, at least by the statistics that are presently available. This movement will no doubt accelerate in the decade of the 1970s, as Common Market firms find it convenient to open production facilities to supply their export markets in Spain.

Tourism

The third "economic reality" pulling Spain closer to the Common Market has been and continues to be tourism. This "industry without smoke" has been exploited to the maximum by the Spanish. Quite literally they have capitalized on sunshine. Over 34 million tourists now visit Spain each year, roughly three-quarters of them escaping the harsh continental climate of Europe; but the tourists are also attracted by Spain's unique art treasures and her language and culture, including the famous *flamenco* and the *fiesta de los toros.*

By 1961 Spain's income from tourism was 650 percent higher than it had been ten years earlier, and this source of hard currency had become a key element in the macroeconomic planning of the Spanish authorities. Spanish dependence on tourism relative to other sources of foreign exchange generation has vastly increased in recent years. According to OECD figures in 1961 its receipts represented 51 percent of visible exports, but in 1972 this figure had jumped to roughly 70 percent.[11] According to official Spanish figures, Spain is now the world's number-one tourist country, having surpassed Italy in this category in 1971. This type of economic dependence, plus the fact that the vast majority of these tourists came from European countries (82 percent in 1967, with 63 percent of the total coming from three countries, France, the United Kingdom, and Germany),[12] has made Spanish policy makers anxious to develop institutional links with the Common Market countries that would protect this vital source of foreign exchange. Such links would serve to legitimize the Spanish regime and help protect it from the periodic attacks that emanate regularly from socialist and trade-union circles, particularly in Belgium and Holland; Spanish officials feel that these attacks have damaged the tourist industry potential, although, surprisingly, in the middle 1960s it was from Belgium and Holland that the largest increases in the Spanish tourist population were being registered, as much as 50 percent per year.[13]

Emigration

The fourth and final force working to move Spain and the Common Market closer together has been the flow of Spanish workers to the various Common Market countries. Historically Spanish out-migration had been directed toward the various Latin American daughter republics, but this pattern changed considerably after World War II. From 1951 to 1960 only one-third of the Spanish emigration settled overseas, principally in Latin America, while two-thirds moved to continental countries, a net migration to Europe of roughly one million Spaniards.[14] In 1959, moreover, there began a sharp increase in this movement of workers toward the continent: whereas in 1959 Spanish emigration toward continental countries was 52 percent of total emigration, by 1964 it was 92 percent of the total.[15]

There is some dispute among Spanish experts over the volume of emigration to Europe in the early 1960s. Reliable authorities usually estimate it at 100,000 persons per year net.[16] Exact figures are difficult to come by, however, since many of the Spanish workers emigrated clandestinely, leaving the country on tourist passports not legally valid for work abroad, and other authors hold that the official statistics may be underestimated by 50 percent or more.[17] In any case, Europe absorbed substantial numbers of Spanish workers, anywhere from 150,000 to 250,000 per year between 1959 and 1965. In 1965 the flow diminished sharply, however, actually reversing itself in 1966.

The preference among the emigrating Spanish workers for the Common Market countries was overwhelming. Again, exact figures are not available, although one study indicates that of those workers choosing to emigrate to European countries, 65 percent went to France,* 20 percent to West Germany, 12 percent to Switzerland, and 1.5 percent to the Netherlands.[18] Several factors encouraged Spanish workers to leave their country to seek work in the Common Market. At home, the restrictive measures carried out under the Stabilization Plan had caused a recession in the years 1959-61, which coincided with a relative economic boom in the Common Market countries. Even if work had been available in Spain at the time, the daily wages in the Common Market were three or four times what could be expected at home.[19] The economic gap separating the Spanish worker from his Common Market counterpart was even more apparent in terms of ability to purchase certain items, particularly consumer durables. For example, a refrigerator could be purchased in Germany with 67 hours of labor, while in Spain it would require 339 hours.[20]

In spite of the fact that the Spanish government did not at first encourage the movement of Spanish workers toward Europe and may even have attempted

---

*The figure for France is inflated relative to Germany, since it includes seasonal agricultural laborers crossing into France for brief periods at harvest time.

to discourage it,[21] this movement resulted in certain benefits for the Spanish regime. In the first place it represented an escape valve for the substantial temporary unemployment generated by the 1959 Stabilization Plan, and in the second place the emigrant remittances made foreign exchange contributions to the Spanish balance of payments that greatly aided in the success of the Stabilization Plan measures.

Some idea of the magnitude of these emigrant remittances can be gained from the following data. From 1961 to 1965 the remittances averaged roughly $200 million a year, exceeding the total yearly amount represented by Spanish citrus exports. In 1971 emigrant remittances were running at $300 million a year, more than double the value of Spanish citrus fruit exports.[22]

The policy makers were again afraid this flow of hard currency might be jeopardized by sudden measures taken by the Common Market countries. Although various bilateral labor conventions had been signed with individual countries of the Six, full membership in the Common Market would provide Spain with a voice in the making of social and labor policy within the Brussels bureaucracy, while at the same time allowing active participation in the disbursements of the European Social Fund. The liberalizing and democratizing effect of the returned *gastarbeiter* on Spanish society can only be guessed at, but the cumulative impact is bound to be substantial and largely irreversible in terms of demands for greater participation in political life as well as an eventual share in decision making on the factory floor.

Overwhelming evidence thus seems to demonstrate the progressive interlacing of the Spanish and Common Market economies. Trade and investment and the financial flows generated by tourism and emigrant remittances all served to alert Spanish officials to the necessity of developing an institutional superstructure based on the "economic realities."

Within Spain, perception of these "economic realities" did not result in a unified opinion among informed Spanish citizens about how the country ought to confront such trends. In fact, for the first five years of its existence the Common Market did not elicit a formal communication from the Spanish government itself. Internally the Spanish administration had to deal with a small group of economists identified with Falangist circles who argued that Spain's weak industrial structures would be overcome by the more powerful Common Market economies. These men, while mindful of the need to expand exports, felt that Spain should rely basically on her own resources for economic development and leave foreign trade in a secondary position. If markets were necessary they should be found in Latin America, where ties of language and culture would facilitate Spanish commercial penetration. The Latin American gambit failed to find an echo among responsible policy makers, mainly because trade with this part of the world was insignificant and its potential for increase judged minor. In 1962, the year of Spain's decision for Europe, only 10 percent of her exports and imports were with Latin America.

The Falangist economists were probably arguing not so much against Common Market membership or association as against the structural changes in the Spanish economy that association would bring: a truly different Spain would result from prolonged and intensive economic interconnection with Western Europe. A rather detailed study making this point was done in 1966 by the Department of Economics of the University of Madrid and funded in part by the Ford Foundation. The study indicated that the island provinces of Spain, the Balearics and the Canaries, and the Levant regions would reap greater benefits from association than the center of Spain, Catalonia, and the Basque provinces. Spain would face an association with the Common Market with the novel prospect of having relatively developed economic sections in jeopardy while poorer regions stood to make substantial gains in living standards. A government economist, not identified with the Falangists but writing anonymously, agreed with the study's conclusion and added emphasis indicating that association with the Common Market would result in a complete overturning of the actual economic structure of Spain.[23]

Under the circumstances it was not surprising that many regional and sectoral interest groups felt threatened by association and brought their fears to the attention of the Spanish negotiating team in Brussels. In fact, during the almost eight years of discussions, these diplomats spent more sessions placating the domestic critics of association than they actually spent negotiating with their Common Market counterparts in working out the complex preferential agreement.

ALTERNATIVES TO THE COMMON MARKET

La Apertura al Este

By 1970-72, due to a confluence of economic circumstances, Spain was very anxious to expand her exports to the Communist nations.[24] Spanish citrus exports to the Common Market faced compensating levies if prices should fall because of temporary increases in supply; expanding markets in the East would help alleviate this problem and also provide a hedge for production that might not be saleable in the United Kingdom once Britain's low agricultural tariffs were harmonized with the higher Common Market levels. Spain's industrialization program, begun in earnest in 1959, was now producing a substantial volume of consumer goods for export. These same goods are in short supply in the Eastern bloc countries and might be exchanged for the raw materials and crude oil needed by Spain. A potential in the East for broadening the tourist industry, presently based on travel from Western Europe, was also noted by the Spanish authorities.

In terms of the above expectations, the reality of Spanish economic relations with the East, unfortunately, does not seem especially promising. In 1971 imports from Spain by the Eastern bloc were down by 3 percent to 1.4 percent of the Spanish total of exports. Exports to Spain from the Eastern bloc were down 13 percent, to 2.8 percent of total Spanish imports.[25] The ostensible reason for this fall-off was that Spanish trade with some Eastern countries was being moved to a convertible basis in 1971 and the Communists preferred not to spend their hard currencies, dollars and sterling, for consumer goods, oranges and shoes.[26] Trade figures for 1972 indicate that Spain's trade with the East had recovered enormously in percentage terms but had swung from surplus to deficit. Spanish exports to the East had grown 40 percent from the previous year, twice as fast as the growth recorded for all exports. Imports from the East rose 104 percent from 1971, while all imports rose only 25 percent. The large percentage increases, however, tend to obscure the relatively small absolute amounts in question. For example, Spanish exports to all Communist countries were only 3.3 percent of their global exports in 1972, or roughly $135 million, out of total exports of $4 billion. Trade figures for the first six months of 1975 indicate that the hope of diversifying Spain's geographic trade dependence by means of the much-vaunted *apertura al este* have so far proven a chimera. During this period, exports to Comecon were 3.4 percent of total Spanish exports while imports from Comecon were only 3.2 percent of Spain's total imports.[27]

The Americas

In general, the future of U.S.-Spanish relations, while good, does not approximate the mutual feelings that existed in the 1950s, when U.S. aid filled much of the gap in the Spanish trade deficit and the United States was looked upon as Spain's major future client.

Today the United States accounts for only 15 percent of Spain's total foreign trade, about the same percentage it accounted for in the 1950s. Spain's commercial future seems to be not with the United States but rather with Europe.

In terms of foreign investment, the same shift toward Europe has already been noted. Between 1945 and 1969 U.S. business invested in excess of $540 million in Spain, all but $100 million of which was fresh outside capital;[28] but in 1969 U.S. investments in Spain were only 2.9 percent of the total of U.S. investments in all of Western Europe and only .9 percent of the total of all U.S. foreign investments. These percentages seem to have remained constant since 1966, moreover,[29] suggesting that a plateau of interest in Spain has been reached on the part of U.S. business.

The statistics for tourism do not seem to indicate any closer U.S.-Spanish relationship, either. Of the total number of tourists who visited Spain in 1973, only about 4 percent were from the United States, while roughly 70 percent came from Europe.[30] Though U.S. tourists no doubt spend more per capita than do the Europeans, they will never be so important to the Spanish economy as Spain's neighbors to the north.

CONCLUSION

Given the economic stakes involved, the Spanish have never had a viable alternative to forming some link with the Common Market. The technocrats then in command of Spanish economic and foreign policy recognized this and sought the best available conditions in Brussels. The EEC has not granted the full membership desired by Madrid, however, and in fact, the preamble to the 1970 commercial treaty disappointingly places Spain in the context of the EEC's "Mediterranean policy." High officials of the permanent staff of the Council of Ministers have expressed the off-the-record opinion that Spain would be the first country to leave the *cadre méditerranean*. Further, informed sources within the EEC indicated that a document prepared for the council by the commission on the association policy of the EEC did not formally place Spain in the category of countries affected by its Mediterranean policy. According to the same document, the EEC considers the policy of concluding association agreements and preferential trade pacts *in Europe proper* within the "cadre général de l'élargissement." Thus it would seem that the EEC had taken favorable note of Spain's special status as a contiguous nation and that at the appropriate moment it would acknowledge politically the link that is so visible economically.

At the end of 1972 Spain was able to reach agreement with the EEC on an "additional protocol" for their preferential accord. This was not the broader renegotiation, falling just short of full membership, that Spain had been demanding; in fact, the protocol was an agreement to disagree, to postpone substantive negotiations for a year. At this writing these negotiations have been suspended as a result of adverse European reaction to the Spanish execution of terrorists in September 1975.

General Franco is now in his eighties, but he still manages to fulfill most of his duties as Chief of State. His comportment during his 1973 end-of-the-year television message was exceptional for a man so old, particularly coming so soon upon the assassination of his newly designated head of government and long-time comrade-at-arms, Luis Carrero Blanco. Franco suffered a serious illness in July 1974, and it is clear to most observers that there will soon be a change of the guard at the apex of Spain's political hierarchy. Franco's passing from power should have an enormous symbolic impact on Spain's relations with the EEC, making it infinitely less difficult for Spanish diplomats to present a modernized Cortez as the equivalent of a parliament on the Western European model.

Initially, Arias Navarro, the newly-named premier and successor to Carrero, made promising moves in the direction of political liberalization. His speech to the Cortez that laid down his cabinet's program included the following sentence widely noticed in the European press: "The Spain of today boasts a society which is, in great measure, healthy, literate, developed and unprejudiced, with very few divisive, upsetting minorities, and therefore, the Government expresses its confidence in the maturity of the Spanish people to prevent those minorities from stalling the process of participation that must needs be completed."[31] Arias thus seemed likely to implement the rather minor institutional changes and proceed with that modicum of political face lifting that would make Spain a partner acceptable to the Common Market members. Unfortunately the new emphasis on political participation, which would have been so useful in softening European resistance to Spanish membership in the EEC, has been superceded by events in the government's escalated confrontation with the Catholic Church over a relatively innocuous pastoral letter circulated by the bishop in Bilbao and in the refusal of clemency by Franco in the cases of 5 of 11 convicted terrorists, resulting in their execution by firing squads in September 1975.

Serious though the above setbacks may seem for the pro-European policies of the new Spanish leadership, one must not forget that the EEC members themselves are troubled by both political and economic problems at home and are therefore less and less inclined to be critical of the Spanish candidacy. In addition, hard-core anti-Franco sentiments are dying out with those European generations that have firsthand memories of the Civil War period. The economic forces that have led to such a remarkable degree of integration between Spain and her European neighbors are operating as strongly in the 1970s as they did in the 1960s, and to this observer there seems to be every likelihood that toward the end of this decade Spain's "special relationship" with the EEC will become institutionalized, with Spain finally becoming a full member of that growing organization.

NOTES

1. For an analysis of Spanish public opinion and the Common Market, see William T. Salisbury, "Spain and the Common Market 1957-1967," unpublished dissertation, The School of Advanced International Studies, Johns Hopkins University, Washington, D.C., 1972, Chapters 4 and 8.

2. Organization for Economic Cooperation and Development, *Technical Assistance and the Economic Development of Spain* (Paris: OECD, 1968), p. 13.

3. Ramon Tamames, *Estructura economica de España,* 5th ed. (Madrid: Guardiana de Publicaciónes, 1970), p. 563.

4. Banco Exterior de Commercio, *Hechos y cifras de la economía española* (Madrid: el Banco, 1972), p. 676. Hereafter *Hechos y cifras*.

5. *Hechos y cifras* (1960), pp. 43 and 46.

6. *Hechos y cifras* (1969), pp. 538 and 561. The last import figure is for 1968.

7. Enricho Fontela Montes, *Commerce extérieur et développement économique: Espagne, cas particulier* (Geneva: Droz, 1962), p. 18.

8. Ministerio de Asuntos Exteriores, "Déclaration de la délégation de l'Espagne à la première séance de ses conversations avec la commission de La Communauté Economique Européenne," mimeographed (Madrid, 1964), p. 12.

9. *Estudio de la vinculacion de la industria española con respecto a paises extrajeras* (Geneva: Common Market Business Reports, 1969), p. 21.

10. *Hechos y cifras*, various years, author's calculations from published data.

11. OECD figures.

12. Tamames, op. cit., p. 515.

13. *Hechos y cifras* (1966), p. 580.

14. Tamames, op. cit., p. 23.

15. Angel Villaneuva, "Causas y estructura de la emigración exterior," in *Horizante Español*, vol. 2 (Paris: Ruedo Ibérico, 1966): 383.

16. Miguel Siguan, "Emigración y desarrollo económico en España," *Arbor* (March 1964), p, 110.

17. Villaneuva, op. cit., p. 382.

18. Jesus Garcia Fernandez, *La Migración exterior de España* (Madrid: Ariel, 1965), cited by Villaneuva, op. cit., p. 405.

19. Fernando Barrera, "Efectos sociales del mercado commun en Espana," *Boletin de Estudios Economicos* (Bilbao, January-April 1962), p. 95.

20. Organización Sindical, *Capacidad de Compra por Tiempo de Trabajo*, confidencial (Madrid: Syndicatos organization, October 1966), Cuadro 1.

21. Barrera, op. cit., pp. 88-89.

22. *Hechos y cifras*, various years.

23. O.F. [pseud.] , "L'Espagne et l'integration européenne," *Les Problèms de l'Europe*, no. 35 (First Quarter 1967), p. 47.

24. On the subject of Spain's relations with the East see William T. Salisbury, "Spain's Ostpolitik: East-West Thaw on the Edge of Europe," paper prepared for delivery at the International Studies Association annual meeting, Panel on the Non-Military aspects of European International Politics, New York City, March 19, 1973.

25. *Información Española*, no. 6940, Oficina de Informacion Diplomatica, Madrid, February 10, 1973.

26. This point was made by Felipe de la Morena, Foreign Ministry official in charge of Spain's East-West relations, in an interview by the author on January 4, 1973.

27. Banco Exterior de España, *Last Week in Spain*, Madrid, Sept. 1, 1975 and Sept. 8, 1975.

28. Stanford Research Institute, *American Investments in Spain* (Madrid: U.S. Chamber of Commerce, 1972), p. 10.

29. Ibid., Table 3.

30. *Hechos y cifras* (1973), p. 691.

31. Madrid, Diplomatic Information Office, *Spain 74,* no. 8, year 2 (March 1974), p. 2.

PART

II

THE CHANGING
NATURE OF
SPANISH SOCIETY

4

**RURAL LIFE
IN SPAIN:
CONTINUITY
AND CHANGE**
Michael Kenny

Anthropologists should not be relegated solely to the rural, in Spain or anywhere else, any more than they should be thought of as associated mainly with old bones and stones. They have, however, gained a deserved reputation for a specially intensive form of microstudy based on various kinds of participation and observation over a lengthy period in "the field," rural or urban. Unlike other disciplines in the social sciences, anthropology is concerned primarily with a horizontal view of society in which the relationships are purposively sought (in sampling) among the economic, political, religious, and other facets of society. Anthropologists are less concerned with, though they do not disregard, the vertical links that other disciplines explore with their own characteristic thoroughness from, for example, local to national. Every anthropologist is to some extent a contemporary historian, but unlike the social historian, the anthropologist tends to synthesize data by seeking generalizations regarding a single set of problems. Nevertheless, since the anthropologist attempts to understand the whole rather than its separate parts alone, the larger the whole he is called upon to understand, the less grasp he feels he can have, and the less dependable the models that even he constructs. Thus, while the economist generally sacrifices the exceptional and the local variation for the sake of his national or regional model, the anthropologist constantly revises his models in the light of these very dynamic variations.

A first suggestion in any interdisciplinary effort would be to seek, if not agreement, then at least mutual understanding, and to articulate points of coincidence in our respective criteria. In this study we break down our information about Spain into divisions for study, whether these are studied for evidence of change or for other reasons. After some consideration of such divisions, given the enormity of the general task, it is apparent that one necessary area of focus is on some internal and external elements of continuity and change in rural Spain with special reference to asymmetrical relationships. Particular emphasis should be put on the contrasts reflected in peasant social structures and economies, patronage and associational models, and the values that underlie these, from the 1950s to the 1960s to the 1970s. The main concern should be to distinguish areas of society that are resistant to certain kinds of change from those that are not. Finally, no such treatment would be complete today without mention of that double-edged phenomenon, mobility, in the forms of emigration and tourism.

The classification of areas and sub-areas in Spain depends on their size and type and on the number of criteria used to define them. A division of Spain into wet and dry climatological areas tells us little until these are correlated with other variables, such as minifundia and latifundia. Excessive reliance on an assumed cultural homogeneity may thwart analysis, but on the other hand, meticulous delineation of cultural heterogeneity may make comparative analysis unnecessarily cumbersome, if not impossible. For their basic units of analysis, political scientists may prefer the region, anthropologists the cultural or subcultural area, and sociologists the *comarca* or social area, if only out of greater familiarity with the criteria and data they each employ. Linz's and de Miguel's typology of the "eight Spains"[1] comes the closest to combining a variety of criteria to satisfy the greater number of disciplinary approaches; theirs, too, has the advantage of permitting inter-nation sub-area comparison. However, their study does not contain enough social and cultural data to satisfy the anthropologist.

In fact, anthropologists have not as yet dared to formulate a typology of Spain, although brave attempts have been made to delineate subcultures[2] and to suggest a preliminary and tentative breakdown into types of rural communities.[3] The acid test for such a typology is, can it be used both as heuristic device and also as one that will aid in producing hypotheses, the working out of which will eventually modify that same typology?

Epic songs tell us that the division of Spain into separate kingdoms was regarded as a temporary evil that God would remedy. It was Menendez Pidal who noted that the romantic idealism of the local region nevertheless encouraged the tendency for insistence on local rights and privileges at times of great national weakness.[4] His theory, however, was that the causes of localism were not the ethnological, psychological, and linguistic differences but rather the reverse, the uniformity of a character universally individualistic, that "Iberianism" persisted as a result of, not despite, the various but continued superstructures imposed on localities since Roman times, causing an asymmetry that has characterized national-local and, by extension, urban-rural relations. This is not likely to change in the 1970s.

If this is true, then it is questionable whether this unilateral "looking down" at infrastructures has affected the approach to study. For instance, until recent decades the Spanish countryside has been characterized as hermetically resistant to national influence and change. Looking at the situation asymmetrically, this might be explained at times by blaming a corrupt and inefficient national bureaucracy that, in effect, stimulated such resistance; yet that might be only half the story if one did not take into consideration the local landlords and caciques, whose control over change is only strengthened by a remote bureaucracy. Similarly, if one accepts the blanketing Great Tradition of Roman Catholicism in accounting for the absence of mutually exclusive sects such as were found in the free Protestantism of Britain (especially after the Industrial Revolution), the wealth of Little Traditions in the countryside, which certainly make Spanish peasants far less "papist than the Pope," would be ignored.

There is an obvious anomaly in regarding peasant life both as a culture and as a part- or half-culture at the same time. If peasant life is indeed a part of something, then it is not part of urban or city culture but part of the state, a complex of cultures, which is the decisive criterion of power dominance. The general argument, therefore, would be that studies of change must take into account the mutual interplay of the local and the national (and rural and urban— for example, the peasantization of cities in the form of in-migrant slums). Moreover, the process of change itself may link two climates of sensibility or systems of thought peculiar to two successive historical periods. These linking processes may be the better plotted by correlating sets of cultural values with the interplay of local and national interest, both as to their recurrent (short-range) and directional (long-range) effects.

PEASANT LIFE AND VALUES

One could hardly wish for a better description of peasant life (in 1898) than that by Vicent Blasco Ibañez in *La Barraca;*[5] yet that was a Valencian garden-type cultivation of rice and citrus fruits subject to an extraordinarily complicated system of irrigation canals that had long required ancient tribunals (Cort de la Seo) to settle disputes. Here the unity of ownership is the land *together with the water rights,* and the highly complex nature of the irrigation ecology seems to be conducive to a vigorous communal organization. Moreover, the products of this intensive cultivation are mainly destined for a large city's markets nearby or perhaps even for export, at national and international prices over which the local growers have virtually no control.

Again, the lease-owner of trees (not the owner of the land on which they grow) does not exert any control from below on the market prices of his products. The lessee of a modest-size olive grove in Andalusia would probably be wryly surprised to learn that more than 2 million pounds of olive oil yearly are now going to an ex-enemy, the Soviet Union, in return for petroleum under an agreement of 1967. His lease is most likely a short-term one, and he is acutely aware of his dependence on his absentee patron. He has no strong communal organization to support him, and his greatest fear is of becoming unemployed like so many of his landless contemporaries.

The current owners of the Feixes, the small holdings of reclaimed land peculiar to Ibeza and granted to commoners to encourage repopulation, still make the *sensal* payment to the heirs of the original owners after seven centuries, even though in token form today. Even in the 1970s custom and practice, rather than any later royal order, similarly govern the rights to a common patrimony in many villages in the province of Soria, whereby each qualified household head receives his bounty in pines by lottery every year. The qualifications for bounty rights are highly complicated and have been handed down bilaterally in traditional inheritance for centuries.

Such common patrimonies lend a certain stability to village economy, although they, like seasonal migration, often supply but one of several income fragments in a plural employment. Indeed, by the 1960s the municipal economy of certain villages in Segovia seemed to depend on the income from the pine leases,[6] but their stability, nevertheless, was also dependent to a degree on the international prices of resin, over which the pine owners have no control. Similar inducements from the distant past to free peasants and serfs resulted in a foral land tenure system (a form of hereditary emphyteusis) in Galicia, where excessive subdivision, *cacicazgo,* and also emigration seem to have characterized the provincial minifundia.

Pairalisme (allegiance to paternal house) in Catalonia, and similar ethics in much of northern Spain, point up the dynamic nature of a primogeniture inheritance system under which the key to success of both landholdings and individual careers lay in the joint enterprise of the family and not just the efforts of the eldest son. Such local traditions may be quite at variance with the national norm, and it must be remembered that rural folk are more community-oriented than nation-oriented.

The above is enough to show not only the diversity of rural life in Spain, which would be obvious to the myopic, but also to indicate that by focusing on merely a few variables, such as unit of ownership, inheritance system, and cash drop price, extremely complicated forms of societal living may be revealed in rural Spain. The fact that they have remained in some sort of integrated equilibrium for so long says much for the dynamic forms of social control at the local level, the subtleties of which are not always recognized by national representatives. When unprecedented external forces, such as those at work in the 1960s and 1970s, make their impact, then the delicate local balance is often lost. A simple case will illustrate this point.

Lack of adequate housing is cited as the greatest single reason for re-emigration among returnees from Europe, and with good cause: the returning emigrants may even find themselves competing with their siblings for houses that could be more profitably rented to tourists. Savings earned abroad have encouraged young men to disregard the integrity of the once-inviolate family home and establish independent households of their own. If the value of the family property has risen, perhaps because of foreign tourists or because of developmental interest in the area, inheritance battles may cause bitter sibling rivalry. The returnees may force a division of the family property by recourse to the Spanish civil code (the national law which requires equal inheritance among all children) in defiance of customary laws, such as those among Basques, whereby the parents select one heir, causing all other siblings to leave, which passed farms on intact from one generation to another.[7]

If it were ever true, it certainly is no longer true to state as does the Banco Español de Crédito in its Classification 4, which is the least important, for towns in the 1,000 to 3,000 population category, that they are "municipalities which possess a commercial value which is practically nil, . . . thus constituting a strong indicator of self-sufficiency which characterizes the greater part of the rural Spanish zones."[8] Here is the familiar but falsely assumed homogeneity, and here, too, is the superiority of the national asymmetrical view, which sees the "greater part" of the countryside as useless for its purposes (commercial, but certainly not military). Is it to be assumed that Spanish villages have no surplus and do not hew to classical theories of maximization?* If they do have a surplus, is it to be assumed that this surplus and their energies are dissipated in meaningless ritual and endless fiestas? This is surely of the same ethnocentric order as any ancient Greek citizen's view of the backward barbarian; yet how persistent it is.

It is suggested here, as well as elsewhere,[9] that there is always an informal power structure that is parallel to that of the official, formal structure. Whether this informal structure, in reality a number of "structures," is merely less visible or is extralegal but accepted as inevitable by the state, it is a phenomenon that rural- and local-level societies in Spain (not necessarily the same thing) fully exploit. At the individual level it can be summed up by the proposition that if Society compromises the individual, then the individual will seek ways to compromise Society.

It is an accepted truth that in every society there is opposition in one form or another to the official value structure, and that in addition to the main theme there is always a series of conflicting themes or counterpoints that strive for expression, preferably in institutionalized form. Social scientists will find at least an echo of this statement in the so-called factional or conflict schools of

---

*The theory of maximization, incidentally, tells us little about what is maximized.

theory. It is also true that just as a national system requires a complex hierarchy of official units and subunits—provinces, cities, counties, towns, districts, villages, hamlets—that lead power and authority to the apex, so, too, paralleling this hierarchy, may be found a set of unofficial units that mirror the natural development of the modern state—subcultural regions, ancient provinces, *comarcas*—all of which have a strong emotional, if informal, pull on the citizens, who resist the homogenizing impersonalization of a central government. This is surely true of Spain.

SPANISH PATRONAGE AND ASSOCIATIONAL MODELS

I contend that a model for understanding the resolution of these conflicting themes or counterpoints can be found in the institution of patronage in Spain and that an explanation for the subcultural pull may be sought in the multiple forms of communal and associational types of local-level organizations. Furthermore both models, patronage and association, have been subjected to special kinds of external and internal change in the 1950s and 1960s and in the 1970s are suffering even greater influences.

Certain aspects of both models are selected here in order to highlight and document this position. If patronage is a strategic device for personalizing relationships, then the classic dilemma in patronage may be put succinctly: How does one resolve conflicting obligations of honor to one's family and friends, to whom one is expected to be partial, and to one's office, wherein one is supposed to be impartial? In the past this conflict was at least narrowed in its range. The vassalage ties to a lord in the medieval *mesnada* groupings were never fully substituted by the new subject-king relationship in the nation-state. In the Restoration period of the 1870s, Canovas propagated the tutelage of the state as an organizing principle, whereas Romero Robledo used familism as a positive tactic (he was reputed to know the leading five families in every village by name). The manipulation of human and economic resources, for good or evil, by caciques is well known, and it is significant that caciquismo as an institution has continued to prosper under the Franco regime.[10]

The religious model of patronage (through the saints) complements and strengthens the temporal model. Patronage, in effect, arms peasants and others with a device that "plugs into" otherwise unattainable sources of power. It permeates all aspects of life, not simply the political. In such of its different forms as sponsorship and brokership, it becomes a link and offsets otherwise asymmetrical relationships among different classes or different types and levels of society, rural to urban, local to national. It can be assumed that the strategic bookkeeping of patronage thrives where the formal institutional structure of society is weak and cannot or does not supply a regular stream of goods and efficient services to its lowest levels; it will thrive where there are no corporate (lineal or village) groups or associational organizations to offer alternative services or influence; it will thrive when patrons of whatever type live in close contact with the peasantry. The prime rule of patronage is reciprocity, and this must conform to informal sanction on both parties. In the 1960s and 1970s there has been far less dependence on patronage in rural Spain for the supply of goods and services, for a variety of reasons, outstanding among which are (1) that the State is supplying more goods and services and, in effect, more patronage by taking over obligations previously handled by kin or local groups, as in medical care and prevention; (2) that patrons no longer hold the monopoly that high rates of illiteracy and low mobility once afforded them; and (3) that clients cannot be so easily mobilized or exploited by patrons, since the clients are so mobile that they have migrated out of their patrons' spheres of influence. In the same manner, one might make a similar case for a decline in spiritual patronage.

This trend is continuing in the 1970s to the extent that classical rural patronage is not entirely disappearing but is being transformed by new roles of sponsorship, brokerage, or intermediation, the recruitment to which is by no means so exclusive or controlled as it was under the old patronage. Mediation has, in fact, become a common part-time employment. An authoritarian but personalistic regime will not lessen the need for patronage but rather confirm it. It may be taken for granted that the more powerful the local elite, the more concentrated and effective is the patronage and the social control it exercises. Thus it will vary considerably from region to region.

As to the associational model, a striking decline is noted in the effectiveness, indeed the very life, of communal-type organizations in rural Spain in the 1960s and 1970s. Voluntary-type associations have or have had a political function—the large landowners' associations, such as the Instituto de San Isidro in Catalonia, and the counter peasant leagues or the contemporary regional guerrilla groups, which even if they draw their symbols and symbolism from the countryside, seem to be created in or operated from cities. Leaving these aside, reference can be made to the long history of municipal cooperatives, the *cofradías* and *hermiandades,* many of which were the direct outcome of agricultural or pastoral communes created by *carta puebla* or *fuero municipal,* largely in northern Spain.

A distinction must be made between public works, which are institutionalized communal tasks, and more informal but now more common cooperation among individuals, such as at harvest time. The latter is clearly more often resorted to at the cost of the former, for it is voluntary and is based on a one-to-one relationship intended for a particular task, which supposes no long-term commitment. In 1969, in Valle de Manrés, the local mayor of Gema tried but failed to revive, once more, the *bediau,* an institutionalized system of communal tasks such as repairing bridges or irrigation conduits, clearing fields and cattle

tracks. Several communitywide activities were thereby affected, including the
fiesta mayor (the same is true for the province of Soria). Sheep farming, too, has
been abandoned for lack of the cooperative support so common until just
recently. The *salia*, the furnishing by rote of supplies to cowherds on the high
summer grazing land, is one of the very few such surviving communal institutions.[11] The reasons appear to be an almost complete disinterest in the traditional and in identification with a collective unity. It should be added that this
is one of many villages in the Spanish Pyrennees that are now jostled by hydroelectric plants and ski lifts, where the local population has been swelled by
industrial immigrants and tourists.

Conversely, cases are found where a traditional but moribund collectivist
institution has been revived to meet external inducement. In 1970, in the
Castilian village of Becedas, the Government Extension Service freely provided
gasoline sprayers and insecticide for fruit trees for the first treatment and was
prepared to subsidize, partially, subsequent treatments if the villagers organized
themselves. Individuals could have done their own spraying, though this would
have been more costly, so organization and cooperation among the fruit tree
owners was not strictly necessary in order to get the job done. However, a
traditional model of cooperation had existed in the village. The new model was
successful (at least 75 percent participation) because the benefits were visible in
the short term and because participation was voluntary and not obligatory.[12]

Where more tangible and immediate rights, rather than obligations, are
involved, as they are in a municipal bounty such as the "pine luck" in villages in
the province of Soria, then the institution persists but with declining importance. In 1948 in a small mountain village in Soria, over eighty arrests were made
of men in open revolt against abuse of their exclusive and ancient rights in the
surrounding pine forests. It is doubtful that they would bother in the 1970s,
for the income derived from the annual sorting by lot of the pines constitutes an
increasingly smaller proportion of the total income. Nevertheless it is a bounty,
however modest now, that every son of the pueblo can return to enjoy should he
fail in his new role as migrant.

Other more voluntary associations, such as mutual-aid-in-burial societies or
strictly religious *cofradías* (sodalities), are moribund or may be flogged to life
once a year for the patronal fiestas—or for a visiting TV team. Others with more
of an economic function still exist as a form of mutual security for their members and for the purpose of regulating certain occupational conditions. In the
1950s the fishermen's brotherhood in Conil de la Frontera (Cadiz) had about
400 members and a governing council to administer its own warehouse and to
control and apportion the fishing grounds by lot.[13] Such cooperatives were common in the 1940s, but now they are the exception. Certainly in the major ports
they have been taken over by the large private commercial corporations, which
provide the vessels and equipment and hire the fishermen on a fixed wages basis
rather than on the traditional sharecropping system that the brotherhood administered.

According to Juan J. Linz, in provinces with a number of associations above the national average, 50 percent of the associations had been founded since 1950, and the number of all types of associations varies directly with per capita income and industrialization.[14] Linz's study confirms the rapid and sudden rise of comparatively new forms of associational life that eschew the more traditional social organization based on propinquity and need. New associational forms are therefore marked by a novel element of volunteering and by a "community" based on mutual interest rather than on locality. However, they appear to be largely an urban phenomenon. To put it another way, since the terms "rural" and "urban" are misleading ("agro-town" nicely straddles both categories), the new associations seem to demand a certain minimum-size population with a predominance of nonagricultural occupations. As a working hypothesis I will assume that (new) voluntary associations provide a structure by linking traditional concepts with social functions that are modern and thus provide a means for minimizing the uncertainties and disruptions connected with rapid cultural change. It is likely that the trend of forming associations in the cities will continue strongly throughout the 1970s as new subclasses form and that these will make only a tentative appearance in the countryside, where they will mainly be types of organization that demand a minimum of cooperation from their members and provide maximum and visible short-term benefits, such as rotating credit associations, Hermandades de Labradores and Ganaderos.

RESISTANCE TO CHANGE

Spanish countrymen, like most other countrymen, are wary of and resistant to changes that commit them to new social relationships in the long term. Romer's Rule states that the initial survival value of change is conservative because it renders possible the maintenance of a traditional way of life in the face of changed circumstances. Changes are also selectively made. There are external pressures for change over which the peasant has little control; other changes are internally stimulated. Distinctions are made, of course, among degenerative change, growth without development, and socioeconomic development itself. It is assumed that development is not inevitable but that socioeconomic change is. Moreover, despite monumental efforts by the Spanish government in developmental plans, including the Badajoz and other hydroelectric plants and the developmental *polos* and *poligonos* described in Chapter 2, there may occur a backwash effect that only increases regional inequality.

Even so, the Land Concentration Program for consolidating farms, begun in 1953, has had steady success, with voluntary petitions exceeding the capacity of the program to deal with them. So, too, the efforts of the Instituto Nacional de Colonización have settled thousands in newly created irrigation areas since

the early 1950s. Since 1939 more land has been brought under irrigation than in
the last two thousand years. Such plans, by establishing regional centers (*centros
comareales*) and concentrating rural services, are aimed at reducing rural depopulation. In the long run the Spanish peasant is willy-nilly becoming a farmer, or
may become a "parkkeeper peasant" in those areas where governmental pressure
is toward the encouragement of tourism and the "cultural landscape" rather than
toward industrial or agricultural development. The Spanish peasant has neither
the inclination nor indeed the talent (as does the gypsy, who has in any case
taken his entertainment to the city) to amuse the foreign tourist, however, and
has never felt the need or obligation to put himself out for his compatriot on
vacation. Instead, he has been increasingly conscious, especially since the late
1950s, of the benefits he might enjoy by transferring himself to the lands from
which these foreign visitors can afford to travel. In the past, the Spanish peasant
could do little but despair of his poverty or perhaps undertake that long-term
and somewhat perilous adventure of migration to the new world. It took the
combination of an emergent prosperity in the 1950s, plus the presence of
thousands of foreign tourists representative of cultures the peasants swiftly
learned to envy, to uproot them in a short-term continental migration to the
northern European countries.

RURAL MIGRATION

There is evidence from economists and others that the peasants in Western
Europe have generally tended to stay at home in times of economic depression,
despite the myth to the contrary.[15] It is surely no coincidence that while foreign
tourists pour into Spain there is also an exodus of Spaniards, both rural and
urban, emigrating to the very countries in which these tourists originate. The
evident attraction exerted by host cultures that needed a cheap labor force, such
as Germany, Switzerland, or France, cannot be denied. For Spain it is an investment in human capital, but Spain benefits in foreign exchange from the
remittances sent home by her emigrants, whose labor abroad also helps produce
the assets the German, Swiss, and French tourists spend in Spain. However, since
heavy migration from rural areas to the cities in Spain and abroad is taking place
at a time when the standard of living in villages has never been higher, one can
only conclude that the villager is making a conscious and planned breakout from
one life in favor of another.

It would be wrong to assume that the countryman is reacting like a
puppet, solely to the tugs of external influences. Migration has never been characterized by recklessness or, for that matter, by lack of planning on the part of
the individual, as chain migration testifies—a reality that classical push and pull
theories have ignored. The creation of the Spanish Institute of Emigration in

1956 also supposed a governmentally organized and planned migration in groups. Moreover, while older peasants crossed themselves and luxuriated in the growing prosperity of the 1950s, younger peasants slowly but irreverently discarded the values traditionally associated with the agricultural round. One by one the younger set, once so committed to the family home, slipped away to neighboring cities or to factories abroad, establishing a beachhead for those who were to follow. At first this migration of the 1950s was a highly individual and tentative affair, since definitive return to the natal home was the norm and the rural family integrity was not unduly threatened; nor indeed did the migrant at that time thoroughly immerse himself in the urban ethos, except for that part that sustained his occupational interests. To this extent the migrants of the 1950s and early 1960s were conforming to a conservative pattern, in the sense that migration became just another aspect of a traditional plural employment, supplying a welcome though unfamiliar income fragment. By the 1970s, however, having gained the confidence of mobility and founded a support group away from home, the peasant migrant tended to move with his family, determined to acquire a totally new life style in many spheres other than just the economic.

In the 1970s, in fact, there is the phenomenon of the migrant committed to a more permanent and revolutionary break with his peasant background, no matter whether he stems from the third-world countryside of poorer Andalusia or from the fertile regions of Catalonia and the Basque provinces. If it is recalled that 3,162,121, or approximately one out of every ten, Spaniards were living abroad in 1970, there is the realization that in that historic decade of the 1960s, the number of returnees from abroad for the first time exceeded those who emigrated. Along with these returnees, there stream into Spain over 30 million foreign tourists every year, a figure roughly equivalent to Spain's total population. This staggering influx of foreign visitors, though largely seasonal, is not only notably changing the face of rural Spain but has created a situation whereby the returned Spanish emigrant must compete with foreigners in his own country for some of those very improvements in life he had sought to achieve by his temporary expatriation abroad, particularly better housing.

CONCLUSION

Little more can be done here[16] than to point out that despite the visibly growing prosperity in rural Spain, more and more returned emigrants find their restlessness unsatisfied by their new television sets and tiled bathrooms. They move away permanently to the cities in Spain if they do not reemigrate abroad, for they have become used to an urban style of living. As their numbers increase, so too will their disaffection. Governmental agencies in Greece and Turkey are already operating programs designed to ease the economic readjustment of their returned emigrants, and Spain is expected to do the same. Such programs, however, should also stress easing the social as well as the economic adjustment of the returnees and acknowledge the fact that they are peasants no more.

NOTES

1. Juan J. Linz and Amando de Miguel, "Within Nation Differences and Comparisons: The Eight Spains," in *Comparing Nations*, ed. Richard L. Merritt and Stein Rokkan (New Haven: Yale University Press, 1966).

2. Carmelo Lison Tolosana, "Sobre áreas culturales en España," in *Ensayos de antropología social* (Madrid: Editorial Ayuso, 1973).

3. Juan Vicente Palerm, "Notas para una tipología de comunidades rurales," (Madrid, 1973, unpublished manuscript).

4. Ramon Menendez Pidal, *Los españoles en la historia* (Buenos Aires: Espasa-Calpe Argentina, 1959), p. 115.

5. Vicent Blasco Ibañez, *La Barraca*. (Valencia Spring: F. Sempre y compania, 1898).

6. Joseph Aceves, *Social Change in a Spanish Village* (Cambridge, Mass.: Schenkman Publishing Co., 1971).

7. Davydd J. Greenwood, "Tourism as an agent of change," *Ethnology* 11, no. 1 (1972).

8. Banco Español de Crédito, *Anuario del mercado español* (Madrid: el Banco, 1966), pp. 80-81.

9. Michael Kenny, "Parallel Power Structures in Castile, Spain: The Patron-Client Balance," in *Proceedings of the Mediterranean Sociological Conference*, ed. John J. Peristiany (Paris: Mouton, 1965).

10. See the superb novel *El Cacique* (Barcelona: Planeta, 1963) by the Catalan, Luis Romero.

11. M. A. Redclift, "The Future of Agriculture in a Spanish Pyrenean Village and the Decline of Communal Institutions" (London, 1969, unpublished manuscript).

12. Personal communication with Stanley Brandes, 1973.

13. George Foster, *Culture and Conquest* Viking Fund Publications in Anthropology, no. 27 (New York: Wenner-gren Foundation for Anthropological Research, 1960), p. 84.

14. See Juan J. Linz, "An Authoritarian Regime: Spain," in *Cleavages, Ideologies and Party Systems: Contributions to Comparative Political Sociology*, ed. E. Allardt and Y. Littunen (Helsinki, Transactions of the Westermarck Society, 1964).

15. Brinley Thomas, *Migration and Economic Growth* (Cambridge, England: 1954).

16. For a more detailed treatment of this subject, see Michael Kenny, "The Return of the Spanish Emigrant," *Nord Nytt* (Stockholm) 2 (1972).

THE POLITICS
OF CHURCH-STATE
RELATIONS IN SPAIN
Tad Szulc

"I'm an atheist, thank God," a Barcelonian once exclaimed, thus summing up the characteristically ambivalent Spanish attitude toward religion and the Roman Catholic Church. Officially, Spain is the "most Catholic of nations"; statistically, it is overwhelmingly Catholic. Under a 1953 concordat with the Vatican, Catholicism was again recognized as the official religion of Spain—the "true one"—and the Church was reconfirmed in its prewar privilege of owning property. In 1962 there were 42,129 churches in Spain, one for every 750 Spaniards. There were 33,352 priests and fathers of religious orders; 5,440 convents; 1,427 monasteries; 72,783 nuns; 29,873 monks; 510,077 pupils in women's religious educational institutions; and 332,052 pupils in the 1,698 men's religious institutions. These numbers have shrunk somewhat by the 1970s, particularly for seminary students, but they remain impressive. The vast hierarchy is headed by the Primate of Spain in Toledo, three other cardinals, thirteen archbishops (four of them also cardinals), fifty-one diocesan bishops, fourteen auxiliary bishops, one military archbishop (in charge of the chaplains), and one bishop heading military religious orders. It is a formidable structure that reaches from the village parish to the twelve permanent episcopal commissions, including one for radio and television, and the ruling National Episcopal Conference. Nevertheless, the 33 million nominal Spanish Catholics are deeply divided about their religion, and the Spanish Church is deeply divided about itself.

RELIGION AND ANTICLERICALISM

The religious division dates from the late 18th century, when anticlericalism first emerged as a militant movement in Spain. This anticlericalism was not born of atheism but of a profound feeling that the Spanish Church was not living up to its original spiritual teaching of universal justice. It was a reaction to the alliance between the Church, the monarchy, and the oppressive noble landlords. The Spaniard had always believed that he owned God, and the Church as well, and he simply felt betrayed. When he killed a priest or burned a church, therefore, he saw himself as purifying religion. The Spaniard is the genuine *Old Christian*, which is why he has rejected Protestantism as a possible alternative.

In 1967 a law on religious freedom was put into effect that required the registration of Protestant and Jewish congregations. Although there are reported to be over 150 Protestant missionaries in Spain from the United States alone, the impact of Protestantism on Spain is very small. Recent surveys indicates that approximately 98 percent of the Spanish population identifies itself as Roman Catholic, with the number of Protestants variously estimated to be in the neighborhood of 25,000-30,000.[1]

The intensity of devotion varies widely in Spain. A comprehensive national survey of Spanish attitudes on social issues that was undertaken in 1970 reported that 77 percent of Spanish housewives identified themselves as either "practicing" or "very good" Catholics. However, there was a significant number, 22 percent, who identified themselves as "not very practicing," "nonpracticing," or "indifferent."[2] Thus a process of turning away from religion seems once more to be occurring in Spain. This affects other groups in the population to an even greater extent than housewives. Some 56 percent of the university students indicated that they were only loosely tied to the Church, if at all, and the percentage rose to 64 among workers and employees.[3]

One Spanish sociologist makes a distinction between devotion, or the practice of religion, and faith.

> In Spain there is much devotion but little faith. Millions of Spaniards, and especially Spanish women, are devoted to the Virgen del Carmen, of Monserrat, of the Macarena; millions of women pray to Santa Rita, . . . thousands of students pray before their examinations, thousands of ill people offer candles to a particular saint asking for a cure. But is this faith?[4]

On the other hand a relative lack of faith does not mean that an individual Spaniard is an atheist or opposed to the church. A clear distinction must be made between anticlericalism, which does not question God, and atheism, which does. There are probably few atheists in mystical Spain. Passengers of Spanish airlines cross themselves before takeoff, although the chances are good that most of the men among them are not churchgoers. Spanish prostitutes wear religious medals around their necks. The Spanish shout of approval at a bullfight is *Olé!* from the Arabic *Wa-Allah!* which means, "Oh, God!" The bullfighter prays to his favorite saint before he goes into the ring. The name of God—*por Dios*—is invoked in every other sentence, both by churchgoers and by those who claim to be atheists.

THE LIBERAL AND THE CONSERVATIVE CHURCH

In Franco's new Spain, the Church (not the religion) is the major source of national controversy. Times have changed since 1937, when the Spanish hierarchy proclaimed, in an open letter to the bishops of the world, that the Nationalist "crusade" was "theologically just." Even in the 1950s the Spanish church was an almost monolithic pillar of the regime, along with the army, the National Movement, and the moneyed classes. Today, however, this pillar is badly cracked. The young clergy, inspired by the Vatican Council, is outspokenly opposed to the Franco regime and its political, economic, and social structure. The younger bishops are openly siding with the liberals. The conservative hierarchy, unable to cope with the rebellion, is not only hedging its bets but is adopting an increasingly antiregime attitude, as in the case of the official efforts in 1974 to expel from the country the Bishop of Bilbao for advocating greater freedom for the Basques. As a Spanish bishop remarked to the author, "We cannot afford to be nailed down to Franco's coffin." In other words, the Spanish Church has begun to realize that unless it adopts a more progressive attitude toward national life, it may face another anticlerical explosion when the Caudillo is gone. The hierarchy is painfully aware that church attendance has been plummeting and that the priesthood is no longer a desirable career in Spain.

Over time, the absolute number of the clergy and its ratio to the total Spanish population has been declining. In the 16th century as much as 25 percent of the adult population may have been in the clergy (including members of religious orders).[5] In the last 200 years the ratio of priests to population is reported to have declined over ninefold.[6]

In 1961 there were 21,615 men preparing to be ordained at Spain's 64 seminaries, but by 1967 the total had dropped to an estimated 15,000. In 1967 the seminaries in Barcelona, San Sebastián, and Seville were unable to graduate their students because of strikes against the superiors.

In the mid-1960s it would have been absurd to imagine a priest being arrested by the Franco regime; yet by 1970 arrests and trials of priests had become commonplace, as had the spectacle of priests and monks leading students and workers in antiregime demonstrations. The progressive clergy today is the nearest thing to an organized anti-Franco underground movement in Spain. Not surprisingly, official repression has daily been winning the movement new converts. The government has been so heavy-handed in dealing with rebels of all kinds that in recent years some bishops and archbishops have issued pastoral letters condemning the regime's repressive practices, along with its social policiès, or lack of them. In a Holy Year message on 1 April 1974, Barcelona's Narciso Cardinal Yubañy issued a ringing demand to the government to let the church "defend human rights."

FRANCO'S REACTION

Franco has shown himself singularly unresponsive to this growing rebellion. He has evidently chosen to ignore the profound spiritual considerations motivating what he regards simply as breaches of law and order. Having identified himself politically with the Catholic Kings, he has followed their religious example by punishing the new heretics in a way that has made even the Vatican wince. His own conventional displays of piety also have the royal touch. At the annual rites for the dead monarchs of Spain at the old Escorial monastery, Franco sits, not with his ministers in the front row of pews, but in a thronelike chair to the right of the main altar—on the same level as the officiants. He seems far from the reality of Spain's new Church.

FRANCO'S DOMINANCE OF THE CHURCH

Franco has dominated the Spanish Church since 1939, as he has dominated everything else in Spain. In fact, he made the Church a part of his regime, directly supporting it through grants and what amounted to the payment of priests' salaries.* In effect, the church had become an economic hostage of the regime, with the Spanish government providing subsidies that have been reported to total $95 million per year.[7]

To further strengthen ties between the church and the state, Franco included the senior cardinal in the Council of the Realm, the handpicked group without any real authority that, in 1969, rubber-stamped the selection of Prince Juan Carlos to be the future king. Three archbishops are ex officio members of the Cortes, and chaplains have been appointed not only to the armed forces but also to the Falange, the regime-run labor unions, and the schools.

The 1953 concordat with the Vatican guaranteed in effect that any bishop appointed to a see in Spain would be politically acceptable to the Spanish government. Under this arrangement, Franco submits six names to the Vatican and the Vatican selects three, from among whom Franco chooses the bishop.

---

*One of the first recommendations made by a group of rebel churchmen late in 1966 was that Spanish priests refuse to accept these salaries.

In the late 1960s, however, the question of the Pope's freedom to name bishops became a major point of controversy between Madrid and Rome. Even Spanish bishops began to demand a revision of the concordat to eliminate the political clause. However, Franco has followed the Spanish tradition of ignoring the Pope's wishes if they do not accord with the views or policies of Spain's temporal rulers. This centuries-long conflict has ranged from the sublime to the ridiculous: the Catholic Kings and Charles V turned a deaf ear to Papal entreaties for less passion and cruelty in carrying out the Inquisition, and later Spanish priests ignored a Vatican ban on their attendance at bullfights by watching them from behind the pillars of the bull ring.

THE "NEW" CHURCH

In recent years, protest has become crystallized among younger bishops inclined toward the liberal cause, church intellectuals impressed by the liberal ideas that emanated from the Vatican Council, and simple parish priests from the villages of Andalusia and the slums of Madrid to the factory districts of Bilbao and Barcelona. Regionalism, especially in the Catalonian and Basque areas, is another focus of confrontation. The priests stand firmly behind the regional groups, which are seeking at least cultural autonomy.

In 1970 I met an active participant in the rebellion of the "New Church" in Spain, a 33-year-old priest who had studied abroad for many years, spoke several foreign languages, and was well known and respected in Madrid's intellectual community. He was a sophisticated if somewhat cynical man, and he expressed an intellectual's contempt for the coarse politicians who make up most of the Spanish hierarchy. He said:

Unfortunately, our church is polluted with imbeciles in high places. I mean priests, bishops, archbishops, and cardinals who simply refuse to understand, or cannot understand, that the world and Spain have changed since the Civil War; that we have a new generation of people who are not going to put up with the pious nonsense they are dishing out. The new generation doesn't want to hear about 1936 and the "Catholic Crusade" of Franco. They don't want to be told that all a good Catholic has to do is go to Mass, confess himself once a week, and keep his mouth shut about everything else that is happening around him.

You must have heard all the lamentations of our bishops in their pastoral letters and sermons about the new wave of anticlericalism, de-Christianization, and alienation from the church. They complain that students and workers are turning their backs on the

Church and religion. Well, they are right about the backs being turned on the Church, but they are wrong that people reject religion. You see, we Spaniards are peculiar people. We can be against the church because it's no good, and still be for religion. When I say that bishops are imbeciles, I mean that they bring on anticlericalism and the alienation from the church by their own actions. They don't think, and they don't understand.

I happen to believe that, particularly with the coming of the Vatican Council, the church in Spain is at the crossroads. Either it will change its ways quickly and survive, or it will remain as it is and die with Franco. Then you'll have a wave of anticlericalism—not as violent, perhaps, but deeper—worse than we had in the thirties, when they burned the churches and killed the priests and nuns.* My private opinion is that the church in Spain can and should fulfill a positive and constructive role, on all the great changes that are occurring in our society.

One of the ecclesiastic centers of the "New Church" rebellion is the ancient Abbey of Montserrat, not far from Barcelona. It crowns a volcanic mountain 4,000 feet high, and much of it was built by the founders of the Benedictine Order in the year 986. Montserrat became an independent abbey in 1410 and has remained one ever since, in every sense of the word. In the 1960s the antiregime sentiment of the Montserrat Benedictines contrasted sharply with that of the Benedictines in charge of the great monastery at the Valley of the Fallen, who have the reputation of being reactionary and thoroughly pro-Franco. The Montserrat liberalism was in large measure inspired by Father Aurelio Escarré, the former abbot and a man of independent and original thought. Under him, the monks quietly began to encourage liberal attitudes in the Catalonian clergy and to advocate cultural autonomy for the Catalans. The abbey's monthly magazine, *Serra d'Or* (Golden Mountain), which emphasized Catalan culture and was, at the time, the only periodical regularly published in the Catalan language, was constantly in trouble with the censors in Madrid. Early in 1965 Abbot Escarré granted an interview to a Paris newspaper and spoke critically of the regime. Arrangements were made to remove him from the abbey, and he went to live in Milan in virtual exile. However, his successors have kept the Montserrat spirit alive.

---

*According to Hugh Thomas, 7,937 clergy, including 12 bishops, 283 nuns, 2,492 friars, and 5,255 priests, were killed during the Civil War.[8]

OPUS DEI

One of the elements of the Church in Spain is the Sacerdotal Society of the Holy Cross and Opus Dei, commonly known as Opus Dei (God's Work). It describes itself as an organization of Catholic men dedicated to a true Christian life and to good works. It has 50,000 members in 67 countries, in which it runs scores of schools, student homes, and neighborhood associations. In Spain it also has vast political power. Why Franco handed Opus Dei members such power, including key cabinet posts, has never been explained. In 1971 the Economic Planning Ministry, which directs the entire Spanish economy, was in the hands of Laureano López Rodó, the Foreign Ministry in the hands of Grégorio López Bravo, and the Education Ministry in the hands of José Luís Villar Palasi; all three were full-fledged Opus Dei members. The premier, Luís Carrero Blanco (murdered in 1973) was believed to be at least an Opus Dei "cooperator" (something like an associate member). The Information Minister, Alfredo Sánchez Bella, was close to the society, and his brother Florencio, a priest, was a director of the Opus Dei in Spain. After Carrero Blanco's death the new Premier, Carlos Arías Navarro, prevailed on Franco to dislodge most of the Opus Dei ministers.

Full members of Opus Dei, the numerarii, take vows of poverty, chastity, and obedience. They are expected to assign a large portion of their earnings to Opus Dei and to live modest lives.

Opus Dei members are guided by a small book of maxims called *Camino,* or "The Way," written by the order's founder in 1933. It is now in its 90th edition in 22 languages, with total sales of over 2 million copies.[9] One critic has likened the book's message to an ounce of St. Ignatius and a pound of Dale Carnegie, because of the organization's concentration on "techniques, tactics and neo-masonic mutual aid."[10] In fact, one Catholic phosopher has described the order's religious message as neither good nor bad, simply nonexistent.

The society insists that its members are not bound in any way by the politics of its directors and that in all temporal matters they enjoy "the greatest possible freedom." This claim is borne out to a considerable extent by the fact that the membership includes both top officials of Franco's regime and some of its strongest opponents. A Madrid afternoon newspaper owned by Opus Dei members was repeatedly seized, fined by the government, and finally closed for its outspoken criticism. A domestic news agency, likewise controlled by members of the society, has also been an outlet for repressive government policies. Opus Dei members have been arrested for antiregime activities.

The society's enemies see it as a sinister organization bent on controlling Spain's political and economic life. Although Opus Dei has no more than 25,000 full-fledged members in Spain, plus perhaps 100,000 cooperators and sympathizers, it is considered a formidable force. Catholics of other persuasions, ranging from pro-Franco conservatives to opposition Christian Democrats and church rebels, tend to regard Opus Dei with vast suspicion, if not downright hate. In

Franco's camp, the Falangists and monarchists fear and resent it as a powerful rival. Except for Opus Dei figures who themselves oppose the regime, the opposition thinks of Opus Dei as part of a Franco conspiracy to perpetuate his type of rule after his death. They point to the fact that Opus Dei member López Rodó and Opus Dei cooperator Carrero Blanco were, for a time, the principal contenders for the premiership whenever that post was reactivated.

Opus Dei has been variously accused of being a "white Freemasonry," a "neocapitalist" scheme, a church Mafia, and a latter-day version of the Society of Jesus. The Jesuits and other religious orders abhor it, too, because they see Opus Dei as competition even though it is a secular organization. Being demonologically-minded, millions of Spaniards are very simply afraid of Opus Dei.

The society remains an exclusive club, with members or supporters to be found among the country's top executives, bankers, economists, and publishers. It is also believed to control vast wealth, but how this wealth is amassed, used, or manipulated is among Spain's best-kept secrets. It is known that a former naval captain is Opus Dei's chief financial officer and works out of the society's central office for Spain on Madrid's Calle de Diego de León, but very few outsiders have met him. Well-informed Spaniards have reason to believe that Opus Dei owns or controls at least two major banks in Spain, as well as an unknown number of other profitable businesses. Spokesmen for Opus Dei readily admit that the society has financial holdings that allow it to run the University of Navarra in Pamplona, as well as schools and other organizations, but they refuse to confirm or deny allegations concerning the magnitude of its portfolio. Spanish businessmen claim, however, that Opus Dei is acquisitive and has a precise program for taking over attractive properties.

The society was founded in 1928 by Josemaría Escrivá de Balaguer y Albas, an Aragonese priest who, at the time, administered a parish in one of Madrid's poorest areas. Presently a monsignor, he has lived in Rome since 1946 but makes regular visits to Spain. It was during one of these visits, in the autumn of 1966, that the society's efficient director of public affairs drove me to an Opus Dei residence near Barcelona where Monsignor Escrivá was spending that day. The gate to the mansion's garden was guarded by quiet young men who looked like karate experts, and other young men patrolled the grounds and steps of the building.

Monsignor Escrivá is rotund and expansive, but his almost jocular demeanor seems to conceal powerful inner tensions and a strong vein of mysticism. He was 65 years old at the time I met him, but he looked and acted younger. The only other people present during my two-hour talk with him were Opus Dei's secretary-general, the Reverend Alvaro del Portillo, once a highway engineer, and the public affairs director. Monsignor Escrivá embarked on reminiscences, anecdotes, and explanations of Opus Dei. He spoke of his days as a parish priest in Madrid and of his traumatic experience during the Civil War, when the Loyalists killed another priest believing it was he. Speaking of his life in Rome, he said with a little laugh that in the basement of his palazzo a sarcophagus awaited his death and burial.

Monsignor Escrivá is a skilled conversationalist. He successfully avoided revealing his political beliefs and his sentiments about Franco's regime. "Opus Dei has no political or economic orientation in Spain or elsewhere," he said, adding that Opus Dei members "are led by Christ's teachings always to defend personal freedoms and the rights of all men. . . . This includes the right to be treated as befits free men and citizens." He also said that Opus Dei was charged with being political perhaps because of the "subconscious prejudice engendered by a one-party mentality . . . in politics or in the spiritual realm." Were these criticisms of the Franco regime?

Monsignor Escrivá shed no light on Franco's favoritism toward Opus Dei members. Had the Caudillo been attracted by the society's spiritual message (which seems unlikely, given his pragmatism), or had he been won over by the professional talents of the administrators who are members of the Opus Dei (which appears more reasonable)? Whatever the explanation, Franco defended some of his Opus Dei men even through the Matesa affair of 1969, which was Spain's greatest modern political and financial scandal.

Matesa, a Catalonian textile machinery company, was owned by José Villa Reyes, who was a close friend of certain Opus Dei figures. The company had been granted $200 million in export credits by the government before it was discovered that most of its exports were fictitious. Matesa declared bankruptcy, and Franco immediately fired the finance minister, who was not an Opus Dei man, and the minister of commerce and the president of the Bank of Spain, who were. All three were indicted, and Opus Dei's enemies happily anticipated the end of the society's sway in the affairs of state. Surprisingly, however, Franco kept on Opus Dei member López Bravo, who, as the minister of industries at the time, was at least partly responsible for extending the credits to Matesa. The education minister, Villar Palasi, an Opus Dei man who was close to Matesa's owner and had been his lawyer, also escaped unscathed. López Rodó, Spain's economic czar and then Opus Dei's brightest star, was never touched by the scandal. In 1971 the Spanish Supreme Court ruled that there were no grounds to indict Villar Palasi and López Rodó. In the same year Franco fired the military governor of Granada for criticizing Opus Dei publicly. In 1973, however, Carrero reduced the influence of the society somewhat, and after his assassination even López Rodó lost his cabinet slot. So the Opus Dei mystery persists. (Further discussion of Opus Dei appears in the third section of Chapter 8.)

CURRENT CHURCH-STATE RELATIONS

There is much less mystery surrounding the positions taken by other elements within the Spanish Church. In fact, in recent years various branches have been speaking out with embarrassing frequency. When Franco held a nationwide referendum on a new Spanish consititution in December 1966, the hierarchy of the Church astounded a great many Spaniards, and presumably the regime itself, by issuing a pastoral letter urging Catholics to arrive "freely" at their decision on how to vote. The regime had counted on either the hierarchy's endorsement of the constitution or at least its silence. Considering the formidable government propaganda campaign for "yes" votes, the church's stand seemed almost subversive.

The battle between the progressive churchmen and the Franco regime has continued, and by 1974 the Spanish church was as deeply split as it has ever been in modern history.

In September 1971 the first assembly of bishops and priests ever held in Spain took place. This was a larger body than the permanent Spanish Episcopal Conference, and during the two years of preparation for this conference, surveys were carried out and meetings held involving over 15,000 priests throughout Spain. The assembly recommended the severing of links between the church and the state. It specifically recommended an end to acceptance of official posts by the clergy, a drastic reduction in the number of chaplains assigned to official bodies such as the labor syndicates, and separation of military chaplains from the army hierarchy. The assembly also criticized the quality of Catholic life in Spain, saying that Spanish Christians "must be preoccupied by the insufficient scope given human rights and the persistence of grave economic and social inequalities." It favored a more active role for the church in society, including the right to comment on political matters, since it was alleged that silence on such inequalities makes the church a guilty accomplice.

The most significant position taken by the assembly was that by which the body declared that the Church might have acted wrongly during the Civil War when it issued a manifesto stating that Franco's uprising was a theologically justified crusade. The resolution read, "We humbly recognize and regret the fact that we did not play our true role as ministers of reconciliation among our people when they were divided by a fratricidal war." Although this resolution did not receive the two-thirds vote required to make it an official motion of the assembly, it was passed by a substantial majority.

The Vatican supported this meeting of church clergy, although various conservative elements of the clergy within Spain did not. The Spanish government also took exception to the assembly's independent stand. In his traditional end-of-the-year message, Franco warned the Church that antigovernment actions would not be tolerated. "The state," he said, "could not cross its arms before the determined temporal attitudes of some clergymen." Nevertheless, in a 1974 message Barcelona's Cardinal Yubany urged the regime to allow "Christ to exercise a purifying effect on the society." "Do not crucify him again," he said.

The conflict between the Franco government and the Spanish Church has continued and will probably not be resolved until a new concordat is drawn up to replace the 1953 document, which is now outdated, or until there is a basic change in the Spanish political system. The existing concordat has been largely overtaken by events, particularly by the deliberations of Vatican II, which ruled against political interference by governments in appointing bishops. Priests were also asked to renounce their civil positions. Negotiations to modify or replace the concordat began in early 1968, when Pope Paul wrote Franco concerning Vatican II. A draft revision allowing Franco to veto the Pope's choice of bishops was rejected by the Spanish Church hierarchy in early 1971. Discussions have since moved from the unofficial to the official level, but the cabinet change in the wake of Carrero Blanco's assassination and a serious dispute between the new Arías Navarro government and the bishop of Bilbao over an alleged attack by the latter in a sermon urging greater freedom for the Basques may prove to be serious impediments. The government threatened the bishop with expulsion and reportedly told the Vatican that it was considering cancellation of the present condordat, thus ending all privileges and state subsidies to the Spanish church and clergy. By lobbying behind the scenes and even discussing the matter with Franco's wife, the bishops were able to prevail over the hard-line conservative elements in the government. Franco temporarily backed away from an open split with the Spanish Church and the Vatican, leaving the impression that the liberal majority of bishops in Spain's postconciliar Church had won a significant and perhaps lasting victory. Marcelo Cardinal Gonzales of Toledo, the Primate of Spain, was frankly on the liberal side.

A fundamental division now exists within the Church itself between those clergy who view the institution primarily as a bulwark of the government and those who see it as a source of strength in creating a new society. The depth of this split is suggested by a recent survey of priests in Madrid that showed that roughly 62 percent of the priests in the Spanish capital were critical of the social and political conduct of the Catholic Church.[11] The junior clergy often come from the poorer economic classes and have fewer political inhibitions. The liberal bishops themselves, however, are engaged in an effort to catch up with other more advanced sectors of the lower clergy. A paradoxical situation exists in which the bishops draw much of their present power from the very concordat they oppose, since it allows them a certain freedom of maneuvering and guarantees various rights and privileges.

In the long run, the real danger to Spanish Catholicism may not come from attacks by the conservative wing of the Church, although resistance by reactionary elements in the clergy must not be underestimated. As one observer has put it, the real danger may come from a "neo-clerical triumphalism among the conciliar bishops, who do not seem to be fully aware of the dechristianization that threatens a traditionally Christian society, like Spain, perhaps more radically than a more secularized (and, therefore, better immunized) one."[12] In any event, the Church is bound to play a major role in the overall evolution of Spain toward the modern age.

NOTES

1. "A Survey of Europe" (London: The Readers Digest Association Limited, 1970), p. 88.

2. Fomento de Estudios Sociales y de Sociología Aplicado, *Informe socio-logico sobre la situación social de España, 1970* (Madrid: Euramerica, 1970), p. 442.

3. Ibid.

4. Jose Gironella, *Cien españoles y Dios* (Barcelona: Ediciónes Nauta, 1969), p. 257, cited in Charles F. Gallagher, "Religion, Class, and Family in Spain," *American Universities Field Staff Reports*, West Europe Staff Reports, West Europe Series 8, no. 4 (1973): 3.

5. William Ebenstein, *Church and State in Franco Spain* (Princeton, N.J.: Center of International Studies, 1960), p. 11.

6. Ibid., p. 22.

7. Alain Woodrow, "The Candle and the Stick: Post-Conciliar Catholicism: Spain," *Commonweal* 98 (13 April 1973), p. 130.

8. See Hugh Thomas, *The Spanish Civil War* (New York: Harpers, 1961), p. 173.

9. "Opus Dei: Holy Mafia," *Church and State* (October 1970), p. 9

10. "Oeropus Dei," *The Economist* 222, no. 6437 (7 January 1967), p. 31.

11. "Unpredictable Priests," *The Economist* 240, no. 6683 (25 September 1971).

12. Alain Woodrow, *op. cit.*, p. 131.

6

REGIONAL
NATIONALISM:
THE BASQUES
AND CATALANS
Stanley G. Payne

REGIONALISM AND THE FRANCO REGIME

Regional nationalism has proven to be one of the three or four most difficult civic problems in 20th-century Spain, because of the peculiar weight of regionalist interests in Spanish affairs. The modern central policy of Spain has tended to a large degree to rest on the support and leadership of its central regions; that is, its north-central, central, and southern regions, those that comprised the historic kingdom of Castile. Until recently, however, these were among the least modernized areas of Spain, both socially and economically. Spain's geographic position, its lack of involvement in the main European diplomatic and geopolitical rivalries, its physical obstacles to internal unity, and the undynamic pace of its modern culture all discouraged the development of any strong sense of unified Spanish nationalism. The social and economic transformation came to be led above all by Catalonia and the Basque territory, regions that to some extent had distinct languages and cultural and civic traditions. It was more the conflicts and stresses of modernization, however, than the weight of historical tradition that led to the emergence of modern Basque and Catalan nationalism in the 20th century. The genesis and history of both movements have been extremely complex, but their basic rationale has been that Catalonia and the Basque country constitute separate national cultures that are repressed and exploited by the Spanish system in politics, economics, and culture. The height of regionalist dissidence occurred in the years 1934-37 and was a major factor in the coming of the Civil War, though the more conservative sectors of both regionalist movements came to support Franco's Spanish Nationalists in 1936.

The nationalism of the Franco government was essentially defensive and counterrevolutionary, a response to the divisiveness and revolutionary antitraditionalism of the Left, more than the expression of a spontaneous and unified assertion of Spanish nationalism on the peninsular or international level. Thus the government has proven psychologically and culturally unable to absorb the sympathies of regional nationalists on the peripheries of Spain, despite, or because of, the coercive means at its disposal. Nonetheless, since the regionalist movements have been essentially lower-middle-class and nonrevolutionary, they played only a secondary role in the major resistance against the regime during the 1940s, and regionalist opposition only entered the limelight in the late 1960s due to the growth of a radical opposition among the Basques.

The future strength of regionalism will depend in good measure on the continuation of structural uniqueness and the propagation of regional culture. The processes of social and economic change that made the Basque country one of the two most modern and distinctive regions in Spain, at first accelerated under the Franco regime. Thanks in part to the care taken by the nationalists, the Civil War did not wreck Basque industry, and the two industrial provinces immediately reassumed their elite role in the Spanish economy. All special tax advantages for Vizcaya and Guipuzcoa were lost, but this proved to be little handicap.

Navarre and Alava alone of the 52 Spanish provinces have enjoyed certain special rights of autonomous corporative (right-wing) self-government and special tax provisions under the Franco regime.[1] The advantages from this began to accrue during the general Spanish economic expansion of the 1950s, when both provinces adopted an accelerated program of attracting new industry and soon began to lose their overwhelmingly rural character. Moreover, by the 1960s Navarre had developed the best provincial road network in Spain and in some respects enjoyed superior government services, particularly in health facilities.

During the late 1940s and early 1950s, the industrial base and technical skills of the economies of Vizcaya and Guipuzcoa, together with certain incentives of the system of autarchy then in effect, enabled those provinces not merely to sustain their lead but perhaps to widen the gap even further. Precise figures for earlier periods are not available, but the middle years of the 20th century may have been the time of widest lead in the per income of the Basques over the general Spanish norms. During the 1950s and 1960s the productivity and income of Basque industry continued to increase, but at a rate lower than the norm of other developing regions, and the proportionate Basque income no longer greatly overshadowed that of the other advanced provinces. (See Table 6.1.)

TABLE 6.1

Evolution of Regional per Capita Income Compared to the Spanish Average, 1949-67
(average individual income = 100)

Region	1949	1960	1967
Basque country	180	165	148
Barcelona	133	154	142
Madrid	133	151	153
Asturias	148	116	96
The rest of Catalonia	122	116	122
The Balearics	111	108	128
Navarre	116	117	125
The Levant	101	116	96
Inner Galicia	79	58	64

Source: Fundación FOESSA, *Informe sociológico sobre la situación social de España, 1970* (Madrid: la Fundación, 1970), p. 338, Table 4.59.

SHIFTS IN REGIONAL INCOME DISTRIBUTION

This dramatic change in income balances among several of the more developed regions was a result of the industrialization and diversification of the economy of Madrid and several other provinces. State planning was partially responsible for this, since government investment was systematically shunted away from the Basque country. In part this was intended to elevate the most backward regions, but this was not the entire reason, since state investment reenforced growth in the other developed regions much more than in the Basque country, as Table 6.2, concerning the place of state industrial investment in various regions, shows.

Despite the proportionate change in gross income figures compared with Madrid, the western Basque provinces continued to enjoy the strongest overall

TABLE 6.2

Number of National Institute of Industry (INI) Employees per 1,000 Active Employees in Industry and Services, by Region, 1965

Region	Number of INI Employees
Murcia	29
Coastal Galicia	28
Madrid	26
Aragon	25
West Andalusia	25
Barcelona	15
Navarre	12
Central Spain	10
Basque country	0.4

Source: Fundación FOESSA, *Informe sociológico subre la situación social de España, 1970* (Madrid: la Fundación, 1970), p. 341, Table 4.63.

TABLE 6.3

Per Capita Disposable Income in Pesetas, 1967

Province	Disposable Income
Guipuzcoa	57,154
Vizcaya	54,545
Alava	53,028
Barcelona	52,377
Madrid	51,623
Navarre	47,266
Average	39,789

Source: Banco de Bilbao, *Renta Nacional de España y su distribución provincial* (Bilbao: el Banco, 1967), 29, in Milton M. da Silva, "Modernization and Ethnic Conflict: The Case of the Basques," *Comparative Politics* 7, no. 2 (January 1975): 240.

TABLE 6.4

Distribution of Active Population by Occupation

Region	Agriculture and Fishing	Industry	Services
Madrid	5	40	55
Barcelona	5	56	39
Basque country	14	55	31
Navarre	35	36	29
Inner Galicia	67	15	18
Extremadura	60	20	20

Source: Fundación FOESSA, *Informe sociológico sobre la situación social de España, 1970* (Madrid: la Fundación, 1970), p. 172, Table 3.64.

financial and industrial position in Spain. The proportionate number of individual bank and savings accounts was greater than anywhere else, and after corrections were made for taxation and indebtedness, the per capita "disposable" income was still higher than anywhere else, including Madrid, according to a 1967 study of the Banco de Bilbao. (See Table 6.3.)

As late as 1964 Barcelona and the three northwestern Basque provinces were the only parts of Spain in which the majority of the active population was employed in industry, as indicated in Table 6.4.

By 1971, when the average proportion of agrarian workers to Spain's entire active population was 25 percent, the figures for Vizcaya were 7 percent; Guipuzcoa, 1 percent; Alava, 15 percent; and Navarre, 26 percent.[2] Conversely in terms of the proportion of the total active population employed by firms with more than 100 employees, the Spanish average was 12.8 percent, while in Vizcaya it was 28.2 percent; Guipuzcoa, 28.1 percent; Alava, 22.7 percent; and Navarre, 12.1 percent.[3]

DEMOGRAPHIC CHANGE AND IMMIGRATION

Primarily as a result of steadily advancing industrialization, the population has continued to increase rapidly.

The Basque percentage of the total Spanish population also continued to climb steadily (Table 6.5), though not so dramatically as the population of the provinces of Madrid and Barcelona, as shown in Table 6.6.

TABLE 6.5

Population of the Basque Provinces, 1945-68

Province	Population 1945	Population 1960	Population 1968	Number of Persons per Square Kilometer
Alava	117,500	138,934	202,891	51
Guipuzcoa	370,114	478,337	660,208	264
Vizcaya	579,978	754,383	1,086,369	375
Navarre	347,369	402,042	443,714	40

Sources: Pedro González Blasco, "Modern Nationalism in Old Nations as a Consequence of Earlier State-Building: The Case of the Basques in Spain" in W. Bell and Walter E. Freeman, ed., Ethnicity and Nationbuilding (Beverly Hills: Sage Publications, 1974), Table 1; and Anuario estadístico (Madrid: Instituro Nacional de Estadistica, 1970), pp. 477-78.

TABLE 6.6

Population, by Region, as a Percentage of Total Population

Region	1887	1920	1950	1960	1965	1968	1971
Madrid	3.9	5.0	6.7	8.6	10.0	10.3	11.5
Barcelona	5.1	6.3	8.0	9.5	10.6	11.1	11.6
Basque country	2.9	3.6	3.8	4.5	5.2	5.3	5.8
Navarre	1.7	1.5	1.4	1.3	1.4	1.3	1.3
Valencian region	8.3	8.2	8.3	8.2	8.7	8.7	8.9
Coastal Galicia	6.0	5.8	5.8	5.5	5.5	5.3	5.2
Inner Galicia	4.8	3.9	3.5	3.1	2.8	2.7	2.5

Source: Amando de Miguel and Juan Salcedo, Dinámica del desarrollo industrial de las regiones españoles (Madrid: Tecnos, 1972), p. 52.

TABLE 6.7

Total Number of Immigrants, by Province, 1901-69

Province	1901-10	1911-20	1921-30	1931-40	1941-50	1951-60	1961-69
Alava	−9,203	−7,293	−5,210	−1,350	203	7,073	32,653
Barcelona	57,112	203,174	376,081	95,597	241,906	479,613	458,528
Guipuzcoa	6,159	8,173	12,732	3,964	16,567	48,754	59,909
Madrid	72,161	158,682	219,650	106,899	275,523	411,697	506,333
Navarre	−25,959	−14,485	−21,182	−10,300	−16,836	−20,499	2,655
Vizcaya	−2,958	18,997	18,290	−1,350	18,988	96,399	127,821

Source: Fundación FOESSA, *Informe sociológico sobre la situación social de España, 1970* (Madrid: la Fundación, 1970), p. 580, Table 8.31.

As was true before the Civil War, much of the growth of the "Basque population" has been not really Basque but the product of massive immigration, mainly from other provinces of northern Spain. Immigration thus accelerated enormously after 1950. Total immigration into the three provinces from 1951 to 1960 was 152,226 and reached 220,383 for the years 1961 to 1969.

There has been a notable increase in the proportion of young people in the Basque population during the 1950s and 1960s. In 1940 the proportion of inhabitants of the Basque country less than fifteen years of age was 27.3 percent, compared with 29.9 for all of Spain, and the proportion had remained similar in 1950; yet by 1965 the proportion of children in the Basque country had climbed to 30 percent, compared with a Spanish average of 27.3 percent. The only other regions with more than 30 percent were traditionally backward, high-birthrate areas such as Andalusia and the Canary Islands. The figure for Barcelona remained consistently 6 to 7 percent below the national average, and the figure for Navarre about 1 percent below.[4]

In general the Basque municipalities have maintained and improved upon the superior level of local services that they developed earlier in the century,[5] but nonetheless, rapid urbanization has made it difficult to extend educational facilities at the rate needed, and the same differences by region were noticeable in the 1960s as at the beginning of the century. By 1965 the total percentage of Spanish children between six and thirteen years of age enrolled in school was 82.3. This level was significantly exceeded only in some of the better organized semirural provinces. Madrid, Barcelona, Alava, Guipuzcoa, and Vizcaya only approximated the Spanish average, while Navarre exceeded it by 5 percent.[6]

CHURCH AFFILIATION

The influence of the Church has declined in the industrialized provinces, though it has remained little changed in Navarre. Even though their indices of religiosity have fallen well below those of Navarre, Guipuzcoa and Vizcaya remain much more Catholic than the other highly urbanized or industrialized regions of Spain as indicated in Table 6.8. If the figures for the Basque country

TABLE 6.8

Percentage of Population Who Declare Themselves "Practicing Catholics," by Region

Region	Number of "Practicing Catholics"
Navarre	95
Inner Galicia	93
Murcia	91
Baleares	89
Old Castile	87
Catalonia, including Barcelona	86
Aragon	86
Leon	82
Basque country	80
Asturias	76
Center	75
West Andalusia	74
East Andalusia and Extremadura	71
Coastal Galicia	68
Levant	67
Madrid	64
Barcelona	58

Source: Fundación FOESSA, *Informe sociológico sobre la situación social de España, 1970* (Madrid: la Fundación, 1970), p. 449.

were broken down to differentiate native Basque from non-Basque families, the percentage of practicing Catholics among the former would undoubtedly be higher. Over all, the figures are probably somewhat too high, but at least they give some measurement of continuing regional differences.

Navarre was the only province in Spain that maintained the same ratio of total population to priests, 273 to 1, between 1915 and 1967. In the other Basque provinces together, the ratio rose from 331 to 575, and in Spain as a whole it grew from 535 to 910.[7]

The 1970 FOESSA (Formento de Estudios Sociales y de Sociologia Aplicada) study constructed a "felicity calculus" to measure the degree of contentment in various regions, the results of which are given in Table 6.9.

TABLE 6.9

Index of Felicity of Housewives, by Region

Region	Index of Felicity	Percent who Consider Themselves "Very Happy"	Regional per Capita Income Rank
Navarre	.85	60	8
Baleares	.85	58	4
The rest of Catalonia	.85	55	7
Barcelona	.84	52	2
Basque country	.81	45	3
Asturias	.80	50	5
Aragon	.78	35	9
Levant	.76	42	6
Castile	.76	33	11
Center	.76	31	16
Madrid	.75	39	1
Murcia	.72	23	12
Coastal Galicia	.70	27	14
West Andalusia	.69	34	10
East Antalusia	.69	30	13
Inner Galicia	.69	20	17
Leon	.66	22	15

Source: Fundación FOESSA, *Informe sociológico sobre la situación social de España, 1970* (Madrid: la Fundacion 1970), p. 623, Table 9.7.

Though the Basque provinces have achieved great economic success during the past generation, their future identity as genuinely "Basque," especially in the industrialized provinces, is open to doubt. The amount of immigration has been so great that by 1966 only 62 percent of the heads of households in the Basque country had been born there,[8] and a small minority of these were not originally of Basque families. Only the provinces of Madrid and Barcelona had a lower proportion of native-born heads of families.

PROVINCIAL DIALECTS

The decline in the use of Euskera, the language of the Basques, has been much greater than the decline of the separate languages of other regions, as shown in Table 6.10. Urbanization is perhaps as important a cause of this decline as immigration. The FOESSA study found that 82 percent of rural housewives could speak the language, but only 51 percent of housewives in cities between 10,000 and 100,000 inhabitants, and only 19 percent in the large cities.

Whereas Galician, Catalan, and the Catalan provincial dialects are functional Romance languages easily adapted to contemporary cultural and technological requirements, Euskera is extremely hard, either to learn or adapt. Non-Catalan speaking immigrants to Catalonia not infrequently achieve some

TABLE 6.10

Percentage of Housewives Familiar with Regional Languages

Region	Understand	Speak	Read	Write
Galicia	96	92	43	24
Balearic Islands	94	91	51	10
Catalonia	90	77	62	38
Valencia	88	69	46	16
Basque country	49	46	25	12

Source: Fundación FOESSA, *Informe sociológico sobre la situación social de España, 1970* (Madrid: la Fundacion 1970), p. 1305 Table 18.46

degree of familiarity with Catalan and tend to become "Catalanized" culturally and psychologically, at least in part.[9] This process is encouraged by the fact that Catalan attitudes are broader and encourage assimilation, whereas Basque loyalties have always been more exclusive and particularistic. Moreover, immigrants into the Basque country come predominantly from the more literate provinces of northern Spain and possess a stronger Castilian culture than have the semiliterate immigrants from the less-developed provinces of southeastern Spain who have composed the bulk of immigrants into Catalonia during the past two or three generations. Conversely, though the rate of marriage of Basques with non-Basques has been somewhat higher than that of Catalans with non-Catalans, the consequence may be to discourage rather than encourage assimilation and lead to further loss of Basque identity, given the linguistic and cultural problems involved.[10]

Another marked difference is that in Catalonia the use of Catalan tends to be associated with upward mobility, and knowledge of the regional language increases according to income and social status. The situation is almost the reverse in the Basque country, where knowledge of Euskera is highest among the lower- and middle-class sectors and lowest among the wealthy and well educated.[11] This serves further to explain why no more than 12 percent of the Basque population is actually able to write in Basque.

Catalan and also Galician have remained more functional languages, useful in current affairs. By contrast, most Basque mothers consider it desirable but not really necessary for their children to learn Euskera in order to function in contemporary society, as illustrated in Table 6.11.

TABLE 6.11

**Attitudes of Housewives toward Their Children
Speaking the Regional Language
(in percent)**

Region	Would Like	Believe It Necessary
Catalonia	97	87
Balearic Islands	91	75
Valencian region	78	50
Galicia	73	49
Basque country	69	31

Source: Fundación FOESSA, *Informe sociológico sobre la situación social de España, 1970* (Madrid: la Fundacion 1970) p. 1306 Table 18 49.

The centralized, Castilian-language educational system of modern Spain has steadily discouraged regional identity, and this trend became much more severe under the Franco regime. During the first years after the Civil War, publication in the regional languages was prohibited almost altogether, and no form of pedagogy in any language other than Castilian was permitted. In Barcelona, street signs at first insisted that Catalans "speak the language of the Empire!"

This situation changed slowly with the relaxation of government restrictions during the 1950s, and regional cultural activity enjoyed a considerable degree of official tolerance after the Galician Manuel Fraga Iribarne became Minister of Information in 1962. During the 1960s Catalan cultural activity expanded enormously,[12] and there were marked revivals in Valencia and Galicia. Basque cultural work also increased notably, though distinctly less than in the case of Catalonia. Whereas nearly all new Catalan cultural publications appeared in Catalan, most new material on Basque history and culture was published in Castilian.

Even under conditions of partial tolerance, cultural proselytization was handicapped by the fact that, except in Guipuzcoa, most schoolteachers in the Basque country were ignorant of Euskera. This was as true of educationally autonomous Alava and Navarre as of centralized Vizcaya, since in the former provinces use of the regional language seemed in danger of vanishing altogether. According to one survey of unspecified data (presumably from the 1960s), Euskera was unknown by 85 percent of the schoolteachers of Alava, 76 percent of those in Vizcaya, 74 percent of those in Navarre, and 19 percent of those in Guipuzcoa.[13]

A drive emerged in the 1960s to open *ikastolas,* parttime Euskera language schools that could give an hour or two of instruction daily. By 1970, more *ikastolas* were in operation than at any previous time in Basque history, but they reached less than 20,000 students: seventy-five were operating in Guipuzcoa with 11,000 pupils; forty in Viscaya with 6,000; thirteen in Alava with 350; and ten in Navarre with an unknown number of pupils.[14] Because of their limited function the long-range influence of the *ikastolas* is problematic. The potentially most far-reaching step was taken by the Diputación de Navarra in 1967 when it approved a plan to have Euskera taught half an hour per day within its autonomous provincial educational system.[15]

BASQUE NATIONALISM

During the 1950s and 1960s, nationalist sentiment in the Basque country remained strong among the same elements that had supported it most directly in the 1930s, the farmers and white-collar workers of the lower middle class and the shopkeepers and smaller entrepreneurs, together with minority elements of skilled workers and/or native Basque Catholics among the urban lower classes. The upper Basque bourgeoisie, on the other hand, had if anything become even more closely associated with the Spanish system and its Madrid connections than before the Civil War. The conservative Basque elite has enjoyed preferential treatment in the economy of Spain under Franco, and the protected position of established Basque industry has produced stronger autarchist-Spanish nationalist feelings among wealthy Basque entrepreneurs than among Spanish businessmen in general. In a study of Spanish businessmen published in 1963, Juan Linz and Amando de Miguel found that 71 percent of the industrial elite in Valencia and Cádiz favored economic integration in Europe, compared with 62 percent of the elite of Madrid but only 45 percent of that of Vizcaya. Compared with business-men elsewhere, it was found that the leaders of Vizcayan heavy industry were more dependent on the Spanish national market, had more links with the central Spanish financial elite, and as a group were more elderly.

Industrial workers have remained dissatisfied and dissident, although in Guipuzcoa and Vizcaya they constitute one of the best-paid sectors of the Spanish labor force. Their traditions of strong union organization and opposition activity have made the workers in the Basque country one of the three or four significant focal points of worker unrest in Franco Spain, but amid the depoliti-cized environment of the past generation, their discontent, like the discontent of most Spanish workers, has been focused on economic rather than on politico-ideological issues. In fact, the suppressed political section of the 1970 FOESSA study* found that in Spain as a whole skilled workers are the least politicized sector of the general Spanish urban population. (See Table 6.12.) The same study found that half the population preferred some form of continuation of the present political system. (See Table 6.13.) Workers were found to be the sector that most preferred political continuity. (See Table 6.14.) Nonetheless, if the sample had been taken exclusively in the Basque country, it is possible that a somewhat greater degree of political disaffection might have been registered, due to particularistic attitudes in the region, the background of worker organization, and even the general level of prosperity. Even so, the above generalizations hold for much of the population of the Basque provinces, though probably to a lesser degree. The same study showed that most voters would prefer a Christian or Social Democratic Party to the Falange. (See Table 6.15.)

Since the 1950s, the discontented and protorevolutionary class, as is normally the case, has not been primarily the industrial workers but rather the radical intelligentsia, including in this case the ultraliberal sector of the younger clergy. During the 1960s the Basque radical intelligentsia became the most

---

*This section of the FOESSA Study on Political Attitudes was written by Amando de Miguel and would have comprised pp. 371-432 of the volume. Mimeographed copies of the data have circulated in Spain.

TABLE 6.12

Index of Political Inertia

	Index
High school students	.34
University graduate students	.19
Lawyers	.16
Doctors	.25
High-level employees	.26
Low-level employees	.36
Skilled workers	.41
Unskilled workers	.29

Source: Fundación FOESSA, *Informe sociológico sobre la situación social de España, 1970* (Madrid: la Fundación, 1970).

TABLE 6.13

Political System Preferred after Franco

System Preferred	Number	Percentage
As now	149	29.8
Monarchy	104	20.8
Republic	247	49.4

Source: Fundación FOESSA, *Informe sociológico sobre la situación social de España, 1970* (Madrid: la Fundación, 1970).

TABLE 6.14

Political System Preferred after Franco, by Vocations
(in percent)

System Preferred	Students	Lawyers	Employees	Doctors	Workers
Present Regime	1	8	37	20	55
Regency	4	5	6	9	4
Bourbon Monarchy	11	23	5	8	5
Carlist Monarchy	3	—	1	1	—
Monarchy	5	10	7	19	6
Republic	76	53	45	43	30

Source: Fundación FOESSA, *Informe Sociológico sobre la situatión social de España, 1970* (Madrid: la Fundación, 1970).

TABLE 6.15

Parties Preferred after Franco

Party	Number	Percentage
Movimiento-Falange	126	21.0
Christian Democratic and Social Democratic	314	52.4
Socialist	98	16.3
Carlist	12	2.0
Nationalist	12	2.0
Other	43	7.3

Source: Fundación FOESSA, *Informe sociológica sobre la situación social de España, 1970* (Madrid: la Fundación, 1970).

dissident element in Spain because of a complex combination of factors, including the greater conflict between problems of values and identities in the Basque country compared with other regions, the continuing sense of particularism (and of nationalism among a minority), the declining status of Euskera, and the slow but at least noticeable growth of secularism in what had been a strongly religious environment. In the 1950s sociologists and political scientists assumed that strong particularism and regional identities were well on their way toward elimination or homogenization in advanced European societies under the pressures of mass society, centralization, economic coordination, and modern communications. The succeeding decade showed that this was far from the case, for the same pressures of modernization led to a growing anomie and to crises of personality, identity, values, and self-definition, which regionalist-nationalist alternatives seemed to promise to alleviate.

THE BASQUE NATIONALIST PARTY AND THE ETA

During the past decade the Basque Nationalist Party (PNV) has reenforced its own stance as a party of middle-class, parliamentarian Christian democracy, the most coherent ideologist for which, among the senior leaders, is the former Alavese Cortes deputy, Francisco Javier de Landaburu. It has continued to define itself exclusively within the Spanish context and to postulate the goal of full autonomy in association within the Spanish state. Some elements of the old guard have remained, however, and their most vocal spokesmen are among the Basque colony in Caracas. On 25 October 1960 the latter issued a "Manifesto de Caracas," demanding a Basque state composed of all seven provinces with its capital in Pamplona.[16] This was disavowed by the PNV.

The PNV completely disassociated itself from nationalist feeling in the French or "continental" Basque country, which had begun to flicker once more in 1945 and finally began to rally modest support during the 1960s. The first faint signs of Basque nationalism in the French Basque country had appeared in the 1890s, but a modest organizational effort was begun only in 1933 and then revived at the end of the war. At that time the most prominent spokesman was Marc Legasse, a somewhat quixotic figure whose position might be described as that of a lower-middle-class anarchist or libertarian nationalist who aimed at the confederation of all seven districts. Legasse was harassed by the French authorities and repudiated by Aguirre's government of Euzkadi in exile, which assured Paris that it was only interested in the autonomy of the Spanish Basque provinces. This brought a sharp letter from Legasse to Aguirre that among other things charged the PNV with having accepted the old Carlist program of regional autonomy in an antiquated and repressive Spanish system.[17]

There are only about 90,000 Euskera-speaking people in the exiguous French Basque country, compared with possibly as many as 600,000 on the

Spanish side.[18] The only notable nationalist group in the French district is Enbata, which emerged in 1960 and was formally organized in 1963. It advocates the unified autonomy of the three French Basque provinces and ultimately the confederation of all seven Basque provinces within the framework of a federal Western Europe. Enbata advocates parliamentary democracy and emphasizes technocratic economic administration and planning, blaming the French government for purposeful neglect of the nonindustrial French Basque region. Enbata received 5 percent of the vote in the French Basque country during the French general elections of 1967, but this dropped to 3 percent under the pressure of resurgent Gaullism in 1968.

In recent years the French government has increasingly placed restrictions on some aspects of the Basque and Breton movements within France. It has tried to prevent radical Spanish Basque nationalists from taking up residence in the French Basque country, and in 1971 several Enbata leaders were sentenced to a month's imprisonment for "inflammatory" and "subversive" activities, in connection with the celebration of the Aberri Eguna (the Basque national day).[19]

It was not surprising that after midcentury the PNV was out-flanked to the left by a new and violent nationalist group based on radical youth politics. The new group was named Euzkadi ta Azkatasuna (ETA), which means Basque Land and Liberty. The ETA apparently originated with a small group of nationalist student radicals in the Jesuit university at Deusto (Bilbao), who founded a clandestine journal called *Ekin* (Action) in 1953-54. They were originally to some extent associated with EGI, the PNV's clandestine youth group, but the founders of *Ekin* did not share the moderate, evolutionary orientation of most of the EGI organization. Small radical elements of EGI, especially the latter's leader, José Luiz Alvarez Emparansa, became increasingly identified with *Ekin.* Alvarez Emparanza was eventually deposed as EGI leader and worked full time with *Ekin,* which was formally reorganized as ETA in 1959-60.

There are three basic differences between the ETA and the PNV. ETA postulates federation, on the basis of municipal and district autonomy, of all seven Basque provinces on both sides of the Pyrenees, in a federal Europe, after the breaking up of the existing structure of the Spanish and French states. It rejects the moderate, parliamentary-oriented tactics of the PNV in favor of revolutionary violence. Whereas the PNV is middle-class reformist and does not go beyond the concept of worker participation in management and a vaguely specified expansion of the public sector of the economy, ETA is social revolutionary and aims at radical syndical organization to achieve some not-well-defined form of Basque socialism.

In a completely apolitical vein, a new nationalist cultural movement called GERO emerged in 1962, devoted to building a spirit of unity and cooperation among all Basques, expanding the knowledge and use of Euskera, and developing Basque culture in all seven provinces.[20] Two tiny Basque socialist groups have appeared during recent years, but neither has been able to mobilize support. The first was named ELNAS (the Basque Workers and Peasants Socialist Party) and stood for an independent Basque republic based on the communal *biltzar*. It called for the "communalization" of land and industry and required that all its members either know Euskera or learn it within two years of joining.[21] After ELNAS faded, a group called ESBA was formed, but did only slightly better.

The great majority of nationalists in the Basque country have remained loyal to the PNV,[22] and the hard-core membership of ETA has probably never been more than a few hundred. At the time of its founding, ETA concentrated on syndical propaganda among industrial workers in Vizcaya and Guipuzcoa, but its top leaders were soon arrested; all were released within less than a year and moved to France in 1961. The first major proclamation of ETA occurred in the following year, differentiating the group from the PNV by pledging to use any means to gain Basque independence and affirming that "violence is necessary," while calling for social democracy and the avoidance of dictatorship whether fascist or communist and indicating willingness to work with other nationalist groups. Jesús María de Leizaola, the new president of the Euzkadi government-in-exile, responded on the occasion of the 1963 Aberri-Eguna celebration in Paris by denouncing ETA and its new journal *Zutik* (Arise) for their radicalism and calls to violence. During 1963 a new program of activities was attempted in Vizcaya and Guipuzcoa with a cadre of some 50 activists, but its efforts were quickly broken up by the police.[23]

From approximately that point the ideology and program of the group moved increasingly toward a sort of Marxism or pseudo-Marxism. ETA had originated as a radical, socialist oriented outgrowth of the PNV youth movement, and the predecessors of the organization of the 1950s had still been somewhat influenced by Catholic residues. In 1963, however, ETA activists cooperated with Basque Communists in setting up the first clandestine opposition *comisión obrera* among the workers in Bilbao. The dominant cadre began to espouse Marxist rhetoric, rejecting any association with religion in favor of determinist materialism, and adopting Basque socialism as the goal of a "war of liberation," though there is no indication that the Communist party has actually exercised any direct control over the ETA organization.*

The fifth assembly of ETA leaders and delegates, held clandestinely in Guipuzcoa at the beginning of 1967, declared the organization to be a "Basque Socialist Movement of National Liberation," establishing the complete victory of the Marxist "ETA-berri" elements over the "ETA-zarra" old guard. The latter was much more nationalist than socialist and still retained Aranist residues. Several of the original leaders then left the party and published a pamphlet, *Por*

---

*By the 1960s the Communist Party of Spain was calling for a "plurinational" rather than a federal system to replace the Franco government, with special statutes for Catalonia, Galicia and the Basque country and lesser autonomies for ordinary provinces.[24]

qué salimos de ETA? The Marxist José María Escubi Larraz became the top leader of ETA in mid-1968 and established closer contact with international Communist groups, which led to a reaction even among the Marxist elements. Escubi was denounced by rivals as an *españolazo,* and his rather arbitrary leadership was overthrown in 1970. However, at the sixth assembly, held that same year, ETA's identity as a "class movement" was firmly asserted. In this it followed the Leninist precedent of a movement of the radical middle- and upper-class intelligentsia arrogating for itself the identity of the working classes.[25]

The key sector of ETA, however, was not the propagandists and ideologues but the *milis,* the direct-action squads led by Juan José Echave Orobengoa. Though some of the ultra-Marxist elements tended to denounce them as petit-bourgeois nationalist terrorists, the *milis* carried out the deeds that in the late 1960s made ETA the most notorious of Spanish political groups.

The increased agitation in the Basque country from the mid-1960s stemmed from a growing mood of particularist dissatisfaction among middle-class youths, which adopted a nationalist form, and also from the militancy of the younger clergy, from the active economic discontent of many workers, and most spectacularly from the terrorist blows of ETA. The Spanish Church leadership first moved to differentiate its position from that of the Franco regime in 1960, but the only members of the clergy that demonstrated militancy were some of the younger priests of Vizcaya and Guipuzcoa. Most Basque priests are of Basque birth, and in general their sympathies with the affirmation of local identity and values has diminished little since the Civil War. In the Basque country the growing social conscience of the younger priests became identified with the cause of local rights and freedoms, all the more attractive because of the high degree of Catholic practice among the Basques. In 1960 a document requesting an independent investigation by the Vatican of the situation in the Basque country was signed by 339 Basque priests.

Meanwhile EGI accelerated its activities among the more "respectable" pronationalist middle-class youth, in an effort to avoid being outdistanced by ETA. In the more relaxed atmosphere of the 1960s, muted Aberri-Eguna celebrations were once more being held. In 1966 the EGI celebrated this occasion at Vitoria, while a separate rally was held by ETA at Irún, where 23 persons were arrested. During the year that followed, activity by both groups of nationalists stepped up, accompanied by protests from younger priests and an accelerated tempo of industrial strikes. By the eve of the Aberri-Eguna celebrations in April 1967, the situation in Vizcaya and Guipuzcoa was the most volatile in any part of Spain for the past 20 years. At that point, under pressure from hard-liners, the Spanish regime reversed the trend of two decades of slow relaxation of pressure by suspending the three principal civil guarantees in the Spanish Bill of Rights (Articles 14, 15, and 18) for the province of Vizcaya during the next three months, reestablishing de jure martial law. During the first week approximately 100 persons, mostly connected with labor agitation, were arrested. One year later, 2,000 special police were moved into San Sebastián to forestall Aberri-Eguna demonstrations there.[26] A unique incident of this period was the arrest of seven Basque mountaineers in November 1967 after their return from an expedition to the Andes. They were charged with having planted the Basque national flag atop one of the mountains they had conquered. Though dissident clergy were occasionally arrested, police repression was primarily concentrated against the leftist activists, some of whom were treated with great brutality, as had been more or less customary for the Spanish police since 1936.

Despite numerous protests over these arbitrary and violent procedures, the only rectification won by the opposition was an order by the Spanish supreme court in April 1968 that removed the civil governor of Guipuzcoa, Manual Valencia Remón, from office, indicting him for arbitrary and illegal acts. Valencia was rescued by the regime, which awarded him a safe seat in the Cortes that carried immunity from such prosecution.[27]

ETA TERRORISM AND THE BURGOS TRIAL

In this atmosphere, ETA terrorists struck their most resounding blow on 2 August 1968, when they assassinated Melitón Manzanas, a leading official of the *brigada social* (political police) in San Sebastián. This was their third killing, but the first that was a significant premeditated assassination, and it constituted a major exception to the tacit rules by which both police and opposition had operated in recent years.

Two days later the regime responded by declaring a state of emergency in Guipuzcoa, where civil guarantees were once more suspended for three months. Within a week approximately 200 people were arrested, including a score of priests. On August 14 the regime reimposed selective martial law in order to repress subversive acts and public disturbances.

At that point direct political opposition was primarily expressed not through strikes—which had become fairly frequent in industrial centers and had even received a degree of legal sanction under new regulations in 1966—but by the clerical and student intelligentsia. Of the 700 clergy in the province of Vizcaya, the liberals numbered from 200 to 300. There were two sit-ins by liberal priests at the diocesan seminary in San Sebastián, and 40 clergy were eventually suspended. On 4 November 1968 a group of liberal priests in Bilbao sent a letter directly to Pope Paul VI calling attention to the grievances of the Basques and urging that the church no longer promote "Castilianization."

The student demonstrations, primarily at the universities of Madrid and Barcelona, were more provocative and violent. They were the most immediate incentive enabling the regime's hard-liners to lead the government to declare a two-month state of emergency in February 1969. Opposition outbursts temporarily diminished, but agitation among the Basque clergy continued. Some 500 Basque priests addressed a collective letter to the Spanish Episcopal Conference of 1969, and in a pastoral letter of May 1969 the bishop of Bilbao, José María Cirarda, drew attention to the persistent violation of the terms of the existing church-state concordat by the government's arrest of priests. On June 6 more than 250 priests in Bilbao signed a statement in support of five of their fellows who were conducting a hunger strike in the diocesan chancery in protest against the repression.[28]

Though they carried out no more assassinations, the ETA militants maintained a high incidence of direct action in 1969-70, concentrating mainly on acts of public sabotage.[29] Scores of nationalists, not all of them from ETA, were arrested and prosecuted by the government in the late 1960s. In addition, 200 young Basques were arrested at Guernica in April 1970 after a protest commemorating the 33rd anniversary of the bombing. The repression was climaxed by the trial of 15 nationalists accused of terrorism, among them several ETA leaders and two priests, before a military tribunal in Burgos in December 1970.

The "Burgos trial" quickly mushroomed into the nearest thing to a political crisis that the Franco regime had seen since the 1940s. It was accompanied by a massive mobilization of liberal and leftist opinion abroad that in some ways resembled the *ferrerada* of 1909. In earlier years most of the nationalist militants would have been quickly prosecuted by court-martial with only minimal public hearings and probably executed. In 1970, considerable care was given to the rights of the accused as far as technical courtroom procedure was concerned. Pro-regime elements in the bureaucracy and the military responded to foreign opinion and continued public protests by workers and intelligentsia at home by mobilizing a massive rally in support of the regime at Madrid, echoed by smaller gatherings in some provincial capitals.

The resonance attained by the Burgos trial was a result of many factors. ETA terrorism, though not usually sanguinary, marked the first revival of violent methods by the leftist opposition in nearly a quarter century. Its sharp repression, together with the intermittent imposition of a state of emergency in Vizcaya and Guipuzcoa and briefly in Spain as a whole, marked a halt or at least a distinct slowdown in the gradual process of moderation and liberalization in Spain. The trial occurred after a decade of increasingly aggressive initiative by the leftist intelligentsia throughout the western world, and by 1970 the Spanish intelligentsia as a whole, especially the young, were more thoroughly leftist than in 1935. Worker dissidence, though frequent, was not much of a political problem, but as usual the intelligentsia was harder to deal with. That one of the twin focal points of ETA militancy was Basque nationalism also presented a serious challenge, since the broader and more diffuse sentiments of regionalism and nationalism proved in some ways to be more resistant to repression than the old myth of class loyalties. In December 1970, the successful kidnapping of the West German consul in San Sebastián as a form of ransom for the Burgos prisoners indicated that the Spanish police were no longer fully in control of the situation. Finally, the recrudescence of an extreme form of regionalist rebellion during the final phase of Franco's life posed a severe question for the unity and continuity of the Spanish regime in the future.

Six of the fifteen accused were found guilty of major acts of "military rebellion," but all were reprieved and given lesser prison terms.[30] In the aftermath, measures were taken to improve the behavior of some sections of the Spanish police and try to embellish their public image.

Economic protest by workers and political protest by university students continued in the early 1970s, but the spotlight was increasingly held by the opposition clergy. At one point late in 1970 at least 26 priests were in jail. In April 1971 the bishop of Pamplona publicly protested the infliction of torture by the police, results of which he claimed to have seen personally. At the end of that year, the conservative Antonio Añoveros, not a Basque, was named bishop of Bilbao which brought about new protest in which 196 priests participated. To a considerable extent the Vatican discreetly supported moderate liberalization in the Spanish hierarchy, and as new bishoprics fell vacant, tended to appoint only auxiliary prelates to avoid having to obtain the regime's approval for a regular nomination as stipulated in the 1953 Concordat. The appointment of José María Setien, a respected moderate liberal and intellectual, as auxiliary bishop of San Sebastián particularly drew the ire of the Spanish state, since it seemed to be a gesture in clear support of the liberal Basque clergy.

CONCLUSION

In general Spain has remained a depoliticized country and the findings of the FOESSA study that much of the population more or less supported some form of continuation of the regime were probably valid. The Burgos trial encouraged a genuine polarization of opinion, since it once more aroused the ire of many Spaniards against regional separatism.

To most Spaniards the persistence and regrowth of regional sentiment in the distinct peripheries of the north and east is as inexplicable as until recently it would have been to most contemporary political science theorists. During the late 1940s and 1950s it was generally held that the process of "modernization" produced increasing atomization and homogeneity and generated an ever-more-inclusive network of social communications that formed common identities and values. Modern society was supposed to result in a natural *gleichschaltung* (harmonization), based on economic interests, education, and entertainment, all of which broke down parochialism while promoting secularization and cosmopolitanism.

During the past decade, however, it has become clear that the dominant political passion of the second half of the 20th century is nationalism, and not any form of social, class, or ideological revolt as such. Nationalism has returned to the center of attention even among totalitarian systems theoretically based on class-conscious internationalism. Regional nationalism among small ethnic groups has gained new momentum all over western Europe.

Modernization may actually exacerbate national consciousness among small ethnic groups instead of diluting and erasing it. In the case of Spain, modernization occurred first and most rapidly in regions of distinct identity and local culture and led to dissociation rather than homogenization. Urbanization sharpened cultural tensions rather than merely transforming them, and the formation of political parties tended to reproduce rather than cut across regional differences. In the Basque country modernization has not even produced the secularization that is supposedly its inevitable concomitant, and to a considerable extent Basque religiosity has fueled Basque nationalism. The modernization process has led to a combination of feelings of superiority and exploitation that has undermined the concept of a Spanish nation-state.[31] Thus Basque nationalists have sometimes interpreted the Franco regime as a not illogical expression of Spanish civil consciousness as a whole, but have insisted that Castilian "backwardness" and authoritarianism will also drag the Basque country down, the moral and civic consciousness of which is held to be of an altogether higher order. As the correspondent Richard Eder quoted one young nationalist in 1968, "We cannot carry Spain on our backs indefinitely. The Castilians, the Andalusians are uneducated and primitive and they are not really ready for democracy. As long as we are tied to Spain, we shall have to endure their dictatorship."[32]

Another paradox of Basque nationalism is that its recent virulence has probably been more a result of the severity of the threat to Basque identity than of the basic strength of Basque nationalism itself. For example, all evidence indicates that a broad sense of Catalanism is more deeply rooted in Catalonia than Basque political and linguistic identity is rooted in the Basque country. The very shrinking of the Basque proportion of the population has encouraged a stronger reaction, and the intensity of the radical nationalists is perhaps not unrelated to the fact that the clergy have always played such an active role in association with the movement. Catalanism, both more secular and more secure, has largely been limited to clandestine assemblies that call for the restoration of the autonomy statute of 1932. The only main difference is that Catalanism was always more collaborationist and less extreme in its demands, and after the frustrations of an exaggerated ultra-Catalanism between 1934 and 1937, many Catalanists no longer have such interest in the extremes of political self-assertion.

It seems undeniable that most political opinion in Vizcaya and Guipuzcoa is opposed to the Franco regime. Opposition attitudes are probably more diffuse and widespread there than anywhere else in Spain except Barcelona province. Participation by heads of families in the 1971 Cortes elections was only 26 percent in Guipuzcoa and 33 percent in Vizcaya.[33] This was the lowest in Spain, whereas under the Republic the Basque provinces had registered the highest electoral participation figures in Spain. Opposition to and alienation from the Franco regime are one thing, however, and positive support for Basque nationalism is another. Without free elections it is impossible to determine the exact extent of the latter, but it seems doubtful that after the unassimilated immigration of recent decades it is any more widespread than in 1936, when nationalism mobilized scarcely half the vote in Vizcaya and Guipuzcoa and less than one-third of the vote in the Spanish Basque region as a whole. Shrinkage of the language base and the rapid decline of the rural population are steadily diminishing the traditionally and incontestably Basque proportion of society. A recent unpublished study by Davydd Greenwood has shown that in part of Guipuzcoa the flight from the land is due mainly to cultural and not economic factors. The lure of urban industrial society is even strong enough to outweigh pure income considerations among some of the more affluent farmers, and has evidently become irreversible.[34]

There is no indication that the great majority of the industrial workers, more numerous than ever before, has any allegiance to nationalism, especially since so many of them are not of Basque origin. Nor will economic conditions necessarily encourage nationalism in the future. All the Basque provinces have continued to benefit from the structure of the Spanish economic system, though in different ways. Navarre and Alava, particularly Alava, have gotten more than they have given to the Spanish state (as shown in Table 6.16), which has promoted their industrialization. Finally, in a semiindustrial Spain the pre-eminence of Vizcaya and Guipuzcoa is no longer so secure. Though they still rank at or near the top in productivity and income, their growth, as in many mature industrial systems, has begun to level off, and their concentration on metals industries may ultimately create new problems of imbalance.[35] Indeed, in the 1960s Asturias surpassed Vizcaya as the leading steel-producing province, although the Basque country as a whole still produces 50 percent of the steel in Spain.

In a similar vein, Victor Alba has argued that because of recent social and economic changes in Catalonia, Spain, and Western Europe the terms of the old Catalan problem have been transcended and that contemporary Catalanism must adjust accordingly.[36]

Nevertheless, although the nationalists as such are likely to remain a minority within the greater Basque region, they are unlikely to fade away or lose their own vigor. With no more than a plurality, nationalism might well reassert itself within a more liberal Spanish system as the leading single factor in the Basque country, resting on the middle classes, the nationalist intelligentsia, and the remaining rural population of Vizcaya and Guipuzcoa. If the opportunity for direct political representation is finally regained, it will not be necessary for nationalism to enroll the bulk of the population in order to regain a broad Basque autonomy, since the principle of autonomy is accepted by all of the

TABLE 6.16

Government Revenue and Direct Expenditures in Catalonia and the Basque Country as Percentages of the Totals for Spain

	Revenue		Expenditures	
Area	1962	1967	1962	1967
Catalonia	23.9	27.4	10.4	12.20
Barcelona province	18.9	22.0	7.3	8.79
Other Catalan provinces	5.0	5.4	3.0	3.41
Basque Country	15.6	14.7	4.6	5.41
Vizcaya	9.6	7.8	2.6	2.98
Guipuzcoa	5.7	6.6	1.5	1.69
Alava	0.3	0.3	0.5	0.54

Source: Juan J. Linz, "Early State-Building and Late Peripheral Nationalisms against the State: The Case of Spain," in *Building States and Nations,* ed. S. N. Eisenstadt and Stein Rokkan (Beverly Hills: Sage Publications, 1973), p. 89.

Spanish left and by much of the Spanish center, and nearly every political group in the Basque region supports some form or degree of autonomy. Some form of serious accommodation of regional feeling is virtually assured if anything approaching liberal or democratic government returns to Spain.[37]

Regional nationalism in the Basque country and Catalonia was born of the contradictions, imbalances, and frustrations in the organization of a modern polity, economy, and culture in Spain. In the past generation these differences have been somewhat assuaged in the economic sector, but the political and cultural frustrations that give rise to Basque and Catalan nationalism remain and are likely to persist for some time to come.

NOTES

1. For Alava, there is a brief exposition by José Badía La Calle, *El concierto economico con Alava* (Bilbao 1965).

2. Amando de Miguel and Juan Salcedo, *Dinámica del desarrollo industrial de las regiones españolas* (Madrid: Tecnos, 1972), p. 160.

3. Ibid., p. 235.

4. Ibid., p. 35.

5. Juan J. Linz and Amando de Miguel, "Within-Nation Differences and Comparisons: The Eight Spains," in *Comparing Nations,* ed. Richard L. Merritt and Stein Rokkan (New Haven: Yale University Press, 1966), pp. 307-309; and the *Anuario estadístico de las corporaciónes locales* (Madrid, 1964-65), cited in Kenneth Medhurst's booklet, *The Basques* (London: Minority Rights Group, 1972), p. 24.

6. De Miguel and Salcedo, op. cit., p. 288.

7. Fundación FOESSA, *Informe sociológico sobre la situación social de España, 1970* (Madrid: la Fundación, 1970), p. 47.

8. Ibid., p. 546.

9. See Francesc Candel, *Els altres catalans* (Barcelona: Edicions 62, 1966).

10. These last two points have been made by Juan J. Linz in "The Party System of Spain: Past and Future," in *Party Systems and Voter Alignments: Cross-National Perspectives,* ed. Seymour M. Lipset and Stein Rokkan (New York: The Free Press, 1967), p. 272.

11. Fundación FOESSA, op. cit., pp. 1305, 1307.

12. On the present extent of Catalan usage and Catalan-language culture, see Josep Melià, *Informe sobre la lenga catalana* (Madrid: Editorial Magistero Español, 1970).

13. Frederico de Arteaga (pseud.), *"ETA" y el Proceso de Burgos* (Madrid: Aguado, 1971).

14. Ibid., pp. 32-34.

15. *Diccionario de Legislación Administrativa y Fiscal de Navarra* (Pamplona: 1969), pp. 1118-19, in Milton da Silva, "The Basque Nationalist Movement: A Case Study in Modernization and Ethnic Conflict" (Ph.D. diss., University of Massachusetts, 1972), p. 156.

16. *Vasconia,* pp. 292, 587.

17. Ibid., pp. 533-37.

18. Manuel de Lecuona, *Literatura oral vasca* (San Sebastián: 1964), p. 8.

19. Erbata has published a good deal of propaganda defining its position, and there is a sketch in J. P. Mogui *La Révolt des Basques* (Paris: 1970) pp. 53-62. On the regionalist problem in France as a whole, see Paul Sérant, *La France des minorités* (Paris: Laffont, 1965); Thiébaut Flory, *Le Mouvement régionaliste français* (Paris: Editions Presses Universitaires de France 1966); Robert Lafont, *La Revolution regionaliste* (Paris: Gallimard 1967).

20. The full text of the 1962 GERO program is given in *Vasconia,* op. cit., pp. 589-602.

21. Ibid., pp. 619-20.

22. Compared with ETA, the PNV has received scant attention in recent years. There is a limited sketch in Sergio Vilar, *Protagonistas de la España*

democrática (Paris: Ediciones sociales Barcelona, Paris, Madrid, 1968), pp. 527-34.

23. There are sketches of the origins of ETA in Arteaga, pp. 239-41; by Juan Pérez del Corral in *Arriba* (Madrid: 1968); and in Mogui, op. cit., pp. 62-75. There is a chronology in Paxti Isaba, *Euzkadi socialiste* (Paris: 1971), pp. 17-20, 158-59.

24. Guy Hermet, *Les Communistes en Espagne* (Paris: Librarie Armand Colin, 1971), p. 170.

25. This account follows Arteaga, op. cit., pp. 242-55.

26. These developments have been followed primarily through the accounts appearing in the New York *Times.*

27. Kepa Salaberri, *El proceso de Euskadi en Burgos* (Paris, 1971), pp. 66-67.

28. The foregoing was gleaned from reports in the New York *Times* and *Alderdi* (a PNV bimonthly), and Da Silva, op. cit., pp. 149-51.

29. A list of terrorist and sabotage activities attributed to ETA down to the close of 1970 is given in Arteaga, op. cit., pp. 379-84.

30. For a full account of the trial and attendant events from the opposition viewpoint, see Salaberri, op. cit., and also G. Halemi, *Le Procès de Burgos* (Paris: 1971). The official Spanish version is in Arteaga, pp. 273-372.

31. There is an excellent discussion of the ways in which Basque nationalism and other contemporary movements have confounded the older political science theories in Da Silva, op. cit., pp. 211-15, passim.

32. New York *Times,* 3 December 1968.

33. *La Gaceta del Norte* (Bilbao), 31 September 1971, in Medhurst.

34. Certain aspects of contemporary Basque village mores have been studied by William A. Douglass, *Death in Murélaga* (Seattle: University of Washington Press, 1969).

35. See Gonzalo Sáenz de Buruaga *Ordenación del territorio. El caso del País Vasco y su zona de influencia* (Madrid: Guardiana, 1969), pp. 274-80.

36. Víctor Alba, *Catalunya sense cap ni peus* (Barcelona: Editorial Portic, 1971).

37. An overview of the broad, if varying, support for regional autonomy in Italy and the efforts to implement it is provided in L. B. Weinberg, "The Regions and the Parties" (Ph.D. diss., Syracuse University, 1968).

7

FRANCO'S RULE: INSTITUTIONALIZATION AND PROSPECTS OF SUCCESSION

Vincente R. Pilapil

Two months after the outbreak of the Civil War in July 1936, military considerations made it imperative to establish a unified command of the insurgent forces. Because of his command of the Army of Africa, his popularity abroad, and his seniority to General Mola, the planner and director of the conspiracy, Francisco Franco was named *generalisimo* by the provisional National Defense Junta. Shortly thereafter, some monarchist* generals master-minded a veritable coup that catapulted Franco into becoming also the chief of state. They considered him the safer bet among the leading contenders, which also included the republican generals Mola and Queipo de Llano. Aside from the statements he made that gave comfort to the monarchists, Franco had a personal fondness for the exiled King Alfonso XIII, who had shown him many favors. Like many others, he could claim that he had accepted the Second Republic because the king's depature provided no alternative.

POLITICAL CONTENDERS IN THE FRANCO GOVERNMENT

At the time of his elevation to the supreme civil and military position, Franco was a political neophyte, lacking in strong ideological convictions. Like the dictator before him, General Primo de Rivera, Franco despised politics and politicians, understood mostly in the context of Spanish parliamentary

---

*Though there were two branches of the monarchy, the Alfonsine and the Carlist, the term "monarchist" is used here for the sake of convenience to refer to the former. The latter will be referred to as Carlists or Traditionalists.

democracy; even today, after many years of rule, Franco claims that he does not dabble in politics. His decision to commit himself to the military conspiracy at virtually the last minute was motivated, apart from the Republic's attitude toward the military caste, by what he considered the government's weakness in confronting civil disturbances, national disintegration, and growing "Bolshevization."

When he became the new *caudillo*, Franco's main task was to win the war, and his regime was without a political substructure. However, the failure of the November offensive to capture Madrid presaged a much longer war than the conspirators had allowed for, and it became necessary to organize the civilian aspect of government. For this task, Franco mainly relied on his more politically conscious brother, Nicolás. Even more important was his brother-in-law, Ramón Serrano Suñer, who managed to escape from Madrid in February 1937 and take up residence in Franco's headquarters. Serrano Suñer had been active in the ranks of the pre-Civil War CEDA (Confederación Española de Aerechas Autónmas) party, organizing its youth branch. He dedicated himself to the task of giving Franco's rule a political framework. The contrast between the political sophistication of Serrano Suñer and Franco's initial naiveté must have been the factor that led Serrano Suñer to say that one spoke of Franco "as one would of a moronic servant."

The principal task was to organize around and subordinate under the person of Franco the various political forces. The two main parties on the insurgent side that had organized popular followings and their own militia were the Falange Española and the Traditionalists. Both tended to act independently of the central command, but to Franco's advantage, they were vulnerable. The Falange was without a strong leader since the execution of its founder, José Antonio, by the Loyalists in November 1936. It was also split internally, mainly between its old and new adherents. The former, the *camisas viejas* (Old Shirts), were true to the radical social ideals of José Antonio, but the great upsurge of party following during the Civil War brought in members who wanted to water down the original Falange doctrines. Serrano Suñer's Falange-Edista orientation was an example. As for the Carlists, though their ideology was fairly intact, their handicap lay in having a limited regional base, mainly centered in the province of Navarre. Notwithstanding the fact that the Carlists looked toward the establishment of a "traditional monarchy" while the Falange was fascist, Franco decreed their merging into the one legal political party, with the unwieldy title of *Falange Española Tradicionalista y de las JONS* (Juntas de Ofensiva Nacional-Sindicalista).

Commentators have often taken this point as the real beginning of Franco's totalitarian rule, since in addition to being the head of state and of the armed forces, he was now the leader of the state party. The realities of the situation are less clear-cut, however; Franco was not the undisputed master of the groups making up the Nationalist side. His control of power depended on the skillful balancing and juggling of those forces, taking care not to alienate any one group completely nor to allow any one group to gain too much influence.

FRANCO'S EARLY CABINETS

The composition of Franco's first cabinet (1938) reflected this balancing and was extremely eclectic. The Falangists, the Traditionalists, the Monarchists, and the military were represented. There was only one person who could be classified as a technician, a type that would be used increasingly as time went on, whose position depended merely on success in an assigned task. With this first cabinet began the practice of what might be termed authoritarian pluralism, a pluralism within a definitely circumscribed system that excluded groups hostile to the regime. The representation of the various groups in the cabinet depended on internal and external conditions, and other groups would also be brought in with the changing times.

In August 1939, after the conclusion of the Civil War, Franco reorganized the cabinet, with the same groups represented as had been in the first. The outbreak of World War II and the triumphant march of Axis troops throughout battle-torn Europe, however, increased the power of Serrano Suñer and the new Falangists in the minor ministerial changes that followed. The height of the Axis victories was also the height of the influence of Serrano Suñer, commonly dubbed the *cuñadísimo*. Franco, however, was loath to allow any individual or group to be preponderant, and in May 1941, while the German might and chances of victory were still impressive (notwithstanding the failure of the Battle of Britain), the Caudillo reshuffled his cabinet to put some counterweight to his brother-in-law's power by bringing in Old Falangists. In the autumn of 1942 the changing fortunes of war impelled the complete removal of Serrano Suñer, who had become an ideological embarrassment. Serrano Suñer's fall also marked the beginning of the eclipse of the Falange as a state party, which degenerated into a kind of bureaucratic machinery (without monopoly of patronage), though parts of its ideological framework were preserved. Further downgrading of the party came after Allied victory; its name was neutralized to "Movimiento Nacional."

Franco constituted the third government on the tenth anniversary of the outbreak of the Civil War. The change was dictated, not only by the expediency of dissociating the regime from Fascism, but by two other considerations, one related to the monarchists. First, in January 1944 Don Juan, the son and heir of Alfonso XIII, had publicized his condemnation of the Franco regime, and the following year he had called for immediate restoration of the monarchy. The second consideration pertained to the decision of the San Francisco Conference in June 1945 to exclude Franco Spain from membership in the United Nations. The 1945 cabinet consequently excluded monarchists and brought in the

Catholic group as a means of breaking Spain's international isolation. In order to avoid the complete alienation of the monarchists and as a sop to international opinion, the Law of Succession was decreed in 1947, as described in the fourth section of this chapter.

The new foreign minister was Alberto Martín Artajo, leader of the lay society, Catholic Action. He emphasized Spain's Catholicism and anticommunism as a bond with other nations. Particular appeal was made to Spanish-American countries, where cultural ties were also underlined. Argentina, the Latin American country with the strongest economic ties with Spain prior to the Civil War, responded generously, especially since the Peronist government felt a kinship with that of Franco. Perón, in defiance of the general spirit of anti-Francoism, presented the Spanish Caudillo with the highest Argentine decoration and extended to Spain a very advantageous commercial agreement. The 1945 cabinet survived through the most trying years of ostracism and autarchy.

The duration of Franco's first post-Civil War cabinet had been almost six years. When the 1945 government reached its sixth year, therefore, Franco named a new one; there was, of course, the added consideration of the desire to exploit the fact that the Cold War had erupted into the Korean War. In 1951, it was safe to give more representation to the emasculated Falange (besides, Franco meant to revive some of its social doctrines) and to place a monarchist in the cabinet.* However, the weight of this government was still in Catholic Action hands. The Catholic suggestion of a policy of national reconciliation with repentant Spaniards who had been in the opposing camp during the Civil War was now favored by Franco. Moreover, Catholic Action had proven to be useful in the effort to escape international isolation. Its usefulness was increased by the fact that what Franco most wanted was an agreement with the Vatican.

THE CHURCH AND OPUS DEI

The Catholic Church in Spain had, in general, been one of the strongest supporters of the Nationalist regime during the Civil War, but the Holy See had acted circumspectly. After the fall of the Basque country to the Rebels had eliminated a major obstacle, the Vatican confined itself to recognizing the Franco government in 1938. A full-scale regularization of the church-state relationship in the form of a concordat, which Franco pressed for, was avoided. Franco's urgency for coming to an agreement with the Vatican became greater as

---

*Moreover, Luís Carrero Blanco, an Admiral who had served as Under Secretary of the Presidency of the government since 1940, now saw that post elevated to a ministerial rank. First and foremost a *Franquista*, Carrero worked to secure the restoration of the monarchy during his Cromwellian master's lifetime.

negotiations for the establishment of U.S. bases in Spain were nearing conclusion; the eminent, archconservative Cardinal Segura was fulminating at the bartering of Spain's Catholic conscience for American dollars. As it was, the concordat between Spain and the Vatican was signed none too soon, just a month before the signing of the pact with the United States. The concordat gave tangible benefits to the Church, but Franco, who styled himself "*caudillo,* by the grace of God," now had the Holy See's full recognition. It is noteworthy that both sides are now dissatisfied with the concordat, and serious efforts are now underway to revise it. (See Chapter 6.)

Ironically, the main usefulness of the Catholic group came to an end with the signing of the Concordat, while the Catholic Action brand of liberalization was made the scapegoat for the political unrest of the following years. This points up the fact that the Catholic Action ministers, lacking an autonomous political base, were not in the class of other groups represented in the cabinet. The same fate would befall Opus Dei in 1973 and 1974.

The main problem in the mid-1950s was political turmoil, the most serious to plague Franco since his rise to power. The police and the army successfully contained the disturbances, but it was necessary to deal with the cause of the trouble, which was economic hardship, brought on by that pair of evils, stagnation and inflation, which plagued Spain earlier than they did other European countries. The roots of the economic problem went back to the post-Civil-War years, and its effects were now climaxing, ironically when the country was beginning to emerge from stagnation.

Franco reorganized his cabinet. According to his timetable, it was about time to do so. Moreover, this coincided with the Franco policy of laying the blame on his ministers: even in an authoritarian system such as Franco's, it is not correct to speak of ministerial changes as the mere relieving of some ministers to be substituted by others; changes also respond to crises—in the case, an internal one. Significantly, the Falange's open bid to regain power during the period of disturbance was shunted aside: the prominent feature of the 1957 ministry was the appointment of Opus Dei members to the economic seats of Commerce and Finance.

Opus Dei is a shortened name for the international, secretive, secular-religious *Sociedad Sacerdotal de la Santa Cruz y Opus Dei,* which has aroused much controversy in Spain, where it reached its highest growth and influence. Founded in Spain in the late 1920s, it "took off" during the Civil War years and matured in the late 1940s, when it also received Papal sanction. The majority of its members are laymen, who work for their personal sanctification and carry out their apostolate by excelling in their secular professions. The laymen who belong to the high ranks of the Society are mostly members of the intelligentsia or have prominent social background. Though *opusdeistas* claim that the society is strictly religious, most of its elite share, broadly, a common political and socioeconomic view. They aspire to the highest posts, in fulfillment of their

Society's maxims, "never fail" and persevere "until you have finally scaled the heights of duty"; they also tend to give appointments to fellow members, confident perhaps that these will likewise do their best. Since the 1940s Opus Dei members had been infiltrating the *cátedras* of the universities, the different branches of government, and the business world.

Members of Opus Dei were helped into obtaining seats in the universities and other scholarly bodies by José Ibáñez Martín, an Opus Dei sympathizer who was Minister of Education for nearly 12 years, the longest to be in that post. Opus Dei entry into the cabinet was owed to the regime's *éminence grise*, Luís Carrero Blanco, reputedly the writer of many of Franco's speeches. In the case of Ibáñez Martín, it was a fellow refugee in the Chilean embassy in Madrid during the Civil War, José María Albareda, who attracted him to the society; with Carrero Blanco, it was Laureano López Rodó, whom the former placed under himself as Technical Secretary General of the Presidency of the Government in 1956 (Carrero Blanco was President of the Government, the title of the prime minister in Spain). In this post, López Rodó worked out the most famous and ambitious economic program of the Franco regime, the Development Plan. The inclusion of *opusdeistas* in the 1957 cabinet was met with alarm and resentment in other political and religious sectors, despite denials that Opus Dei had any political aims, including denial by Monsignor Josemaría Escrivá de Balaguer y Albas, the society's founder and president for life.

The Falange, which had to reconcile itself to reality and drop its cry of "Falange sí; Franco, no," shifted its negativism to "Franco, sí; Juan Carlos, no," and latterly, to "Franco, sí; Opus Dei, no." In organized Catholic circles, the Jesuits and Catholic Action are Opus Dei's disgruntled rivals. Some members of the Church establishment looked with disfavor at the tying of the Church with the Franco regime through Opus Dei, at a time when they considered it wise to relax the bond of association. Alarmist reaction ignored two salient factors: first, Opus Dei had no independent base of political backing, and second, the ministerial seats occupied by its members were those normally assigned to technicians. Alberto Ullastres, in Commerce, and Mariano Navarro Rubio, in Finance, produced the Stabilization Plan and worked to relax economic regimentation and open Spain for integration with Europe. Their success was reflected in the 1962 cabinet, when Franco appointed more members of Opus Dei to Industry and Labor, while López Rodó's Development Plan was put into practice with the announcement of the first Four Year Plan in 1963. Though some economists have criticized aspects of the plan, its initial results increased the influence of the Opus Dei. López Rodó was raised to the rank of minister. Rival groups, notably the one around Fraga Iribarne, were overcome despite the implication of some Opus Dei members in a financial scandal. By 1969 the society reached its political apogee in a cabinet that was preponderantly filled by its members. Never had any one group been allowed such control in a Franco cabinet before. (For further discussion of Opus Dei, see Chapter 6.)

THE MONARCHICAL SUCCESSION

Carrero Blanco and López Rodó, in particular, had not only been attending to the systematization of the Development Plan, but also had been working on "Operation Prince," a definitive step in the restoration of the monarchy. As I have mentioned, Carrero Blanco had all along been working behind the scenes for the restoration of the monarchy. In 1957, in one of his rare public utterances, he emphasized that the "installation" of the monarchy could be done in Franco's lifetime and that it would not be incompatible with the Caudillo's continuing exercise of his power.

By 1961 Franco was nearly seventy, and though he reassured Spaniards by pointing out that he came from a line of long-lived ancestors, he must have shared his people's concern about "After Franco, what? " Many wondered whether Franco was not unduly endangering the future by his disinclination to start delegating some of his power. While he was on the scene, Franco could continue to control and juggle the various political groups, but after him, would not the scramble for dominance among these groups lead to chaos and allow the leftists to reemerge? That could mean another civil war, which would leave Spain back where she left off in 1936.

The Caudillo's next move allayed these fears somewhat. A hunting accident toward the end of 1961, when a shotgun exploded in his hand, prodded Franco to raise his oldest companion and oftentimes minister, Augustín Muñoz Grandes, to the rank of vice-president, automatically to take over the presidency after Franco's demise. However, Muñoz Grandes, though a few years younger than Franco, finally had to leave the government in 1967 because of ill health. Carrero Blanco took his place, but his elevation to the vice-presidency was delayed a few months while the post remained vacant. This was a typical Franco gesture of showing that no person in whatever position was indispensable as long as he was around.

It was left also to name a successor as Chief of State. Franco had stated that his regime was not going to be a "parenthesis," that it would lead to the creation of a "new state" and to the *convivencia* of Spaniards—at least a government better than under King Alfonso XIII and the Second Republic. He once justified his continuance in power on the grounds that his rule was the one "which divides us least." "New state" and *convivencia* considerations pointed to other than the continuation of a military dictatorship. There was no one in the military who came close to Franco's prestige, nor was there political homogeneity in the army. The role of the army was clearly to be that of a pillar of the regime rather than its leader. Neither could the Falange fill the needs of the future; it was leaderless and internally divided. Moreover, Franco had always been basically a monarchist. During the Civil War he had prevented the heir of Alfonso XIII from fighting in Spain because, as Franco reasoned, "If there is a

King, he will have to come as a pacifier and should not be numbered with the victors." The monarchy was saved for the healing of wounds, for *convivencia*. As for the continuance of his "new state" within the monarchical system, Franco adopted a phrase that had been used as early as February 1937, when some Falangists and Carlists had tried to reach a political compromise: "the installation, not the restoration" of the monarchy. Later, Franco talked of a "new monarchy" and of a "kingdom . . . born of the decisive action of July 18." The "installed" monarchy would issue out of his system.

Back in 1947, partly to add to his regime's framework and partly to contribute to the mellowing of the hostile international attitude toward him, Franco decreed the Law of Succession. The country was declared a monarchy with a vacant throne; Franco was regent for life with the right to choose the next king. According to later specification, this person whom Franco could propose to the Cortes for its approval had to be male, a Spaniard of royal blood, at least 30 years old, and more importantly, sworn to uphold the regime's fundamental laws. Franco protected himself further with the provision that he could change his mind and revoke his designation of a successor and could, in fact, appoint another regent if there were no apt royal successor. This law was the first to be submitted to a popular referendum, in which it obtained 93 percent of the votes. By a clever stroke, the lifetime Caudillo could claim popular endorsement for his stay in power, while also restoring the monarchy.

Many had learned better than to make predictions about the wily chief of state, and there was enough uncertainty surrounding the restoration not to estrange the antimonarchist Falangists. Furthermore, when the Falange bid for resurgence in the mid-1950s was answered by the appointment of military and Opus Dei members to the cabinet, to placate the Falangists the Law of the Principles of the National Movement was promulgated in 1958. This law confirmed the old Falangist postulates of a Catholic, corporative, syndical, and one-party state. These principles were declared "permanent and unalterable," part of the laws that Franco's successor would have to swear to uphold. The next king could not dismantle the Franco system.

It was easier to declare Spain a monarchy than to choose the next king, for there were a number of rival monarchist groups. The Carlists, whose claim to the throne dated back to the 1830s, had not only fought two civil wars in the 19th century to uphold their views but had formed an important nucleus of government support in the 1936 Civil War. Their claim had to be considered; in addition they had served to "divide and rule" the monarchists when Franco's rule was still uncertain. However, in Franco's pragmatic view of the future the Carlists had never had much of a chance: their base was too regional for the purpose of national unity, and their doctrines too outmoded. Significantly, Franco had never bothered to remove a constitutional obstacle that lay in the path of the Carlist successor: according to the Succession Law the king must be Spanish, but the request of the Carlist pretenders (who had become French citizens) for naturalization was left unattended. In 1964 the present pretender, Carlos Hugo of Bourbon Parma, sought to bolster his claim to the throne by marrying a Dutch princess and then working to mobilize his supporters in Spain. This threat of royal demagogy was removed when Franco ordered Carlos Hugo and his family out of the country in 1968.

The eldest son of Alfonso XIII, named Alfonso, had renounced his rights to the throne in 1933, twice married a commoner, and died in Miami, Florida, in 1938. However, Alfonso of Bourbon Dampierre, whose father was Don Jaime, the second son, remained a minor royal contender. Because of his handicap as a deaf-mute, Don Jaime had renounced his right to the succession and contracted a morganatic marriage that confirmed his ineligibility for the throne. He later revoked the renunciation, and despite his having renounced the throne "for my-self and for whatever descendants I may have," his eldest son laid claim on the crown. Antimonarchists, Falangists in particular, wanting to sow discord in the Alfonsine branch, built up Don Alfonso as an affable, hard-working prince who promptly reported to work every morning. However, his claim was without foundation and was not considered seriously when Franco decided to designate his successor. Recently, however, Don Alfonso has resurfaced as a potential thorn, since his marriage in 1972 to Franco's eldest granddaughter posed some threat to the already designated royal successor. Some political observers remarked that the Caudillo would not have permitted the marriage if he had been as mentally agile as before, while others who see more ambition in Franco's wife lay the blame at her door; scandalmongers are not lacking who explain it differently.

The legitimate heir of the last king of Spain, to whom the latter abdicated his rights a few months before his death in exile, is Don Juan of Bourbon Battenberg, who lives in Estoril, Portugal. As befits a prince who was mostly educated in Britain, Don Juan is of a liberal persuasion. To Don Juan, Franco's refusal to relinquish power after the Civil War meant a usurpation of his own rights; it was Don Juan who called on Franco to step down when Allied armies were victorious in World War II; he denounced Franco's authoritarian rule and criticized aspects of the regime before the dictator himself. Still, Franco hoped that Don Juan would become more amenable, accept the historical validity of his regime, and promise to uphold its principles. However, Don Juan maintained his intransigent stance with the emissaries Franco sent to Estoril: the royal heir judged it harmful for the crown to be tainted by Francoism and would not accept the throne from Franco's hands; he precisely condemned the Law of Succession as "vitiated substantially by its origin." Franco saw his way out of this impasse in a solution favored by Carrero Blanco and López Rodó, a restora-tion of the monarchy in the person of Don Juan's son, Juan Carlos.

Juan Carlos was born in Rome, the final residence in exile of Alfonso XIII, on 5 January 1938 and spent his childhood in Switzerland and Portugal. Since Don Juan wanted his sons to grow up in the country of their heritage, Juan

Carlos was sent to do his schooling in Spain, where he has lived since the age of ten. His secondary studies over, the young prince entered the service academies of the three branches of the army; after this his father wanted Juan Carlos to receive some education abroad, but Franco insisted that he continue to pursue his studies in Spain. As a compromise, Juan Carlos was matriculated at the University of Madrid in return for his being given the Zarzuela Palace as a residence and honors due his rank. After completing graduate studies at the university, Juan Carlos undertook practical training in government, serving in the different ministries. His mentors and advisors were mostly members of Opus Dei, not the Falangists. In 1961 Juan Carlos married Princess Sofía of Greece, who turned out to be an asset to the prince in popular eyes.

Two events in January 1968 directly contributed to Franco's final decision to name his successor. One was the birth of a son, Felipe, to Juan Carlos and Sofía. For the christening, 80 year old Queen Victoria Eugenia, the child's great grandmother, came to Spain from exile. Her return was received with extraordinary enthusiasm in Madrid, and the Francos paid her their respects. Don Juan, too, came to Madrid, was allowed to move and mingle freely about the capital, and had talks with Franco. It is reported that Franco made last-minute efforts to win Don Juan over to his views on the restoration. The other event of that January was that Juan Carlos, reaching the age of 30, the legal age of succession, began to express a change of mind. Where previously he had reiterated his loyalty to his father and his refusal to usurp his father's rights, he now declared that he would accept the crown from Franco even without his father's approval. Though Don Juan denounced his son's decision, he speedily acquiesced in Juan Carlos's designation. He disbanded his private royal council and declared that he did not wish his person to be a source of discord among Spaniards. Relations between father and son are presently cordial. There is speculation about the name Don Carlos will use. Will he be Juan IV, in recognition of his father's rights? Carlos would make him the fifth of that name and confuse him with the Hapsburg Charles V, who was Charles I of Spain. Many Spaniards cavalierly dismiss the question by calling him Juan the Brief.

On 22 July 1969, Franco proposed to the Cortes his choice of Juan Carlos as successor. It was, of course, approved overwhelmingly, with only a few negative votes from Carlists, die-hard Falangists, and strict monarchists who deplored the tampering with the laws of monarchical succession. The following day Juan Carlos appeared before the Cortes and took the oath of loyalty to Franco and the Fundamental Laws of the land. Little was known of this tall, handsome prince; he had been appearing, mute and subservient, by Franco's side in public ceremonies, and many dismissed him as Franco's political stooge and as a person of limited ability. Great was the surprise at the content of his acceptance speech. As if to qualify his promise to uphold Francoism, as if to accentuate the harsh difference presented by his youthful self and that of the aged and bent Caudillo by his side, he said, "I am indeed close to youth. I admire and share its desire to seek a better and more genuine world." Perhaps he had in mind the recent "State of Exception" decreed by the government in response to political disturbances when he continued, "I know that within the rebellion which worries so many persons there lives the fine generosity of those who want an open future, often in the form of unattainable dreams, but always with the noble desire for the best for the people." These are promising words from the man who, when he comes to the throne, will have more power than his contemporary constitutional monarchs; cabinets will depend on him rather than on parliament. Juan Carlos has been given more public exposure since his designation, but his speeches have reverted to harmless platitudes. Since Franco has the option to change his mind about his successor, one cannot expect Juan Carlos to endanger his position by taking an independent line, if that indeed be his design.

CARRERO AND ARÍAS: THE PATH TO THE POST-FRANCO ERA

Franco seemed pleased that he had removed an uncertainty about Spain's political future with a designated king sworn to uphold the regime. In a speech to the Cortes in November 1971, he expressed satisfaction when he said, "Everything is bound—well bound." Furthermore, in 1972, partly because of his doctors' recommendations, he made another step to ensure a smooth transition after his demise. He who had been described as "the sentinel who never goes off duty, the one who watches while others sleep," now decided to delegate an important part of his responsibilities. Where he had before acted both as Chief of State and President of the Government, he now relinquished the latter office. Not the least of the considerations that led to this decision was the availability of one whom he considered ideal for president, Luís Carrero Blanco.

Carrero Blanco had commanded the cruiser division of the Nationalist navy during the Civil War and had been chief of naval operations thereafter. A professional navy man whose sons have also followed a naval career, he was deviated to politics when Franco appointed him undersecretary to the presidency in 1940, a post which was raised to ministerial rank eleven years later and which Carrero held until his promotion to the vice-presidency in 1967. Taciturn and hardworking like Franco, he vigorously seconded the Caudillo's task of protecting Spain from Communism, Freemasonry, and democracy. He himself best described his identification with Franco: "My loyalty to his person and to his work is total, clear, and clean, without a shadow of any personal conditions or a trace of mental reservation." In Carrero, therefore, Franco found his instrument of continuity, a guarantor against liberal deviation from Francoism, and Carrero became Spain's first President of Government after Franco.

Nowhere was the Spanish saying, *"El hombre propone, Dios dispone,"* better demonstrated than when Carrero Blanco was assassinated on 20 December

1973. Terrorists planted under a street a bomb, which could be detonated with precision because of the Admiral's habit of hearing Mass in the same church and at the sime time every morning. The force of the bomb hurled the president's car up five stories, naturally claiming the lives of its occupants. Though the assassination was clearly the work of terrorists—ETA, a Basque terrorist group, claimed responsibility—the hard-liners seized the opportunity to blame advocates of liberalization and called for a declaration of martial law. At Carrero's funeral crowd is reported to have screamed "Assassin, Assassin!" at the liberal Cardinal of Madrid, Alcalá, while placards called for an authoritarian government and reminded the military, "The hour of the sword has come." No political disturbances accompanied the assassination, but Franco's plans were upset and a new president had to be chosen.

Franco selected the 65 year old Carlos Arías Navarro, reportedly the leading candidate among the three recommended to him by the Council of the Realm. Arías Navarro is the first civilian to have risen so high in Franco Spain, but he is definitely a "law and order" man and, like his predecessor, very loyal to the Caudillo. Arías Navarro had served as a public prosecutor with a reputation for toughness against the republican adversaries of Nationalist Spain during the Civil War. In 1957 he became Director General of Security, leaving that post after eight years to become mayor of Madrid, where his credit lay in increasing the city's parks and school facilities. In June 1973 Arías had been chosen to serve as House Minister in Carrero Blanco's first and only cabinet.

Political observers expected the new president to make few ministerial changes, in an emphasis on continuity; apparently that was also Franco's wish. However, Arías Navarro insisted on making extensive changes; twelve ministers were replaced and two were shifted from one post to another. A prominent casualty was the sole opusdeista, López Rodó. With the disappearance of Carrero Blanco and López Rodó, Prince Juan Carlos lost his most ardent supporters. It is unlikely that his position was damaged, however; in 1973, in Franco's traditional year-end speech, the Caudillo had exceptionally warm phrases for the prince.

The new Falangists in the cabinet are not believed to be antimonarchist; although Falangists occupy many seats, they are not of the *camisas viejas* sort. Even Old Falangist Torcuato Fernández Miranda, who was interim president after the assassination of Carrero, was dropped. A number of the new ministers are friends and former subordinates of the new president. They are all loyal to Franco and his principles of government.* In comparing Franco's first cabinet with the cabinet under Arías Navarro, one notes a fundamental change: in the fomer there was meticulous representation of the various political forces that made up the Nationalist camp, but under Arías Navarro this is not the case. Traditionalists and monarchists do not have specific representation, and army

---

*One is reminded of a newly appointed minister in 1970 who, when asked what were the factors that brought about his designation, very simply and candidly replied, "the confidence of His Excellency, the Chief of State."

officers occupy the purely military seats. Franco's program was aimed at the "depoliticization" of the different groups, melting them into a political consensus of a regime that was Catholic, monarchist, conservative-evolutionist, and modern-Falangist. Supposedly the Arías Navarro cabinet members are of this consensus; the question is, whether the structure is real or whether it will crumble into divisive parts.

The program of this cabinet, as outlined by Arías Navarro, emphasizes law and order but also promises to elevate the standard of living and allow more political participation for the people. Much remains to be seen, however. Undoubtedly the government will crack down on terrorism and illegal opposition. The harassment will principally affect the most active underground groups, the Communists and the ETA, but the illegal opposition groups are not very promising of success, being weak, internally divided, and without firm contacts with one another. The Communists, for example, are splintered into Castroite, Maoist, and Russian segments, while the ETA cannot be identified with the general Basque nationalist movement. The more problematic element is how much dissidence will be allowed within the system and how much liberalization is going to be admitted. The government's intentions will be revealed by, among other things, its attitude towards the "a-legal opposition" such as the Christian Democrats; towards the movement to form political associations, as theoretically distinguished from political parties; towards the politicoeconomic activities of the "workers' commissions"; and towards the inflamed atmosphere among intellectuals and university groups.

A PEACEFUL TRANSITION?

Hardly anyone talks anymore of toppling Franco from power, and the question is not really what will happen immediately after Franco passes from the scene: a peaceful transition in the event of Franco's death can reasonably be expected. The problem is whether the Franco system can survive its founder in the long run. In the jockeying of forces for power after Franco, the King's initiative will be significant. His main task, and the main task of his government, will be the not easily reconcilable one of preserving authoritarian rule and allowing liberal evolution. Abrupt liberalization and the resulting disorder would be likely to force the military to intervene, while the absence of any liberalization would ignite the forces that have been restive for so long.

Gradual liberalization will have to be pursued if the government is not to be dependent on the army and the police. In seeking liberalization, the aid of the Church, the symbolic power of which is considerable, could be enlisted. The Church, in general, has tended to separate itself from purely political matters and from the continuing of too close an identification with Francoism. Its desire is for a peaceful transition after Franco to keep it from being confronted with a crucial situation. Especially among the younger clergy, there is a desire for social justice and for a relaxation of the rigid, authoritarian rule. The church could be of valuable assistance in the task of a politicosocial *aggiornamento*. Membership in the European Common Market would also reenforce liberalizing tendencies. For some time Spain has sought entry into the European Economic Community, but some of the latter's members have vetoed Spain's inclusion because of their objection to Franco. When that obstacle is removed, Spain's chances of belonging will be vastly improved.

Strangely, the future seems more uncertain than before. The horrors of the Civil War do not frighten the growing number of Spaniards who have no direct personal recollection of them as did their parents. The propaganda line of keeping Spain as a bulwark against Communism and Freemasonry is no longer very effective, since the menace of these enemies seems less real and threatening in an era of East-West detente, particularly now that Spain herself has opened commercial relations with Communist countries.

The slowing down of economic growth, which was to be expected, is hitting the working classes, while the general European recession is limiting the opportunity of Spaniards to seek employment abroad, and placing great uncertainty on the important tourist industry. The raging inflation is affecting the different classes severely. Franco's regime, which first started with its emphasis on its victory as a religious crusade and later changed its line to emphasizing that the Spaniards had "never had it better" in the material sphere, may find the people's stake in the regime eroded by economic problems.

It is still open to question whether the Franco regime will succeed in institutionalizing the first important non-Communist dictatorship or whether it will merely have been another impermanent, albeit long-lasting, military dictatorship.

PART

III

**SPAIN AND THE WORLD:
FOREIGN POLICY
AND SECURITY ISSUES**

8

SPAIN AND
LATIN AMERICA
Arthur P. Whitaker

Obviously, the course of Spain's post-Franco relations with Latin America depends not only on Spain but also on the 20 Latin American countries. As if that were not uncertain enough, all Latin America is now in a state of ferment, and the agitation is the greatest (and the future, consequently, the most obscure) in precisely those countries that are the most Europeanized and Western, Argentina, Uruguay, and Chile. In view of all this uncertainty, it would be absurd to venture a hard-and-fast prediction, and therefore most of this chapter will be addressed to the less ambitious but more fruitful task of identifying major trends in Spanish relations with Latin America and the factors that seem most likely to intensify or change them.

DEFINITIONS AND BACKGROUND

Spain's goals in Latin America in this century have almost always been primarily cultural and sentimental. They have been economic only in a limited field and to a limited degree, and political mainly as regards the effect within Spain itself. It is a good thing for Spain that this has been so, for otherwise her Latin American policy could be written off as a dismal failure, with little, if any, hope for the future. That policy, best though not fully represented by the term Hispanism (*hispanismo*), has been pursued with relatively few and minor variations ever since 1898. In that year, Spain's otherwise disastrous war with the United States proved a boon in terms of its relations with its former colonies in America, the independent Spanish-American states. Hitherto its relations with

119

them had been soured by Spain's retention of Cuba and Puerto Rico, which, as exhibits of colonialism in action, had kept very much alive the centuries-old "black legend" of Spanish greed and cruelty.

Far from going to pieces after the debacle of 1898, Spain reacted vigorously on two fronts: on the home front, through the so-called Generation of 1898; abroad, with an intensification of Hispanism. The two policies were interrelated in some ways, but separate in most. This chapter will be limited to Hispanism, the focus of which has been as definitely on relations with Hispanic America as the focus of the Generation of 1898 was on the internal renovation of Spain. I use "has been" and "was" because, while the Generation of 1898 has long since passed away, Hispanism is still alive and active.

Hispanism is used here in a broad, nontechnical sense that includes both Spain's conception of the Hispanic world, including Latin America, and also the whole wide spectrum of Spain's aims in Latin America. The conception stresses the unity of the Hispanic world and its race, religion, and language as bonds of unity. The aims, though primarily cultural and sentimental, as already noted, are also political and economic. The relative weight of these components has varied considerably, not only from one time to another, but also from one Spanish group and even from one individual to another. Consequently, the description fits present needs better than a precise definition, which is usually a bore anyway. Still, the description must note how Hispanism and related terms have been defined at various times.

The definition in Fredrick Pike's excellent book on Hispanism during the period 1898-1936, is likewise descriptive-chronological.[1] Summarized, it represents Hispanism as expressing a belief in "the fundamental unity of character of Spaniards and Spanish Americans" and in the right and duty of Mother Spain to take the lead in fostering this unity and maintaining the integrity of the Hispanic character. Views have differed about the name that should be given to the rather amorphous movement associated with this belief: Hispanism, Hispanicamericanism, Iberoamericanism, and Pan Hispanism have been suggested. As to its geographical scope, the main question has been whether it should include Portugal and Brazil; many, especially Portuguese and Brazilians, think not.

Also, and perhaps even more widely, views have differed about its significance in the political field. To cite Pike again, in the period 1898-1936 "most partisans of *hispanismo* viewed the movement as essentially opposed to Pan-Americanism."[2] In its early stages it was led by Spanish liberals, but in the 1920s control passed to conservatives, who from the mid-1930s to the mid-1940s—that is, during the period of the Spanish Civil War and the early years of the Franco regime—gave the movement its strongest political expression and the neological label *Hispanidad.* Interestingly enough, the Spanish originator of this term, Ramiro de Maeztu, in his *Defensa de la Hispanidad* (Madrid: Edicones Fat, 1934), appears to have borrowed it from Argentina by way of a Spanish priest residing in that country and by analogy with *Argentinidad,* a neologism given currency there as far back as 1916 by one of the most noted Argentine writers, Ricardo Rojas. It appears that Rojas himself may have adopted it under Spanish influence, but however that may be, the history of the term illustrates the "copenetration" or reciprocal cultural influence between Spain and Spanish America that is one of the most blameless pleasures of Hispanicists.

The most significant difference between *Hispanidad* and the older Hispanism, according to Pike, was religious rather than social (even Spanish liberal Hispanists being socially conservatives) or, by inference, political.[3] The liberals advocated religious toleration in a secular society, whereas conservative proponents of *Hispanidad* regarded the Catholic Church as the strongest bond of unity of the Spanish race and hence called for "a resurgence among its members of militant, uncompromising, exclusivist Catholicism." It seems clear that this religious motif has strong political implications, if only because in Spanish America religious conservatism has so often gone hand in hand with political conservatism. The point is of considerable consequence to our present inquiry because in both Spain and much of Latin America the Catholic Church is still a force to be reckoned with in public life but is no longer so closely identified with social and political conservatism.

SPAIN'S PRESENT LATIN AMERICAN POLICY

Except for a kind of "opening to the left" totally absent from her domestic policy, Spain's present Latin American policy seems much the same as the one forged by Foreign Minister Alberto Martin Artajo in the late 1940s and early 1950s and continued into the next decade by his successor, Fernando María de Castiella. It was a kind of Neo-Hispanidad purged of the pro-Axis and anti-Yankee connotations of Hispanidad in the prime of Hitler and Mussolini; it was aimed not at hegemony, but at cooperation. Nevertheless, the aims of Neo-Hispanidad were still ambitious. As stated in 1958 by the director of the policy's principal institutional expression, the Institute of Hispanic Culture, its objective was nothing less than the formation of a cultural, economic, and spiritual bloc of Hispanic nations with its own common market. Columbus Day, formerly *Día de la Raza* (Day of the Spanish Race) was officially renamed *Día de la Hispanidad.* Political objectives, though less prominent, were still pursued. Chief among those avowed, after the conclusion in 1953 of the air and naval bases agreement with the United States, was to assist the United States in combating communism in Latin America.[4]

Hispanic America was still given a place of honor in a 1973 comprehensive statement of foreign policy for Foreign Minister Gregorio López Bravo.[5] Bracketing Hispanic America with Gibraltar as of exceptional significance for Spaniards, López Bravo said that they must feel themselves deeply involved in the destiny of the Hispanic American republics and engage in technical and cultural cooperation with them. Spain, he continued, which is passing out of the underdeveloped stage in which most of the Latin American countries remain, can be very useful to them in these fields; and as for their forms of government, Spaniards recognize that, just as the "demoliberal" European model could not be followed by Spain, so the form adopted by each Hispanic American country must be appropriate to its particular situation.

This is an allusion to that "opening to the left" in Spain's Latin American policy to which I have referred. The opening had already been made in the early 1960s in the case of Fidel Castro's Cuban government. It was repeated in favor of the Salvador Allende government brought into office in Chile by the election of 1970. Late in 1972, with considerable fanfare, Foreign Minister López Bravo and Chile's ambassador to Spain signed, in the Palacio Santa Cruz, an "Accord of Financial Cooperation" under which the Spanish government granted Chile credits amounting to more than 2.5 billion pesetas (about $40 million). In January 1973 the ceremony was publicized in the Institute of Hispanic Culture's organ, *Mundo Hispanico.*[6]

An article in the same issue of *Mundo Hispánico* summarized the financial aid, amounting to just over $1 billion, furnished Hispanic America by Spain since the adoption of her new economic policy in 1959. The article forecast that the amount of aid would be tripled by 1980 and closed with a statement breathing the more pragmatic spirit of Neo-Hispanidad. "We hope," it said, "that the beginning of the next century will see us (the Hispanic nations) a united group, independent, prosperous . . . indestructibly united, not by memories of the past, but by the conquest of the future."

In Latin America the Institute of Hispanic Culture is assisted by local institutes, of which there were thirty-one in 1969, including six each in Argentina and Brazil, three each in Chile and Mexico, and one each in most of the other countries. In that year some 12,000 students from Latin America were attending Spanish universities—more Latin American students than in all other European universities combined—attracted by, among other things, the scholarships and special residences provided by the Madrid authorities. These students were drawn from all over the area, but with a concentration-distribution that may seem odd at first sight. The largest number, 13 percent, came from Cuba, as compared with 4 percent from Chile, with a population and stage of economic development about the same as that of Cuba, and only 2.5 percent from the far more populous Mexico, the government of which had never recognized the Franco regime. Venezuela and Colombia accounted for 10 and 9 percent, respectively, as compared with 8 percent from the substantially more populous but also more distant Argentina.[7]

A bird's-eye view of the activities of the parent institute in Madrid in its first 20 years, 1950-70, was provided by *Mundo Hispánico* in its report of the

First Congress of Ibero-American Former Fellows (*Ex-Becarios*). Under the institute's auspices the congress met in Madrid in January 1970. Some 400 *ex-
becarios*, described as only a small fraction of the total number, attended.
Among them, according to the report, were some 30-odd cabinet ministers, 23
rectors of universities, and "we don't know how may ambassadors, university
professors, writers, economists," and so on. Spain's mission in "the greater
fatherland which is the Iberian World" (*la gran patria que es el Mundo Ibérico*),
it continued, is thus revalidated.[8] So also the awareness that Spain is "the ideal
nucleus" and meeting place for the Hispanic American world, "for Spain's only
frontiers with that world are spiritual ones and she is involved in no commercial
rivalries and does not desire to displace any American country" (presumably a
reference to the United States). In closing, the report described the union of
these *ex-becarios* as constituting a common market of the intellectual and moral
elite of Ibero-American that was more promising and more urgent than a
common market of agricultural products and raw materials could be. The
thought was one that befitted a cultural institute.

The concept referred to as Neo-Hispanidad seems much the same as the
"Hispanic Commonwealth" idea discussed in Herbert Goldhamer's 1972 book,
The Foreign Powers in Latin America, cited above.[9] He notes that, by treaties of
double nationality and otherwise, the Spanish government had been pushing this
idea, which has some support among Spaniards and also, though less, among
Latin Americans. These statements of fact are followed by two questionable
comments. The first is that these insistent appeals to ties forged many years ago
show how little Spain's aspirations in Latin America have been fulfilled. In my
opinion they show only that there are people on both sides of the Atlantic who
are not satisfied with what has been accomplished, however, much or little that
may be. To put it another way, they show that Hispanicism is a hardy perennial
that survives in the face of repeated disappointments. Also, in my view, Spanish
aspirations are less closely identified with power politics than Goldhamer seems
to think, and these aspirations are in a sense rewarded, if not fulfilled, by asserting them and striving to achieve them even though the effort fails.

Goldhamer's second comment is that Spain's relatively modest importance
to Latin America as compared with that of Western Europe, the United States,
or even Japan is "a measure of how much commerce, investment, economic and
political power have counted in comparison with the linguistic, religious, and
cultural-historical ties that relate Hispanic America to Spain, past and present."
Again I take exception, this time, to two words: "measure," which gives the
proposition an air of scientific or at least mathematical accuracy that it does not
in fact possess; and "power," because it is no less inadequate a clue to Latin
American opinion and policy over the years than (as suggested above) to the
opinion and policy of Spain.

I enter these dissents with regret because Goldhamer's book, though by no
means focused on Spain, contains other comments and much information that

make it quite useful. Particularly useful are its comparative data on the economic and other relations of foreign powers with Latin America, which do indeed bear out his statement that Spain has fallen far short of realizing its Hispanicist dreams of leadership—that is, they do if measured with an economic yardstick. In trade, for example, it lags far behind the United States and most of Western Europe, even in the Spanish-speaking countries and even in those branches of trade in which a common language is a head start. Thus in Latin America's book imports, the United States ranks first in most countries; among the larger countries Spain is also outranked by one or more European countries except in Chile, Venezuela, and Portugeuese-speaking Brazil. Spain fares even worse in other branches of publishing and communications, being mentioned by Goldhamer as a leading source of movies only in Colombia and Venezuela and not mentioned at all among the principal foreign sources of Latin American imports of newspapers, magazines, press services, radio, and TV.[10]

Stated in this way the results of nearly a century of Pan-Hispanic effort seem quite discouraging; yet instead of being downhearted, the Spaniards keep plugging away at it, apparently with as much determination as ever. Why the Spanish do so, when common sense might tell them to try something else, is a puzzle not to be disposed of by facile references to Don Quixote. Perhaps the answer may lie partly in Spanish confidence that similar value systems will bring success in the long run, but there are other reasons of a more practical kind. The authorities in Spain seem, for example, to have received lasting encouragement from the important role played by the majority of Latin American governments, first in halting reprisals against the Franco regime for its pro-Axis posture just before and early in World War II, and second in getting Spain admitted to the United Nations.[11]

Subsequently, similar evidence of a Hispanic "hands across the sea" and "blood is thicker than water" spirit emerged in the UN debates on colonialism. Thus the Latin Americans' vigorous anticolonialism has been turned on full force in Spain's favor on the hotly debated Gibraltar question[12] (as in 1967, when a mixed bag of Latin American, Communist, and Arab votes carried a pro-Spanish resolution), but has been conveniently forgotten by most of them when the issue arises of Spain's own enclaves in Morocco and elsewhere in Africa. There is also the Madrid meeting, discussed above, of Latin American *ex-becarios*, which brought together a very substantial number of political and cultural leaders from Latin America who had lived in Spain, had presumably been indoctrinated there, and liked the country well enough to return to it for this congress.

Finally, not to make the list too long, the great success of the new economic policy adopted by Spain in 1959 gave its leaders further encouragement to persevere in its Hispanicist policy. Within the following 12 years its gross national product increased threefold and the number of automobiles tenfold, and enough of the prosperity trickled down to make it seem a national achievement, a "Spanish miracle" comparable to the "German miracle" of the 1950s.

For the Hispanic movement the "miracle" is particularly important because it has provided Spain with more resources for carrying out its Hispanic policy and has fortified the Spaniards' confidence in their ability to provide leadership for the Hispanic family. In the latter connection its effect was intensified by the dramatic contrast between the success of Spain's new economic policy and the dismal failure of a similar policy adopted at almost the same time in Argentina, where it not only failed in its economic objectives but was also a major factor in the political disaster that overwhelmed its chief Argentine sponsor, President Arturo Frondizi, and his administration in 1962.[13]

HISPANIC PROSPECTS IN POST-FRANCO SPAIN

Hispanism will continue to receive support from whichever government succeeds the present Caudillo's, just as it has received that of all the assorted governments that have preceded it from the turn of the century to the present—constitutional monarchy, Primo de Rivera dictatorship, Second Republic, Franco dictatorship. Of course, the kind of Hispanism that will be fostered after Franco's passing depends on the kind of government that succeeds his, just as the liberal Hispanism of the period before 1920 gave way to a conservative one, which was soon remodeled as Hispanidad, which in turn gave way to the present Neo-Hispanidad.

So we face the question, what will the post-Franco government of Spain be like? One can expect the *continuismo* of the present Spanish regime to prevail to the extent that in the post-Franco period there will be a high degree of continuity as regards form of government, composition of major interest and power groups, and trends in major policies, both domestic and foreign. There will be change, of course, as there has been under the Franco regime itself, despite all the talk there has been about its immobilism.

Specifically, a continuation of authoritarianism in some form or other can be expected, as well as the preponderance of the armed forces and *la banca* (Spain's Wall Street, so to speak), with the acquiescence if not the support of the country's new large and still-growing business and professional classes. As regards policies at home, the government will adhere to the policies, including the economic policy of mixed private enterprise and state intervention, that are credited with working the country's economic "miracle" since 1959. It will continue the labor policy of just enough concessions to the workers to forestall an explosion. Abroad, there will be a policy of continuing the preferential relationship with the United States of the last 20 years, but with increased efforts to build up an economic and political counterpoise to it. There will probably also be a widening of the opening to the left already begun in Spain's foreign relations.

Another civil war in Spain is not expected. France has never had another since the bloody suppression of the Paris Commune of 1871, and to Spaniards their Civil War of 1936-39 was a Paris Commune of much longer protracted agony. Nor will Franco be followed by a republic, if only because of the widespread fear among Spaniards that the establishment of another republic might bring on another civil war.

The Catholic Church has always been widely regarded, especially by conservatives on both sides, as one of the strongest bonds between Spain and her former American colonies. Consequently, the question arises whether that bond will be weakened by the sweeping change now in progress in the Church's Spanish branch. The process is inspired partly by the watchword of the universal church in the Vatican Council—*aggiornamento*, updating or modernization—but it was also provoked by, and is addressed to, specifically Spanish problems associated with the Franco regime.

From criticism of the regime and a call for separation of church and state, the reformers in Spain have gone on to urge a restructuring of society in the interest of social justice. People cannot be expected to act justly themselves when they are forced to live "under the inhuman weight of unjust systems," a commission of Spanish bishops warned in a report, published in 1972, which has been described as "the severest and most open criticism of the [Franco] regime ever launched by the Spanish Church."[14] Not surprisingly, the government began to prepare charges against the head of the commission, Monsignor Rafael González Moralejo, bishop of Huelva. I spent an inspiring day with Bishop Gonzáles Moralejo in 1959, when he was auxiliary bishop of Valencia, and I admire him greatly for the courageous and enlightened reformer he already was at that time and still is. The fact is, however, that besides promoting the separation of church and state, the reform group of which he is a leader is dividing the church itself. Though now able to carry a majority in Church councils on some important questions, the reformers are opposed by a strong conservative phalanx, and both groups seem to have substantial strength among laymen as well as the clergy.

This ecclesiastical upheaval in Spain could have adverse repercussions overseas, and the likelihood that it might seems all the greater in view of the fact that large numbers of Spanish priests still serve in the chronically understaffed churches of Spanish America. It should be remembered, however, that similar disturbances are shaking the church everywhere and that Latin America is no exception. There too, as I shall show in detail below, strong reform elements are urging programs aimed at profound alterations in society at large for the benefit of the masses, as well as in the Church itself; and the odds are that the upheaval will continue on both sides of the Atlantic for several years, that is (presumably), well into the post-Franco period. Instead of alienating Hispanic America, the ferment in the Spanish church is more likely to keep the two on a parallel if not converging course.

In short, the degree of change, either secular or ecclesiastical, between present and post-Franco Spain will not be sufficient to alter substantially the present course of Spanish relations with Latin America. If any such alteration takes place in the years ahead, it is more likely to have its source in Latin America. What are the prospects there?

PROSPECTS IN LATIN AMERICA

In approaching this aspect of the problem we should begin by defining and reducing the political-geographical area to be considered. If the problem is to be considered exclusively in terms of Hispanicism, the first step should be to drop Haiti, which even the most rabid Hispanicist could hardly keep with a straight face. The next step should be to cancel out the one-half of South America and one-third of all Latin America comprised in Brazil, though many Hispanicists would not agree. Indeed, the proposition would be condemned as rankest heresy by the present high priest of Hispanicism, Julián Marías. In a recent discussion of terminology he rejected the term "Latin America," as well he might, except that it is too well established in universal usage to be abolished now. Instead he prefers "the Spains" (*las Españas*), but says he finds "Hispanic America" and "Ibero-America" equally acceptable on the ground that all three mean the same thing and all three include Portugal and Brazil as well as Spain and Spanish America. For proof he quotes Portugal's great poet Camoëns' description of the Portuguese people as "a most sturdy people of Spain" (*una gente fortissima d'Espanha*).[15] The trouble with this is that Camoëns, besides being a poet, lived in the 16th century and is hardly an authority on the relation of Portugal and Brazil to Hispanicism in the late 20th century. As for Marías himself, he is a convincing writer about his native Spain and an eminent authority on his maestro, José Ortega y Gasset, but he knows Hispanic America mainly through one of its most Hispanic and least typical countries, Argentina.

The present Spanish government apparently takes about the same view of the extended Spanish family as Marías, for as noted above, it has established more Institutes of Hispanic Culture in Brazil than in any other country except Argentina; accordingly, Brazil is included in this discussion of Hispanicism. All the signs, however, indicate that the Brazilians (not to mention the Portuguese) have no intention of being drawn into any Hispanic or Iberian association in which, as Marías puts it, though no orders would be given, Spain would be the *plaza mayor,* the main square and central meeting place of all members of the Hispanic family.[16] The term is typical. No matter how hard he may try, no Spaniard seems to be able to talk or write about the Hispanic family without somehow elevating Spain above the rest. However natural or justifiable this may be, Spanish Americans and Brazilians do not take kindly to it.

Every year that passes makes it less palatable to the latter, for in recent years Brazil has achieved an economic development rivaling the Spanish "miracle." So, with a population three times as large as Spain's and growing faster, and with far greater and more varied natural resources, it is no wonder that Brazilians scoff at Spanish pretensions and confidently expect that Brazil will soon become a major world power—a position Spain has not held for more than three centuries.

Brazil's relations with her nine Spanish-American neighbors in South America add nothing to the credibility of the extended Hispanic family idea. A rivalry with Argentina as old as the nations themselves is only one sign of the wide gap that separates Brazil from all these Spanish American neighbors except perhaps Uruguay. The gap has been closed only on special occasions and in individual cases, as when Brazil and Chile have teamed up against Argentina in the minor league games of South American power politics. In recent years the gap has widened as a result of Brazil's exceptionally rapid growth, which has aggravated Spanish American apprehensions of a Brazilian bid for hegemony.

Spain will no doubt continue to cultivate relations with Brazil regardless of the prospects of Hispanicism in the latter. In doing so, however, Madrid will have to work its way without any of the advantages of common language, literature, and tradition that enable it to keep its head above water in Spanish America. Spain and Brazil do have in common a spectacular economic growth and the authoritarian character of their governments. On the other hand, their respective economies are not interrelated with each other, and despite a common authoritarianism, their governmental systems differ too widely to provide a basis for building anything approaching political or ideological unity between them. There is, in short, no apparent reason to expect any great change, for either the better or the worse, in post-Franco relations between Spain and Hispanicism, on the one hand, and the biggest of the Big Three countries of Latin America, on the other.

PROSPECTS IN SPANISH AMERICA

We must still consider Spain's relations with the 18 Spanish-American states. In Spain's relations with the largest of these, Mexico, it is easy to believe that the post-Franco period may bring about a significant change—for the better, from Spain's point of view. There is a possibility that, after Franco passes from the scene, the addition of some more of the window dressing of self-government with which his system has already been decked out might at last induce the Mexican government to renew completely normal relations with Spain.

The probabilities favor such a change. Much of the animus against the Franco regime is against the man himself; when he is gone, a rather slight liberalization of his regime will be enough to mollify its critics, in Mexico as elsewhere.

Such a liberalization is likely to take place in any case in order to remove the long-standing bar to Spain's admission to the European Common Market—an event that has become doubly desirable to Spain now that Britain has joined it, since Britain is Spain's best customer except for the combined membership of the Common Market itself. One would think that Mexico too would welcome a plausible excuse for ending a rupture that is now nearly 40 years old and has come to seem an anachronism at a time when Nixon has visited Peking and Moscow, when Brezhnev has visited Bonn, and when Franco has furnished aid to a Chilean government well to the left of the left-wing Mexican regime that has kept the breach with Spain open all these years. Keeping it open does Spain no harm and seems to have little effect of any kind except to impede Mexico's efforts (paralleling Spain's, by the way) to diversify her foreign ties so as to keep from becoming too dependent on the United States.

POLITICIZATION AND POLITICAL TRENDS

Some ten years ago Roger Vekemans, and other specialists on Latin America called attention to the spread of "politicization" in Latin America.[17] Now, Herbert Goldhamer, in the book already cited, has produced a brief but perceptive analysis of the phenomenon, which he calls in terms of medical pathology, "political hypertrophy, . . . that is, the hyperpenetration of the political into most organs, functions, and spheres of life."[18] In Goldhamer's explanation of this development, three factors stand out: the colonial heritage of government control; the rapid growth of statism since 1930, as in the displacement of private business by state enterprises; and the lack in most of Latin America, as in other underdeveloped regions, of those partly insulated organs and institutions that, in the more highly developed countries, tend to diffuse power and hence to curb interest in political power. In Latin American societies, on the other hand, "hyperpoliticization . . . drains the attention and efforts of important sectors of society and focuses them on the political arena, . . . and the exercise of power becomes equivalent to the total 'administration' of society, and in some cases, the paralysis of it."[19]

Goldhamer's analysis could have been refined and extended, as no doubt it would have been if the author's main concern had been with Latin America itself instead of with the activities and interests of foreign powers in that area. It seems clear, for instance, that politicization is even more widespread than his brief account might lead one to think. A striking example that bears directly on the subject of this paper is one already mentioned in discussing Spain, the recent rise of a powerful movement among Roman Catholics in favor of demanding extensive changes in the structure of society and the distribution of wealth in the interest of social justice, and asserting the right and duty of the Catholic Church to intervene in public life to bring them about.

This is the most obvious kind of politicization. It is paradoxical that it should be taking place at the same time, and often with support from the same people; that separation of church and state is being strongly urged where it does not already exist, as in Spain, and confirmed where it does, as in Chile. One might say that the Church is leaving politics by the front door only to return by the service entrance.

Consequently the state of the Catholic Church is very important, probably as important in much of Latin America as it is in Spain, though there are wide variations from country to country, in this as in nearly every other respect. Latin Americans make up 35 percent of the world total of some 700 million Catholics, and while the proportion of Latin Americans who practice the faith actively seems to be abnormally low, there are signs that the Church there is very much alive.*

One such sign is that the Church in Latin America is in the midst of a reform movement like the one in the Spanish Church. This parallel development is of particular interest. On the one hand, it may strengthen the bonds of religion between Spain and Spanish America by heightening their sense of common purpose. On the other hand, the reform movement in Latin America is marked by a definite strain of anti-Europeanism that could estrange these Catholic reformers from their counterparts in Spain.

Though this anti-European strain is unmistakable, its strength is impossible to determine at this time, for the Latin American reform movement has begun to assume substantial proportions so recently that studies of it are soon outdated. For example, Ivan Vallier's article, "Church 'Development' in Latin America: A Five-Country Comparison," first published in 1967 and reprinted in 1972, is interesting, even stimulating, and was well-informed for its time; yet by the mid-1970s it is already outdated in important respects.[22] Quite aside from the fact that the concept of development has lost much of the glamor it had when Vallier wrote, his article gives a very inadequate picture of the church reform movement in Latin America at large, which did not get well started until

---

*A dimmer and otherwise different view of the Catholic Church in Latin America is taken by some able writers in leading journals. Two examples, both of which I regard as partly wishful thinking and as typical of Latin American diversity. The first is "La política vaticanista en América Latina," by Carlos M. Rama,[20] to the effect that the church there is "languishing," that the efforts to revive it by reform are really aimed at promoting the designs of the Pentagon and U.S. economic imperialism, and (not very consistently) that the attempt by Pope Paul VI, on a recent visit to Latin America, to *curb* the church reform movement was made in favor of the arch-reactionary sector of Latin American society, an ally of Yankee imperialism.

The second example is Darío Canton, "'Revolucion argentina' de 1966 y proyecto nacional,"[21] which represents the Church in Argentina as still essentially traditionalist, the tardy "movement of as having won little support in the hierarchy, and religion *"como cosa viva"* (as a living thing) as having "no meaning" in Argentina.

the following year at the General Conference of the Latin American Episcopate held at Medellín, Colombia, in August and September 1968.

Furthermore, Vallier's article paints individual Latin American countries in colors that have run since he wrote. Of Argentina, for instance, he asserts that it is one of the countries in which "progressive groups" have attempted to "create and to generalize a meaningful ideology of social change but without important successes."[23] In fact, in 1969 the Argentine bishops held a meeting at which they drew up and published a declaration that followed the guidelines for reform set by the recent Medellín Conference and by the papal encyclicals of John XXIII and Paul VI. In conformity with these, the declaration committed the Church in Argentina not only to sweeping reforms in the Church itself, in such matters as liturgy and organization, but also to structural change in society at large in the interest of social justice.[24] How effective the reform effort will be remains to be seen, but at any rate the effort is being made, with apparent sincerity, in Argentina and other Latin American countries as well.

In several ways the Catholic reform movement in Latin America differs from the one in Spain. For one thing, the former has been marked by more violence, both espoused and practiced. Brazil, of which the people, mythology tells us, are exceptionally pacific, has been uncommonly productive of both varieties. Colombia, however, has produced the most famous exponent of both espoused and practiced violence in Camilo Torres, a priest and a member of an upper-class family.[25] Maintaining that in Colombia violence was the only road to social justice, Torres practiced what he preached, and died practicing it as a guerrilla.

Another difference between the two Hispanic branches of the Catholic reform movement is the already-mentioned strain of anti-Europeanism in the Latin American branch, which has so far been confined largely to that branch's left wing. There it is clearly related to the populistic nationalism that is now rampant in Latin America. In the name of national independence, nationalists of that breed condemn rather indiscriminately every reminder, cultural as well as economic and political, of Latin America's exploitation by "imperialists"—a term that in cultural matters refers primarily to Western Europe.

Unequivocal expression of this anti-European bias is found in a thoughtful and profusely documented position paper, "Currents and Tendencies in Contemporary Latin American Catholicism," prepared in 1970 by an Uruguayan professor of sociology, Cesar A. Aguiar, for the Catholic Inter-American Cooperation Program (CICOP).[26] "The church," wrote Aguiar, "is intimately bound to the social structures of Latin America," and "the key to bring about [imperative] changes in society at large . . . is to eliminate dependence," meaning, of course, dependence on foreign "imperialists."[27] Surveying left-wing Catholic thought on this problem in the years since the Vatican Council, which had had, he said, "a profound impact on the Latin American church," he noted the existence in it of one school that "insisted on continued identification with the masses because of the post-Medellín view of *the need for a social nationalistic and even anti-European protest.*"[28] (Emphasis here and in following sentences is mine.) Again, he attributed to "the avant-garde groups" the rejection, or at least the revision, "except by certain small . . . elitist circles," of the *"European approach* to the theology of secularization."[29] Yet again, he recorded the *"explicitly anti-European"* position taken by the Third World Priests' Association in Argentina and the "great emphasis" now laid on "the need to rethink theology, primarily to cope with the political issues and . . . liberation."[30]

POLITICAL TRENDS IN LATIN AMERICA

This brings us to a direct consideration of the political prospects of post-Franco Spain in Latin America, which so far have been noticed only peripherally. These depend mainly on Latin America. The political trends there are more favorable than one might think for friendly relations on equal terms, but not favorable for a political or economic league or union, least of all one in which the Latin Americans would be subordinated to Spain.

There are two main political trends in Latin America at the present time. One is a kind of fascist militarism; the other, a populistic, civilian Peronism, though not necessarily under that label. I do not regard the former socialist-communist regime under Allende in Chile as the Latin American wave of the future. If it had survived and prospered, it would no doubt have influenced other Latin American countries; but even if its influence had been profound, it would not have been copied by any of them, any more than Castro's Cuba has been. Its influence on them would have been much more likely to promote the two trends mentioned above, by stimulating some people to join Peronist-type movements, while provoking others to rally around the militarists.

The militarist type is discussed, and its bearing on relations with Spain suggested, in an article by Gino Germani, published in 1969 but still timely.[31] After speaking of the various forms of fascism, he notes that "in Latin America attempts have been made since the 1930s, but with greater frequency in the past decade, to set up another, a military, form of fascism, or more precisely, a functional military substitute for fascism."[32] The most advanced Latin American countries, he adds in a footnote, are passing through a situation comparable to that of the Latin countries of Europe between the two world wars, but differences in structural configurations, ideological climates, and other factors tend to generate different forms of fascism from the original, or a functional substitute for it. Also, the ambivalence and incoherence of the Latin American middle class, which remains the key factor, may help to bring about some kind of fascist solution in Latin America. In this situation, concludes Germani, the dynamic factor is represented by the military, whose intervention replaces the massive movements of classic (European) fascism aimed at demobilizing the lower classes and protecting the upper classes against the risks involved in modernization.

Returning to the subject a little later in the same article,[33] Germani makes it clear that he regards the Spain of Franco as not only authoritarian with some totalitarian features, but also as basically fascist in its purposes and historical significance. The case of Spain, he notes, is particularly interesting in relation to Latin America, since "up to a certain point," Spain "is drawing closer to the fascist regimes on the rise in those [Latin American] countries."[34]

I would, however, suggest two emendations to Germani's remarks. One is that not only fascist but also populist regimes are on the rise in Latin America today, and the other, that Spain is seeking to "draw closer" to regimes of both types, civilian populist as well as military fascist.

As already stated, I regard the rise of these populist regimes as one of the two main political trends in Latin America, and I expect them to be predominantly of the Peronist type. This is not the place to go at length into the reasons for thinking so, which I stated in an article published in 1973,[35] but briefly, they are based on the belief that present-day Peronism is the most persuasive form of Latin America's "new nationalism," which is in fact only an updating of one form of the original, protean Peronism of the 1940s. In each country the new nationalism combines a primarily Yankeephobic antiimperialism with a demand for sweeping social reform at the expense of the *"vendepatria"* (country-selling) oligarchy. Among the restless masses and the generally Marxist intellectuals of the left wing, the new nationalism seems to be making an increasingly strong appeal. In Argentina, for example, in 1973 a free election gave the Peronists control of the national government (and nearly all the provincial governments) for the first time since Peron was ousted. Whether the numerous Peronist factions can work together in power remains to be seen.

The concern here is with the bearing of this neonationalist trend on Latin American relations with post-Franco Spain. No such trend, one suspects, would be tolerated in Spain itself, any more after Franco than it is under him, but foreign policy is another matter, and surely a policy flexible enough to accommodate the communist and left-wing socialist regimes in Cuba and Chile would not find it hard to live with a regime of the Peronist persuasion. Indeed, if Perón himself had been personally involved in it, such a regime could reasonably have expected a cordial *abrazo* from Madrid. In the late 1940s Perón's government and Franco's were united in a quasi-alliance, and although this was soon dissolved, any coolness that followed has long since disappeared. Perón spent most of his exile in Spain with the acquiescence, if not the encouragement, of its government, and he formed many ties there. According to some unverified reports, he widened the market for Argentine exports in Spain and elsewhere in Europe.

Le Monde Diplomatique supports this view in an article on Perón's return visit to Argentina in November 1972 by its generally well-informed Latin American correspondent Elena de la Souchère, in which she says in part that, from the

Bolivian revolution of 1952 to the present military regime in Peru, other nationalist leaders "s'inspirent, pour l'essential, du viex fonds péronistes."[36]

Peronism, under whatever label, will probably flourish and spread and become a major factor in Spain's relations with Latin America after Franco. It is also likely to prove compatible with good relations between these two divisions of the Hispanic world; that is, unless the lunatic fringe of Peronism gains control, which is doubtful. Like the new nationalism at large, the Peronist variety is strongly xenophobic, but this should be no impediment to good relations with Spain, since it is directed primarily against foreign interests and activities of an economic character in Latin America; and, as pointed out above, Spain's position in Latin America is weakest in the economic sphere. Thus does weakness become strength, and a liability an asset.

NOTES

1. Fredrick Pike, *Hispanismo, 1898-1936* (Notre Dame, Ind.: Notre Dame University Press, 1971), pp. 1-3.

2. Ibid., p. 3.

3. Ibid., p. 3.

4. A. P. Whitaker, *Spain and Defense of the West* (New York: Frederick A. Praeger, 1961), pp. 342-43.

5. "Política Exterior Española," *Mundo Hispánico* (Madrid), no. 263 (February 1970): 72.

6. "Objectivo Hispanico," *Mundo Hispánico* (Madrid), no. 298 (January 1973): 59.

7. This paragraph is based on Herbert Goldhamer, *The Foreign Powers in Latin America* (Princeton, N.J.: Princeton University Press, 1972), pp. 145-46.

8. "Hoy y Manana de la Hispanidad," *Mundo Hispánica* (Madrid), no. 263 (February 1970): 71-72.

9. Goldhamer, op. cit., pp. 111-12.

10. Ibid., pp. 151-56.

11. Whitaker, op. cit., pp. 344-48.

12. Goldhamer, op. cit., pp. 54-55.

13. A. P. Whitaker, *Argentina* (Englewood Cliffs, N.J.: Prentice Hall, 1964), pp. 61-65.

14. *Ibérica* 20, no. 1 (New York, 15 January 1972): 11.

15. Julián Marías, *Esquema de nuestra situación* (Buenos Aires: Editorial Columba, 1970), p. 37.

16. Ibid.

17. Cited in Goldhamer, pp. 288-89.

18. Ibid., pp. 288-89; see also pp. 284-85.

19. Ibid., p. 289.

20. Carlos M. Rama, "La Política Vaticanista en América Latina," *Cuadernos Americanos* 166, no. 5 (September-October 1969): 31-44.

21. Darío Canton, "'Revolucion argentina' de 1966 y proyecto nacional," *Revista Latinoamericana de Sociología* 5, no. 3 (November 1969): 524-43.

22. Ivan Vallier, "Church 'Development' in Latin America: A Five-Country Comparison," in *The Roman Catholic Church in Modern Latin America*, ed. Karl M. Schmitt (New York: Knopf, 1972), pp. 167-93.

23. Ibid., p. 181.

24. Ismael Quiles, S.J., "El Catolicismo en la Argentina, hoy," in *Qué es la Argentina* (Buenos Aires: 1970), pp. 257-310, especially pp. 274-300.

25. Schmitt, op. cit., pp. 139-46, includes selections from the revolutionary writings of Camilo Torres; also, pp. 147-51, a selection from Torres's Brazilian admirer, the archbishop of Olinda and Recife, Hélder Pessoa Camara, who wrote that "the memory of Camilo Torres or of Ché Guevara merits as much respect as that of Martin Luther King" (p. 150).

26. Cesar A. Aguiar, "Currents and Tendencies in Contemporary Latin American Catholicism," *IDOC International,* North American edition, no. 13 (14 November 1970): 50-73.

27. Ibid., p. 60.

28. Ibid.

29. Ibid., p. 62.

30. Ibid.

31. Gino Germani, "Socialización política de la juventud en los régimenes fascistas: Italia y España," *Revista Latinoamericana de Sociología* 5, no. 3 (November 1969): 544-92.

32. Ibid., p. 547.

33. Ibid., p. 549 and note 8.

34. Ibid.

35. Arthur P. Whitaker, "The New Nationalism in Latin America," *Review of Politics* 35, no. 1 (January 1973): 77-90.

36. Elena de la Souchère, "L'Argentine après le retour du 'lider' exilé," *Le Monde Diplomatique,* December 1972, p. 5.

Relations with Spain, perhaps more than with any other country in U.S. history, have veered for three centuries between extreme hostility at certain times and close, even cordial, collaboration at others.

In part, this was the result of geographical propinquity, which during America's revolutionary era often led to friction. In part, it was national dynamics: the Spanish empire was crumbling as the "manifest destiny" of the United States was gathering speed. In part, it has been the result of exigencies of the past quarter-century, during which the United States assumed the defense of the "Free World," and Spain, at first reluctantly but then with accelerating self-interest, fell into line.

For the past 20 years the United States, in its role of world policeman against Soviet aggression, has tended to regard Spain as an important, if occasionally difficult, pawn on the chessboard of global strategy. Spain, on the other hand, has made bilateral relations with the United States the key to its foreign policy, its escape hatch from politicoeconomic isolation and its reintroduction into the family of nations.

Currently, these relationships are subtly changing. No longer is Spain's geographic location at the mouth of the Mediterranean of quite such importance, given the U.S. detente with the USSR, friendship with mainland China, and generally relaxed conditions throughout the world.

Spain's own needs, too, are changing. With $5 billion in convertible currency reserves; with a strong and expanding economy; and with, superficially, at least, domestic stability, Spain now wants integration with Western Europe, particularly the European Economic Community (EEC).

The United States and Spain still need each other, but their need is shifting from the requirements of mutual defense in the Cold War to a more subtle, relaxed relationship embodying tourism, trade, and cultural and scientific exchanges.

Over this relationship hangs the imponderable: which road will Spain pursue when Franco dies? The Caudillo, now in his 82nd year, has ruled Spain for 36 years. The embodiment of law and order, the political manipulator extraordinary, Franco has presided, erratically, even shakily, over an economic miracle. Spain is prospering.

Has there, however, been a concomitant political miracle? Have Spain's traditional political passions finally been drowned in a rising wave of consumerism, of bourgeois comfort, of new job opportunities, of new cars, refrigerators, washing machines, and television?

Will Spaniards too young to have known the bloodbath, hunger, and deprivations of the 1936-39 Civil War meekly accept a continuation of the same rigid rule once Franco has gone, or will they insist on those democratic freedoms enjoyed throughout Western Europe: free elections, political parties, free trade unions, free speech?

It is too soon to tell, but Americans who have closely followed Spanish affairs for many years feel increasingly concerned about the "overidentification" of the United States with the Franco regime; about the U.S. policy dating from the Cold War of concentrating solely on the quick use of military bases to the exclusion of all else.

A new tide is rising in Spain; are the Americans aware of it?

EARLY RELATIONS

Historically the United States and Spain are closely bound. St. Augustine, Florida, founded by Spaniards, is the oldest city in the United States. Santa Fe, New Mexico, also founded by Spaniards, is our oldest state capital.

Arms and money provided during the American Revolution by Charles III of Spain through Beaumarchais, librettist of the opera *Figaro* and one of the great secret agents of modern times, materially helped in the war against Great Britain. Then the pendulum swung: American frontiersmen pushing westward over the Appalachian ranges into the valleys of the Ohio and the Mississippi found the mouth of the great river, their natural outlet to trade, blocked by an often venal, sometimes tyrannical, Spanish power in the then Spanish city of New Orleans.

Frustrated and angry, the frontiersmen, who were preponderantly of Anglo-Saxon Protestant stock, importuned Jefferson to throw the Spanish out or, alternately, backed plots such as those conceived by Aaron Burr to wrest Mexico from Spanish rule.

Napoleon's occupation of Spain and his cynical sale of Spain's Louisiana Territory, overnight doubling the size of the infant United States, staved off a

U.S. clash with Spain. Moreover, it paved the way for the purchase of Spanish Florida in 1819, thus eliminating another point of friction. While the post-Napoleonic revolt of Spain's South American colonies, abetted in many cases by U.S. agents, and the U.S. war with Mexico in 1846 virtually eliminated "Spanish" rule from the New World, insurgents from Spanish oppression in Cuba and Puerto Rico found sympathy and arms in the United States.

The young, thrusting United States expanded geographically, economically, militarily, and some might say arrogantly. Spain, by comparison, declined steadily in U.S. eyes; the once mighty empire was withering. In 1898 came the final spasm.

President McKinley, goaded by jingoistic U.S. newspaper proprietors, by Congressional and public figures proclaiming America's "manifest destiny," and by swashbucklers hungry for spoils, declared war. The mysterious explosion of the U.S.S. Maine in Spanish Havana was only a pretext for war, not a cause.

Within weeks Spain lay stripped of the last shreds of a great empire. Cuba, the "Pearl of the Antilles," Puerto Rico, Guam, and the huge, rich, sprawling Philippines became U.S. possessions, though neither McKinley nor anyone in his entourage had planned to seize or even knew what to do with the 7,000-island Philippine archipelago. In the United States there were victory parades for Admiral Dewey, Teddy Roosevelt, Leonard Wood, and other heroes of the fray, but in Spain there was only anger against the United States, which had declared war even as Spain was signaling fresh concessions over Cuba.

As Spain's soldiers and sailors came home in defeat, there arose an inner conviction that the genesis of Spain's defeat lay in a decadent monarchy and a corrupt political system. The writers, philosophers, poets, and other intellectuals of the "Generation of '98" now called on their countrymen for a cleansing and a renewal, self-discipline, and a renunciation of tawdry imperial "glory." The medicine was harsh, and the debate it provoked rent the Spanish people for years to come.

RELATIONS BETWEEN 1900 AND 1950

For the next half-century, until around 1950, dislike and distrust of the United States was to mark those who, for better or worse, ruled the Spanish; and in truth, many developments in the distant United States adversely affected Spain.

The 1929 Wall Street crash; the protectionist Smoot-Hawley tariff; the continuing U.S. depression; and U.S. credit shortages, stagnating trade, and growing unemployment—all these affected Spain. Soon Spain, like her richer neighbors, Germany and Italy, was faced with a terrible choice in solving its politicoeconomic malaise. The great masses of moderation and reform dithered, and so the choice was Left or Right: Communism or Fascism.

In 1936 Spain became the cockpit of the struggle, and the Spanish Civil War a rehearsal for World War II. Franco, an avowed admirer of much, if not all, in Nazi fascism emerged victor of Spain. This cardinal fact has permeated, if not dominated, Spanish relations with the United States ever since.

The United States has always seen "Franco" when it should have been concentrating on "Spain." There are 35 million Spaniards whose voices one day will be heard; whether in harmony or in cacophony remains to be seen.

In thinking of the Spanish people, as distinct from Franco, I often recall a talk in Madrid in 1962 with the late General Agustín Muñoz Grandes, after Franco the country's ranking military leader. He was already grizzled, ill, stiff with wounds received on battlefields from Morocco to Russia; but he was also a man of conviction and integrity who, had he ever dared risk Franco's displeasure, might have won wide public support. However, utterly loyal to Franco, his comrade-in-arms during the French-Spanish "mopping up" in the Rif in 1925, he deliberately obscured himself.

Muñoz Grandes was reluctant to see any newspaperman at first, but finally agreed, and the meeting was in his simply furnished apartment. There he talked of many things: Africa; the Soviet front where he had commanded Franco's Blue Division; Spain's future; and especially of the United States.

"My generation grew up to hate your country," he said quietly. "You defeated us in 1898 and humbled us. You were hostile to us during and after World War II. But later, during the 1950s, after we'd signed the base agreements, your Pentagon invited me to visit the U.S. Two events changed my opinion of your country. First, visiting Fort Benning one day I saw approaching a group of American soldiers in fatigue uniforms escorted by a non-com. He saluted me but they didn't. My escort officer explained that they were military prisoners who while serving their sentences had lost the 'right' to salute. This surprised me," Munoz Grandes continued, "because it had never occurred to me that a salute was a privilege—a mark of mutual respect between officers and men—and not merely an obligation from soldiers to superiors. I began to ponder this and concluded that you Americans were right.

"Next," he went on, "I was flown to Pearl Harbor, the scene of your great defeat at the hands of the Japanese. I saw the battleship Arizona lying almost submerged, a permanent war memorial to the almost 1,000 men who were trapped and drowned. When I saw that great battleship in the still waters and heard a bugle playing taps one evening, I realized that—contrary to everything I had been brought up to believe—you Americans were people with a heart. I changed my view of you."

Incidents like these, vignettes, explain the imponderables of U.S.-Spanish relations. They are significant because U.S. foreign policy and diplomacy has overemphasized such issues as strategic mobility, mutual security, and defense of the "West." U.S. diplomacy must have a heart, as well as a head.

ENDING OF POSTWAR ISOLATION

Broadly speaking, U.S.-Spanish relations alternate between periods of uneventful normality and periods of international crisis when the United States suddenly recalls the usefulness of Spanish geography.

After Franco's Civil War victory in 1939, U.S. relations with Spain virtually ended. During World War II the Roosevelt Administration regarded Franco's Spain as a satellite of Hitler, providing some oil and wheat to foster independence from Hitler, but otherwise treating Spain with scorn.

After World War II Franco's indifference to the somewhat incongruous calls upon him to resign by the United States, Britain, and the USSR led to such reprisals as the barring of Spain from the United Nations and the severing of trade, credits, and diplomatic ties. This was Franco's darkest moment, but again, circumstances favored a shift in U.S. policy. Soviet aggressiveness soon began to drive a wedge between the wartime allies. The Soviet demands on Iran in 1946 and threats to Greece and Turkey in 1947-48, the widespread Communist subversion in Italy in 1947, the rape of Czechoslovakia in 1948, and the Berlin Blockade of 1949 forged a powerful anti-Soviet alliance, the North Atlantic Treaty Organization.

NATO, created in 1949, was initially only a "paper" alliance, and Western Europe lay exposed to a Soviet land thrust. The explosion of the first Soviet nuclear weapon in 1949 heightened the tension. Then came the sudden North Korean attack on South Korea, a U.S. "protectorate," on 25 June 1950. Would Western Europe be next?

Truman quickly dispatched Eisenhower to be the Supreme Commander, that is, the architect, of the gathering NATO forces, but a year passed before he reluctantly consented to a visit to Franco by Admiral Forrest Sherman, then the U.S. Chief of Naval Operations. The U.S. Navy had long been eyeing bases in Spain, but Truman and Dean Acheson, his Secretary of State, had always opposed. In two hours of private talks on 16 July 1951, Sherman and Franco reached agreement.* Nothing was signed, but their talks were to lead in time to the construction of important U.S. bases across Spain, to the beginning of the economic revival in Spain, and most important of all, to the end of Spain's role as the pariah of Western Europe.

While mutual, U.S. and Spanish interests were also strikingly different. The United States wanted only the use of Spain's geographical position (1) to control the Western access to the Mediterranean and (2) as a fall-back area in the event of a Soviet lunge into Western Europe. Truman wanted no entangling or

---

*By a singular irony of fate, Sherman was to die suddenly a few days later while visiting his friend Admiral "Mick" Carney, NATO commander in Naples; yet the gentlemen's agreement with Franco endured, being based on mutual interest, not paper.

embarrassing ties with a regime that was still anathema to many in Congress and to most American liberals.

Franco, on the other hand, had political, economic, and military goals in mind in aligning Spain with the then foremost power on earth, but as always, he had to steer cautiously. He had, for instance, been vociferous in denouncing the "decadent" democracies, early in World War II. Franco had been proved wrong, and as the Axis began to crumble he had started trimming his sails, but too late and too grudgingly to derive any postwar benefits: the Allies had cast him into outer darkness. Now, four years later, he was proposing to invite onto Spanish Catholic soil the Anglo-Saxon-Protestant hordes with their dubious manners and still more dubious morals.

Franco's generals might perceive the strategic advantages, including money and modern arms, but his cardinals and especially the vast, reactionary Falangist bureaucracy had to be carefully persuaded. Soon after seeing Sherman, Franco accordingly began negotiating a new concordat with the Vatican.

Spain's negotiations with the United States and with the Vatican proceeded cautiously and on parallel tracks. Agreement with each took two years to complete—by then the Korean war was effectively over—and it was characteristic of Franco that the new Vatican concordat was solemnly signed one month before the 1953 defense agreements with the United States.

Since that day Franco has consistently balanced the relations with the United States (the head) that are demanded by tactical or strategic imperatives, with other ties appealing to Spanish emotions (the heart). At first the appeal of emotions was to the Latin Americans and to the Arabs, whose combined votes had helped Spain gain admission to the United Nations in 1955, and since the mid-1960s it has been to Spain's neighbors in Western Europe: France, West Germany, even Great Britain. One day, although perhaps not in Franco's lifetime, it will most likely be their backing that will bring Spain into NATO and into the Common Market.

The signing of the defense accords between the United States and Spain in September 1953 marked the end of Spain's isolation. Between 1953 and 1958 the United States poured about $400 million into Spain to build major SAC bases at Torrejon, near Madrid, at Zaragoza, and at Moron de la Frontera; a 500-mile pipeline was built from Rota, near Cadiz, to Zaragoza; and numerous aerial early-warning and radar sites and naval ammunition facilities were built across Spain.

Most important, a huge submarine base designed for the U.S. navy's new nuclear submarines was built at Rota, on the Atlantic side of the strategic Gibraltar Straits. Apart from Holy Loch in Scotland, Rota is the Navy's major nuclear storage and repair base in the Atlantic for the Polaris, and now the Poseidon, submarines that form the key deterrent to Soviet power.

It must be emphasized, however, that the United States only agreed in 1953 to furnish "support of Spanish defense efforts for agreed purposes; to provide military end-item assistance to Spain."

As Under Secretary of State U. Alexis Johnson testified before Congress in 1970, the U.S. government obligations were limited from the start to providing military equipment, and "no defense commitment was given to Spain either in the agreement *or otherwise.*" (emphasis added) This has remained the pattern, despite Spanish hints to the contrary, and despite 20 years of persistent efforts by Franco and his negotiators to extend U.S. military support, explicitly or implicitly, into a military guarantee for the regime.

In 1953 it might have been thought that the extension of U.S. power onto Spanish soil, the construction of a vast modern military base network across Spain, and the furnishing of modern arms to the Spanish forces would have sufficed Franco at least momentarily, but this would have been misreading Franco. He saw in the United States ties, a springboard for economic and diplomatic triumphs too. He has always been a shrewd negotiator.

During World War II Franco had foiled Hitler's imperious demands that he join the Axis, or alternatively, that he open Spain for a Nazi attack on British Gibraltar, by insisting that "honor" demanded that the Spanish forces themselves first essay the attack. Before this could be done, he had warned, Hitler would have to furnish huge quantities of wheat, oil, and other war-scarce commodities. Hitler had ground his teeth in helpless rage.

Using similar techniques in 1953, Franco insisted that before Spain could play its full role in "Western" defense, the United States must furnish substantial economic aid to repair years of privation. Accordingly, an estimated $1.2 billion in U.S. wheat, cotton, tobacco, oil, and other commodities flowed into Spain after 1953.

Buoyed materially and psychologically by his new ties with the United States, Franco now moved cautiously, if erratically, to liberalize his laggard economy. There was no corresponding liberalization, however, of the regime's rigid political hold; that remained inflexible. In 1957, Franco reshuffled his cabinet, placing the foreign and economic ministries in the hands of "Europeanists" and "technocrats." The emphasis was now on scrapping moribund monopolies, reforming banking and currency restrictions, and soliciting admission into international financial and economic organizations.

ERA OF IMPROVED RELATIONS

Meanwhile, relations with the United States swung between cool and excellent. Eisenhower's visit to Madrid in December 1959 marked the first time that an American president had set foot in Spain, a feather in Franco's cap. On the other hand, the election of John F. Kennedy in 1960 led to strain, not because Kennedy was a Catholic, but because Kennedy was a liberal Catholic. Kennedy's 1961 Bay of Pigs fiasco in Cuba, with which Spain still harbored sentimental ties, despite Castro; the anti-American riots in Panama in 1964; and Lyndon Johnson's intervention into the Dominican Republic in 1965, all evoked critical echoes in Franco's closely controlled press, relations during the 1960s were cool.

Even though Kennedy's skilled handling of the Cuban missile crisis in 1962 proved that the United States, Spain's ally, was still the world's greatest military power, many Spaniards suspected that in another crisis between the United States and the USSR the two superpowers might settle global issues over the heads of, or behind the backs of, smaller powers.

By 1963 the original agreements between the United States and Spain were ready for renewal. Franco still intended to expand them into a full-fledged treaty, and to win over Kennedy he named as his new ambassador in Washington and chief negotiator, Antonio Garrigues. Garrigues, a handsome widower, was not only a family friend of the Kennedys, but also Spain's top international lawyer and the advisor to the leading American firms doing business in Spain. Despite his negotiating skill, however, Kennedy and his advisors remained adamant. Congress was in no mood to extend U.S. commitments abroad, they insisted; the United States still wanted the bases and was willing, within reason, to pay for them, but no more. The result, grudgingly accepted by Franco after round-the-clock cabinet sessions and vociferous protests by his hard-liners, was a "joint declaration" that a threat to the security of either signatory would be a matter of "common concern." This skidded dangerously close to a "commitment" in the eyes of Congress, although not in the eyes of Franco; yet it was the most that Kennedy would concede.

Meanwhile there were other compensations. Spain was now being admitted to such prestigious world organizations as the World Bank, the International Monetary Fund, and the OECD. Great Britain, France, and West Germany had begun competing for the increasingly lucrative Spanish market. Franco, emboldened perhaps by Eisenhower's 1959 visit, had begun scrapping Spain's archaic restrictions against foreign investment, hoping thereby to attract U.S. and other large oil companies to seek oil in the peninsula or in Spain's distant, half-forgotten Sahara. The U.S. interests, he surmised, might yield more than oil; they might provide tacit protection against Spain's rapacious Arab neighbors, Morocco, Algeria, and Mauritania.

ECONOMIC RELATIONS

Since the economic reforms of the late 1950s, Spain has steadily prospered. Its economic growth rate in the 1960s, 7.6 percent, has been second only to Japan's.

By 1960, foreign tourists, now enabled to exchange their money legally and fairly into pesetas at airports or border posts instead of, as previously, on the black market, helped pour a flood of needed foreign reserves into Franco's coffers. What was then a trickle seeking sunny skies, empty beaches, inexpensive food and lodging, and a friendly people, has now become a flood, threatening, if unchecked, to bury Spain alive. In 1961 tourist revenues made up 51 percent of Spain's visible exports; in 1972, approximately 70 percent. In 1973 the tourists numbered 34 million, one for every living Spaniard. Such a large influx has brought Spain money and problems.

Spurred by the tourist demand, Spaniards have swarmed into service industries, and hotels, bars, restaurants, summer villas, and resorts have quickly been built. The tourist hordes have started to swamp local water, sewage, and other facilities, and many Spaniards are now grumbling that the annual tidal wave threatens not only their coastline but their traditional values and way of life.

Nonetheless, tourism in Spain, like so much of recent Spanish development, stems directly from the reforms of the late 1950s and early 1960s, assisted and sponsored in large degree by the United States. In 1962, following a World Bank mission, Spain began its first four-year development plan. Simultaneously, Franco authorized his then Foreign Minister, Castiella, to apply cautiously to the newly formed European Economic Community for "associate" status, as a step toward membership. Spain's request, meticulously worded by Castiella, set the stage for a debate that has gathered intensity in Spain ever since. Spain is still barred from full membership in the EEC, owing essentially to Western European opposition to Franco's regime; yet Spain keeps pushing.

The debate, still raging among Spanish bankers, industrialists, traders, and wide segments of society both for and against Franco, centers around the obligation, implicit and explicit, in the Treaty of Rome (1957) creating the Common Market, that obliges members to adhere to recognized democratic principles such as parliamentary parties, free trade unions, free press, and free speech.

Although Ambassador Garrigues told American audiences in 1962 that Spain was fully aware of "all" the provisions of the Treaty of Rome, there were few who thought Franco would ever accept "democracy" imposed from abroad, and time has proved the skeptics right. Notwithstanding, Spain has steadily increased its trade with the EEC, as it has with the United States, with Latin America, and to a smaller extent with the USSR and Eastern Europe.

Spain's gold and convertible currency reserves stand at over $5 billion. Its annual per capita GNP, which was $300 in 1960, reached $1,250 in 1972 and may rise to $2,000 by 1980, although, of course, by no means every man, woman, or child in Spain receives anything like this share of the national wealth. Still, the overall index is rising, not falling. Spain's exports in 1972 totaled $3.7 billion. Imports stood at $6.6 billion, with the "gap" bridged by tourism, remittances from Spanish workers abroad, and various "invisibles."

The United States remains the dominant foreign economic force in Spain. Private U.S. investment, estimated at $850 million, represents about one-third of all private foreign investment. Spain sold $621 million worth of goods to the United States in 1972, one-third being shoes, and bought back $1.1 billion worth, largely in atomic-energy equipment for peaceful energy production. By contrast, Spain's exports to the EEC-EFTA countries reached $2 billion, or more than one-half of all its exports, and the EEC-EFTA bloc was its greatest supplier. Imports from EEC-EFTA totaled $3.3 billion. Western Europe's boom has not only bolstered the economy of Spain on the southern flank, but has also strengthened Franco's rule.

The older generations, remembering the savagery of the Spanish Civil War, want peace and tranquillity, virtually at any price. The young generations, reared in an atmosphere of strict political discipline, are restive, but it would be erroneous to describe them as rebellious. They know, through tourists and through books, magazines, films, television, and increasing travel, that north of the Pyrenees exist democratic "freedoms": the right to strike, to criticize governments, to form or to join political parties. No doubt the desire for similar "freedoms" in Spain is growing among younger Spaniards, but it still seems largely academic, even philosophical.

Even Spanish workers returning after lucrative years in German, French, Swiss, or Belgian factories seem to hestitate before condemning the regime. They are torn. Around them they see a way of life, despite or possibly because of Franco, that they find in many ways superior to that north of the Pyrenees, even compared with those countries with democratic freedoms. How to explain it?

This innate Spanish pride in things "Spanish" accounts for much of Franco's hold on power. In all his years of rule not a shot has been fired, nor a bomb thrown, at him. Open opposition not only causes Franco to harden, but makes the average Spaniard recoil.

In the spring of 1962, soon after Franco had applied for "associate" membership in the new EEC, there began a wave of half covert maneuverings among opposition groups to embarrass Franco. Their aim was publicly to ask the EEC to bar Spain until Franco had carried out political reforms. The maneuvers failed; the nation's pride was stung; the public rallied to Franco.

Simultaneously, strikes flared across the industrial north, the most widespread since the Civil War. They were economically motivated and largely justifiable, but Franco sent in the Guardia Civil and plainclothes police to crack heads, while behind the scenes he let the mine owners negotiate quiet pay raises. The strikes collapsed, and Franco's prestige remained intact.

In 1955 it was the university students, who demonstrated over longstanding grievances: obscurantist teaching, bored professors, crowded classrooms. Once more the police moved in, and once more the nation looked on. In 1969 it was the military trial of suspected Communists at Burgos that caught world attention (and caused private pleas from the Nixon Administration for clemency), but once again, by a combination of public toughness and behind-the-scenes maneuvering, Franco emerged with his power undiminished.

Despite periodic political ripples, Spain's economic course remains steady. Its foreign exchange reserves are rising, and the Spanish people's standard of living, despite inflation, is improving.

THE LATEST PHASE OF RELATIONS, 1967-73

Phase III in the relations between the United States and Spain began soon after the 1967 Arab-Israeli war, when the U.S. Joint Chiefs of Staff recalled how useful overflight rights and staging facilities in Spain might be in the event of a Middle East crisis. Spain was the only air route into the Mediterranean. The year before, France had pulled out of active NATO participation, thus barring French airspace. Spain, too, had temporarily refused the U.S. overflight rights, following the dumping of four unarmed nuclear weapons on the Mediterranean coast near Palomares. Italy and West Germany wanted no trouble with the Arabs: their airspace was refused.

Meanwhile the Arab defeat was quickly followed, not only by a huge Soviet arms airlift devised to revive Arab morale, but also by a rapid buildup of Soviet naval strength in the Mediterranean. Spain now found herself caught between the temptation to wring fresh concessions from the United States, on the one hand, and, on the other, to "lead" the Mediterranean riparian states into a conference aimed at getting the United States and USSR to reduce their naval power. By seeking to achieve both, however, Spain achieved neither.

By the summer of 1968, with the U.S.-Spanish pacts up for their third successive renewal, Spain's proud foreign minister, Castiella, flew into Washington with instructions from Franco to get a defense treaty and the best supply of new U.S. arms he could negotiate. Spain submitted to the Pentagon a "shopping list" worth $450 million. After much maneuvering, Castiella managed an appointment with Lyndon B. Johnson, which was, as he later told friends, a disaster.

On entering the Oval Office, the tall, courtly Spaniard found President Johnson seated, a telephone under his ear, his feet on his desk, and his ankle-length socks exposing his shanks. Johnson continued his conversation for a quarter-hour. Then, hanging up, he peered at Castiella and barked, "What do you want?" Even Dean Rusk, using all the diplomatic arts he had acquired over many years, was unable to mollify Castiella's outrage during long later talks at the State Department. Johnson, bedeviled by the Vietnam War and by the Soviet invasion of Czechoslovakia, had no time or inclination for Spain. The problem could wait for his successor, Nixon. Castiella flew home empty-handed, angry, and mortified.

Meanwhile Franco, too, had begun to calculate that with Nixon's election Spain might fare better. Nixon had a soft spot for Franco. In 1963, three years after his narrow defeat by Kennedy, he had visited Europe with his old political friend, John David Lodge. Lodge, the younger brother of Henry Cabot Lodge, Nixon's Vice-Presidential running mate, had entered Congress from Connecticut in 1946 and had served with Nixon. Lodge had later become governor of Connecticut and, under Eisenhower, U.S. Ambassador to Madrid.

During that trip Nixon was rebuffed by the Soviet leaders, who considered him politically finished. De Gaulle received him, however, and Franco interrupted a summer vacation to meet Nixon in Barcelona and to offer him and his family courtesies. From then on, Nixon had admired Franco and considered Spain strategically important to the United States.

Conscious that the U.S. agreements with Spain had expired and were only being continued by an informal gentlemen's agreement, Nixon persuaded another long-time political friend, Robert C. Hill, former U.S. Ambassador to Mexico, to become his new ambassador to Spain and to negotiate a new base agreement. Hill, aware of Nixon's personal interest and backing, agreed.

At first the Nixon Administration exhibited too much interest in Spain. No less than 18 Nixon officials of cabinet rank visited Madrid in 1969-70; Secretary of State Rogers no less than three times. Franco's price went up. But as the months of hard bargaining followed, it was evident again that Congress, and notably William Fulbright, would not accept a "defense" commitment, nor for that matter new major arms supplies.

By the end of 1969 Franco had begun to conclude that with a new team in the White House he, too, needed a new negotiator. Castiella had served 12 grueling years as foreign minister; he was tired, and rigid. He had pinned his hopes on expelling Britain from Gibraltar, and now he urged cutting off the Americans too, sending them packing if they would concede neither a "treaty" nor arms.

By October 1969 Franco took the occasion of a major financial scandal (in which Castiella was not involved) to reshuffle the cabinet, and he named as his new foreign minister the young, keen, and highly flexible Lopez Bravo. To spur the Americans to greater effort, meanwhile, he allowed Lopez Bravo to conclude a defense pact with France that called for joint training and arms manufacture but not, insofar as could be seen, for any French commitment to defend Spain.

Unmoved by Franco's flirtation with France, the Nixon Administration stuck to its guns: no "treaty of defense," no major arms supplies, but, to placate Fulbright, a new "Agreement of Friendship and Cooperation" in which, for the first time, U.S.-Spanish cultural, educational, scientific, environmental, and even "public information" ties would take precedence ahead of defense. The agreement was signed in August 1970, to run for five years. In October President Nixon himself visited Franco in Madrid, and with characteristic hyperbole described Spain publicly as an "indispensable pillar of peace in the Mediterranean."

In Washington the Administration stalwart, U. Alexis Johnson, solemnly assured the Senators that there was still "no commitment" such as existed in NATO, in the Southeast Asia Collective Defense Treaty, in the Security Treaty with Australia and New Zealand, or in various bilateral mutual defense treaties around the world. The United States, said Johnson, had 10,000 military men in Spain. For 17 years the U.S. "joint bases" had supported important missions of SAC, MAC, Air Defense, antisubmarine warfare units, the Sixth Fleet, and most significantly, the Polaris submarine force.

Continuing U.S. use of these facilities in Spain was important, he insisted, (1) to maintain the general U.S. "deterrent" posture in the Mediterranean; (2) to provide infrastructure to support forces deployed in Europe and the Mediterranean; and (3) to contribute to worldwide U.S. strategic and tactical mobility. "All our facilities in Spain are defensive and deterrent in nature, and," he pledged, "will contribute to the maintenance of peace and avoidance of conflict."[1]

To ram home the lastest U.S.-Spanish five-year extension before Fulbright could insist on a treaty, General Earle "Buzz" Wheeler, Chairman of the U.S. Joint Chiefs of Staff, was hurried up to Capitol Hill to tell the Senators, somewhat infelicitously, that the mere presence of U.S. troops in Spain was a greater deterrent than a "piece of paper." The Senate went along, albeit reluctantly.

For Spain there were at best minor concessions. The "joint-use" bases became U.S. facilities on "Spanish" bases; the United States relinquished the Rota-Zaragoza pipeline; and it agreed to spend $35 million in USAF funds modernizing the U.S. aerial warning and communications system in Spain and to grant Spain $26 million worth of excess arms.

The United States promised $120 million in EXIM (Export Import Bank) credits for Spain's purchases of U.S. arms; Spain later protested the 7.5 percent interest rate and eventually agreed to buy $60 million in arms herself when the United States agreed to lend the remaining $60 million at 6 percent. Finally, for education, culture, and science there was to be $3 million per year for five years.

Despite initial Spanish grumbles about the condition of 54 U.S. M-48 tanks being donated and the sorry state of three excess U.S. destroyers back from Vietnam, by 1973 the arms program appeared to be going reasonably well. About $2 million remained to be delivered, and the Spanish forces had already taken delivery of forty-eight 105 mm howitzers, eighteen 155 mm howitzers, twelve 175 mm guns, sixty armored personnel carriers, and machine tools for ammunition manufacture. Through EXIM credits, its own funds, and some grants, Spain has also acquired two U.S. submarines, some minesweepers and other naval auxiliaries, thirty-six F-4 Phantom jets, two KC-130 air-refueling freighters, and twenty-four helicopters.

The Spanish government, however, began tightening restrictions on the use of Rota by U.S. Poseidon nuclear submarines. The motives are unclear, but the thought of "pressure" for a defense treaty in 1975 when the current agreement expires has crossed not a few minds in the Pentagon.

In April 1973 Lopez Bravo flew into Washington with a personal letter from Franco to Nixon. Suggestions for the visit, first broached by Spain in January, had been coolly received by the White House. At first it was suggested that Franco's letter be transmitted via the U.S. Embassy, but finally the White House relented and offered Lopez Bravo "three minutes" with the Chief Executive. Lopez Bravo had a twenty-minute interview and again relayed Franco's interest in a defense treaty in 1975. Obviously the aging Caudillo would like, before he passes on, to maintain U.S. and Spanish defense ties for another five-year period after they expire in 1975. This would be a suitable legacy for young Juan Carlos, the future king. However, the prospects seem less and less propitious. The current detente between the United States and the USSR, the end of U.S. involvement in Vietnam, the U.S. friendliness toward China, the renewal of the SALT talks, MBFT, and even the relative quietness of the Soviet fleet in the Mediterranean all diminish Spain's strategic value.

What the United States would like, and has been trying in vain to achieve for 20 years, is for Spain to become a member of NATO, thus letting the fifteen-nation alliance share the burden of modernizing Spain's armed forces and integrating Spain into the defense of the West. The memory of the Spanish Civil War, especially Franco's merciless treatment of thousands of Spanish socialists and other leftists, seems stronger today in some Western European chancelleries than in Spain itself, however.

Belgium, Holland, Denmark, and Norway, as well as the British Labour Party, all continue to oppose Spain's membership in NATO, presumably because of Franco. The bias is emotional, and thus stronger and more implacable than if it were logical; as in the example of a mixed NATO squadron comprising five warships, each of a different NATO nationality including one Norwegian, that completed maneuvers at Naples in 1973 and set course for a week's rest and recreation at Barcelona, a historic "liberty" port in the Mediterranean. Norway's foreign ministry refused to allow any Norwegian warship to enter a Spanish port and furthermore argued that it was unthinkable for any NATO formation to enter Spanish waters: the squadron meekly took its leave elsewhere. This lingering anti-Francoism also finds widespread echoes in the U.S. government and in wide segments of Congress and impedes the development of closer ties between the two countries.

"Each time renewal of the Spanish base agreements come up it costs us more—not just in money—but in Congressional and public disapproval," said a senior American official. "This autumn, at the UN General Assembly, we'll be looking at the advantages and disadvantages more closely than we ever have before!"

Apart from the base agreements, only trade and the Law of the Sea complicate U.S.-Spanish ties. Trade is the more immediate issue. In 1970 Franco negotiated with the EEC a six-year preferential trade agreement that gave Spain a 60 percent tariff cut on a relatively small range of its industrial exports, while Spain gave the EEC a 25 percent tariff cut on a broader range of industrial imports. The United States, however, protested to GATT (The General Agreement on Trade and Tariffs) that the treaty violated GATT principles. In addition, it complained that some Florida citrus exports to the EEC have been jeopardized and reiterated its faith in "globalized" preferences, though as everyone knows these were momentarily dead.

By 1973 Spain was about to renegotiate its 1970 arrangement with the EEC, not only in view of the recent entry of Great Britain and other states but also to seek concessions no less favorable than those enjoyed by such non-applicant EFTA members as Austria, Sweden, Switzerland, and Portugal.

In the unlikely event that the Spanish-EEC negotiations should result in full membership for Spain, the United States would approve, officials say. However, the United States does not approve the expansion of the EEC through "preferential" arrangements that are at the expense of nonmembers and of dubious legality under GATT. To the hard-pressed Nixon Administration, this smacked of EEC economic warfare against the United States.

The Law of the Sea Treaty was due to be considered by more than 100 UN members states during 1974. The United States and Spain were at loggerheads. By a curious irony, the United States, the USSR, and such other maritime powers as Great Britain and France are united against Spain and such of its allies as Malaysia, Singapore, and Indonesia that border on international straits.

The United States and the maritime powers insist on the unfettered right to "free" passage; that is, to send their surface ships, submarines, or aircraft through, under or over international straits with neither let nor hindrance. Spain, its eyes fixed on Gibraltar, is leading the move to permit only "innocent" passage. This means, essentially, that submarines must transit on the surface and that the 150 ships of varied nationality that daily transit the Gibraltar Straits, including, of course, those of Great Britain, at least tacitly acknowledge Spain's "sovereignty."

What the maritime powers foresee, of course, is that "tacit" acceptance of Spain's sovereignty may quickly become "de facto" recognition. Thus, conceivably, Spain might begin insisting on tangible "recognition," such as tolls, fees, or certificates, and the process could escalate until either all passers-by agreed, or risked an armed confrontation. Spain, furthermore, might well be copied by other states that dominate important straits, such as Malaysia, Singapore, Morocco, and Egypt.

It is likely that Spain will lose her struggle against the United States, the USSR, and other "Big Navy" powers for the right to "control" the Straits of Gibraltar. Even her hopes of winning the "moral" support of fellow riparian powers such as Morocco collapsed recently when Morocco unilaterally extended her own territorial sea to 70 miles, thus putting several thousand Spanish fishermen out of work.

In conclusion, U.S.-Spanish relations are "correct." Spain fears U.S. import restrictions against its shoe exports, while the United States fears the loss of Spain's growing market to the enlarged EEC. Compared, however, with past disputes these issues seem manageable. What most concerns American students of Spain is the internal political situation. They see the regime developing economically, but stagnating politically. Once Franco is gone, some suspect, pent-up frustrations may erupt. Spain's post-Franco transition, the *salida suave*, may collapse. It is too early to say what the United States could, or should, do then.

Many close students of U.S.-Spanish affairs fear that in recent years the U.S. Embassy in Madrid, acting under the orders of successive regimes in Washington, has deliberately stopped its ears to, and cut itself off from, "opposition" voices. The United States obviously has no responsibility for Spain's internal politics; but it should, and must, know what is happening. It cannot remain totally identified with an obsolescent regime, from which even the venerable Spanish Church is turning, merely to retain "instant" use of the bases in a crisis. "The U.S. is seen by [moderate opposition] groups," wrote a keen analyst of Spanish affairs not long ago, "as the last powerful institution on earth which still works in close harmony with the Franco regime."

NOTE

1. U. Alexis Johnson, Under Secretary for Political Affairs, Department of State Hearing before the Committee on Foreign Relations, United States Senate, second session on Agreement of Friendship and Cooperation between the United States of America and Spain (U.S. Government Printing Office, 26 August 1970), p. 11.

10

SPAIN
AND NATO

James G. Holland, Jr.
Gregory A. Raymond

To paraphrase an old saw about Britain and Europe, one can describe Spain's relation to the North Atlantic Treaty as being of NATO if not in NATO.* Within the alliance structure there is a wide variety of views on the problem, ranging from the position of those who see an immediate requirement

---

*The attitude of the Spanish government toward Spain's position among western nations is summarized in the following quotation from a speech by Foreign Minister López Bravo:

> Although Spain does not belong to any [political] bloc, she is definitely a part of the Western World by virtue of her moral and ideological affinities. And, without renouncing her freedom of action, she is part of the defense of the West through the Iberian Pact with Portugal and the Agreement of Friendship and Cooperation with the United States, although the aid provided by the United States is not considered satisfactory. The perspective opened by the speech made on April 23 by presidential adviser Henry Kissinger about the reform of the Atlantic Alliance, Japan's participation, and a general reorganization of the international economic system on a more equitable basis, is undoubtedly attractive for Spain. With reference to the United States in particular, that country's disposition towards Spain is favorable and can be structured upon two postulates: intensifying the political and security ties, which while tightening the links with other Western countries, does not imply that Spain should advance her candidacy as a NATO member, and increasing economic collaboration in the commercial and investment field and even in monetary matters. This very same policy toward Spain is being followed by Portugal, West Germany, France, and Italy.[1]

for Spain to be integrated into NATO through that of the United States, favoring but not pushing for Spanish membership, to the other extreme of the socialist states of Western Europe, who, still rankled by the dictatorship of the aging Caudillo, adamantly oppose any effort to include Spain formally within the security pact. From the other side of the Pyrenees it appears that Spain's position is that little could be gained other than considerable expense if her ties to the alliance were made more formal.

What makes the old problem of Spain and NATO of immediate interest is the changing nature of international politics, as we proceed into an era of complex multipolarity. Whether or not one agrees with the view of an emerging Western Europe as one of five power centers, along with the United States, the USSR, Japan, and China, there is little doubt that the considerable progress that has taken place within the Common Market has been accentuated by the growth from the Inner Six to the Nine. Western Europe is obviously becoming a major actor on the international scene, and Spain has clearly identified her European interests as primary.[2]

Other indicators of the changing nature of international politics in the 1970s have included President Nixon's efforts to normalize the U.S. relationship with China, the SALT talks, the MBFR (Mutual Balanced Force Reductions) discussions, the preparatory talks for the European Security Conference, and the 1973 appeal by Henry Kissinger for a joint NATO effort to create "new approaches" to deal with the new realities.[3] Among the new approaches suggested by the Nixon Administration was the idea of including Japan as a principal partner. While the European governments' initial response to the U.S. call for a revitalized Atlantic relationship shared with Japan was rather cautious, should Nixon's suggestions ultimately meet with success, there surely must be included a redefined role for Spain.

Some would have us believe that Europeanizing the problems of European security is "not a valid option,"[4] while others see that solution as "the best evolution we might expect."[5] Still in an age of change and much-hoped-for creativity, American military guarantees remain the essence of security for her partners. In short, the American elephant still rules the forest: "His awareness of the fact is not acute, as he complains of his internal problems and recovers from the wound of Vietnam. The margin of his strength is somewhat impaired as other countries grow and prosper. But he is still the ranking animal."[6]

However, the dominant American position does not hide the fact that security arrangements in the North Atlantic region are extremely uneven and far from the unified picture NATO presents to the popular mind. NATO is most frequently depicted as in the central region of Allied Command Europe, where seven NATO nations and the troops of their political ally, France, present a picture of integrated or cooperative defense. Few people seem aware that in Norway, Denmark, Portugal, Italy, Greece, and Turkey, NATO is represented almost exclusively by each nation's armed forces.

The first fact one should learn about NATO is that it is an association of independent, sovereign states, some of whom, like Norway, which in 1972 voted not to join the Common Market, have one foot in NATO at best. Norway's "base and ban" policy excludes bases for foreign troops on Norwegian soil and bans nuclear weapons. Another attitude toward NATO membership is exemplified by Italy, which has only one Alpine battalion committed to NATO defense outside of Italian borders, and still another by Portugal, which has committed no troops for NATO defense outside of her national boundaries.

On the other hand, Spain, through her bilateral arrangements with Portugal in the Iberian Pact and the Agreement of Friendship and Cooperation with the United States, might be said to be more of a NATO "member" than some of the Fifteen. Given the impact on Europe of the change in the nature of international politics and the imminent possibility of Franco's demise, the triad of Spain, the United States, and NATO appears to have acquired new significance.

Spain's strategically significant geography is the focus of this triangular relationship. Resting securely behind the Pyrenees, Spain appeared as potential haven to Western strategists when the question facing a newborn NATO was, When will the Soviets attack? Its strategic importance to naval operations is followed closely by the tactical and logistical depth Spain adds to the doctrinaire defense of Western Europe. Her climate is a great asset to the tactical training of air crews. With the withdrawal of France from NATO, all of these factors have assumed increased importance.

Although even de Gaulle could not change the realities of European geography and France's place therein, he could take significant depth from the traditional European battlefield by withdrawing France from the military organization of NATO. The politics were as clear as the strategic implications—de Gaulle was not getting his way in the North Atlantic Council. Integration efforts in NATO were an anathema to this godfather of the modern nation-state. The changes in American strategy from massive retaliation to selective response and the concept of the "pause," together with the concomitant delay in planned use of nuclear weapons for European and French defense, were unacceptable to de Gaulle. Removing France from NATO robbed the alliance planners of tactical depth; required lines of communication to run parallel to the battlefield; and if de Gaulle was correct, required earlier decisions on the use of nuclear weapons.

Spanish writers have likewise underscored the strategic implications of their *situación de privilegio*,[7] and they have also pointed to their country's utility as a bridge connecting three continents. For instance, *Ya* (Madrid) has editorialized that "it is not only that we have a need of returning to the international community, [but] the international community has an equal need of Spain, a European community which serves as a bridge toward those nations which each day assert themselves with greater strength, the iberian-american and arab lands."[8] In addition to the "bridge" argument, a conception of an

Ibero-American community has also been forwarded. "The times are past when one could speak of national development. The very concept of 'nation' is in crisis. Nations, as free and sovereign unities, are beginning to be replaced by *patrias,* as supranational unities. The modern world is a world of *patrias* not of nations."[9]

One approach to conceptualizing the relationship between Spain and Latin America is to view the former as an element comprising the periphery of the Latin American subordinate state system. Not only are there structural similarities between these actors,[10] but empirical studies have shown notable exchanges occurring between them.[11] Regardless of Spain's affinities for Latin America, however, and whether or not *L'Afrique commence aux Pyrenées,*[12] Madrid has looked toward Europe and North America when dealing with economics and national security. As José María De Areilza has remarked, "Spain is a member of Europe. Its problems . . . are problems of a European type. Contrary to the tourist slogan, Spain, in this aspect, is not different."[13]

Spain can be characterized as a four-sided house in which the inhabitants are looking from their northern window for security purposes.[14] What, then, are the ramifications for the Atlantic Alliance? In order to probe this question, the initial step that will be taken here involves the analytic partitioning of the trigon of Spain, the United States, and NATO into those double components of which Madrid is a constituent element: that is, the dyads of Spain with the United States and of Spain with the European NATO members. Subsequently, upon scrutinizing the foreign-policy posture of each actor toward the other, exchange theory will be utilized to examine the strategic importance of Spain in the context of Western defensive efforts.

Examining national security policy is methodologically difficult, since "political formulas such as 'national interest' or 'national security' . . . may not mean the same thing to different people."[15] This sociopsychological enigma is further complicated by the impact of Franco's idiosyncrasies. As a Galician tradition has it, "No one knows what goes on in his head. No one can be sure what he will do next. And when he has done it, it is often hard to tell what has happened."[16] To help overcome these dilemmas, one may view security policy from the *exchange* perspective, which interprets defense efforts as the collective supply of public goods.[17]

THE STRAIN OF "GOING IT WITH OTHERS"

Spain and the United States

"There is nothing stranger or more curious in the annals of United States foreign policy," observes Carlton Hayes, "than the story of . . . [Washington's]

relations with Spain."[18] One of the most remarkable chapters within this story
concerns the metamorphosis of Hispano-American interaction between Spain's
accession to the Anti-Comintern Pact in 1939 and the signing of the 1953 Pact
of Madrid. Whereas under the banner of *Hispanidad* the Franco regime had previously declared that "the warships of Mexico and Peru, [plus] the airplanes of
Chile, Argentina, or Spain . . . [would] defend one great Empire,"[19] nowadays
one often hears discrete asides mentioning that "if Spain were a member of
NATO, it would be ready to station troops in Germany in peacetime under the
orders of the Supreme Allied Commander, Europe, . . . as well as . . . place its
warships under the orders of the Commander in Chief, Allied Forces, Southern
Europe."[20] In essence, not only has Spain been able to weather the international
ostracism resulting from its earlier cooperation with the Axis, but "The Spain of
Franco has been converted into a decisive part of the American strategic network."[21]

Military partnership with Franco Spain represented a foreign policy
venture both novel and controversial for the United States. When viewed from
the traditional "billiard ball" perspective of state behavior, the acquisition of
Spanish bases represented a rational response of a unitary, value-maximizing
actor to the ominous specter of Soviet expansion. From the vantage point of
Allison's bureaucratic politics model, however,[22] American behavior toward
Spain was a consequence of (1) collegial bargaining between individuals of
unequal political influence and diverse interests within the country's governmental hierarchy; plus (2) the interaction of the two states' structurally diver-
gent political systems through side payments gained by an individual in one
nation as a result of the performance of officials in the other.

A primary example of the impact of the former foreign policy determinant
can be seen in the role of the "Spanish lobby" role in influencing the formula-
tion and conduct of Washington's postwar orientation toward Madrid.

The prospect of military ties with Spain had little support during 1948.
President Truman was opposed to the fascist nature of the Franco regime; the
Air Force was interested in an intercontinental bombing capability that would
obviate the need for foreign bases, and the Army had disregarded the prospect of
employing Spanish troops in defense of Europe. The following groups, collec-
tively labeled the "Spanish lobby," exerted considerable pressure on the executive branch in favor of improving U.S. relations with Spain: (1) Catholics;
(2) anti-Communists; (3) anti-Trumanists; (4) Southern cotton interests; and
(5) individuals who feared that without Spanish bases the Navy's position in the
Mediterranean with regard to Great Britain would be weakened. According to
Lowi, "These elements gave the 'Spanish lobby' a surprisingly bipartisan, supra-
sectional, supra-religious and supra-economic appearance."[23]

By way of contrast, the tacit coalition between U.S. Air Force General
Burchinal and his Spanish counterparts during the 1968 base renewal negotiations is illustrative of the second variable in the bureaucratic politics model.

Robert O. Keohane describes these negotiations as a "classic case" of one sector of the U.S. government (the military) pitted against another (the state department).[24] According to Keohane, the U.S. Navy and Air Force tend to take a more favorable view of the U.S. military positions in Spain than does the Department of State.[25]

The incorporation of Madrid into the U.S. defensive network was a complete but controvertible about-face for Spanish foreign policy. Overtures had been made as early as 1944, though the possibility of obtaining bases in Spain was not voiced for three more years. By 1948 the Spanish argued that "the Marshall Plan and European Union will economically save Europe, but it is necessary to save Europe militarily as well . . . from whence the necessity for a military alliance arises."[26] However, Madrid's exclusion from NATO forced the Caudillo to follow the bilateral route that eventually resulted in the Pact of Madrid.

As a consequence of Spain's economic gains, Arthur P. Whitaker notes that "despite the existence of strong but necessarily muted opposition to the alliance, there seems no doubt that at the outset it did enjoy rather widespread popularity."[27] Nevertheless the agreements were later questioned. Liberal Spaniards began to ask ruefully whether the United States would have acted so swiftly to aid a liberal or social-democratic regime financially,[28] while at the opposite end of the political spectrum, Franco declared that the partnership needed "to be studied afresh and brought up to date."[29] Although the first decade of the pact had proven to be fiscally lucrative for Madrid, it subsequently fell below Spanish economic expectations. López Bravo, in referring to the 1970 Agreement of Friendship and Cooperation, said in 1973, "The offer of aid from North America has not been satisfactory."[30] (See Table 10.1 for the total amount of U.S. assistance rendered, 1950-71.) A survey in *The Economist* reported that "between 1953 and 1961 alone, Spain received $618 m in direct aid and a further $404 m in loans from the United States. But the level of American aid sagged later on. Between 1962 and 1968, direct aid amounted to only about $60 m, while most of the $420 m worth of credits was channelled through the Export-Import Bank . . . and tied to purchases from the United States."[31] Moreover, though the Caudillo had hoped to transform the quasi-alliance of 1953 into a formal defense commitment in 1963, he was only able to secure the following joint declaration (my emphasis): "A menace to either country or to the installations that provide for mutual defense would be considered *something* of concern to both countries, and each country would take the action *it* considered appropriate within the framework of its constitutional procedures."[32] Consequently, prior to the renegotiation of the agreements in 1968, Madrid began to stress Washington's exploitation of Spain. According to E. Inman Fox, by government propaganda at this time, the Spaniard was reminded . . . that his country had been denied inclusion in the Marshall plan and [that] through 1968 American aid to Spain had amounted to only $2.1 billion, of which almost 40 percent was in the form of loans, half of which ($400 million) was to be spent in the United States. By the same date the United States had given $5.6 billion to Turkey, $4.2 billion to Greece, and $3.1 billion to Yugoslavia. The United States had not even produced all of the $100 million in economic aid promised in 1963. It was also argued that relations with the United States are of little value to Spain's international diplomacy: they alienate Spain from many of the Latin American countries and from much of the Arab World, and they certainly have produced no support for what Spaniards consider their legitimate claim to Gibraltar.[33]

The Madrid government also stressed the dangers from nuclear accidents such as the one at Palomares and the risks confronting Spain's major cities in the eventuality of a Soviet thermonuclear strike against the American bases.

TABLE 10.1

Military Assistance and Foreign Military Sales for Fiscal Years 1950-71 (in thousands of dollars)

Type of Assistance	Total
Military assistance plan	626,226
Foreign military sales	357,716
Cash	355,416
Credit	2,300
Excess stocks acquisition value	60,392

Source: *Greece, Spain, and the Southern NATO Strategy,* Hearings before the Subcommittee on Europe of the House Committee on Foreign Affairs, 92nd cong., 1st sess., July 12, 14, 19, 21; August 3; September 9, 15, 1971 (Washington, D.C.: Government Printing Office, 1971), p. 260.

According to Antonio Sánchez Gijón, "the hidden objective of this complaint would become clearer further on: to force the United States to negotiate a new type of agreement on the basis of new conditions."[34] Although 1970 marked the finalization of a new bases agreement, it did not likewise signify the termination of Spanish dissatisfactions concerning the amount of aid the country was to receive and the quality of the military hardware Spain had purchased.[35] In the words of one commentator, "We do not believe it an exaggeration to say that in 1970 relations between Spain and the United States have been substantially modified in our favor."[36]

So far we have abstracted two salient themes that are woven throughout the fabric of Spain's partnership with the United States, (1) the heterogeneity that has characterized the groups advocating intimate Hispano-American relations* and (2) the Spanish desire to forge a more tangible bond with Washington. However, several other political strands complicate the texture of this quasi-alliance. On the one hand, though security considerations have appeared to be the common denominator that accords a degree of unity to the multifarious interests in the United States that favor military bases in Spain, the question has been raised whether the type of operation the United States has employed has anything to do with combat defense. Colonel Edward King, for instance, has criticized the excessive number of personnel assigned to the Joint U.S. Military Group—Military Assistance Advisory Group, declaring that "they are maintained more to provide pleasant overseas military duty stations than to defend the security of all Americans."[37]

On the other hand, as Arthur P. Whitaker has pointed out, "the Franco regime's constancy in defense of the West wavers when the defense does not coincide with Spain's interests as the regime sees them."[38] With regard to Cuba, for example, Franco has been able to maintain a *modus vivendi* with Castro despite the claim that Spain "represents in today's world an undisputed position for having been the first, and until now the only nation in Europe that . . . had engaged in battle with communism and won."[39] On 13 March 1962, Madrid and Havana established a commercial agreement marketing Cuban tobacco and sugar for Spanish olive oil. Twenty months later a three-year agreement was concluded exchanging 300,000 tons of sugar for manufactured goods and machinery. The total commerce between the two countries amounted to $8.4 million in 1962 and $30.8 million in 1963; by May of 1964 it had reached $21 million.[40] This inconstant policy is also shown in former Foreign Minister Castiella's suggestion that all Mediterranean fleets be withdrawn.[41]

---

*Besides the "Spanish lobby," a good example of this diversity is the camaraderie that surrounded the individual visits Senators Robert Kennedy and Barry Goldwater made to Spain during the spring of 1965.

In spite of the inconsistencies in Franco's U.S. policy, President Nixon labeled Spanish-American cooperation an "indispensable pillar for peace in the Mediterranean,"[42] stressed the significance of the 1970 Agreement of Friendship and Cooperation (see Figure 10.1 for its military provisions and Figure 10.2 for other military agreements not superseded by the 1970 Agreement), and called for Spain's admission to NATO.[43]

The accomplishment of this last objective, however, is contingent upon the positions taken by NATO's European members. Hence, before analyzing the strategic costs and benefits of Spain's addition to the alliance, we will turn to an overview of the "stresses and strains" in Madrid's relations with Europe.

Spain and the European NATO Members

"The Europeanization of Spain," admits López Bravo, "has in the past been a program . . . never realized through lack of the minimum premises for achieving it."[44] Although on the commercial level, for example, trade between Spain and Western Europe has increased, on the social-psychological level many individuals north of the Pyrenees have not yet forgotten the Spanish labyrinth.[45] Nonetheless, various public opinion surveys have suggested the growth of mutual relevance on the attitudinal plane. Werner J. Feld's research indicates EEC support for developing ties with Madrid,[46] and a recent elite survey has revealed a strong Spanish desire to become aligned with Western Europe.* In view of these findings, what are the prospects for closer military ties between Spain and the NATO members in Europe?

Like the United States, France has made an about-face in her policy toward the Franco regime. In 1946 the Franco-Spanish border was closed, and Spain was threatened with invasion by a combined force of French *maquis* and Spanish exiles.[48] By 1964, however, the Gaullist daily *Paris-Presse* declared that diplomatically the Pyrenees no longer existed,[49] and the Fifth Republic proclaimed, "The French Government especially understands the growing importance of the role that Spain is called to play with respect to everything which concerns the economic development and military defense of Europe.[50]

This *rapprochement* was not particularly bold; for example, *Le Figaro* observed, "One cannot pretend, in addition, that Paris had demonstrated any special audacity in the matter, Washington with Eisenhower and McNamara,

---

*Of the 389 respondents, 72 percent favored Spain's alignment with Western Europe. Moreover, despite 74 percent believing the United States to be the world's most potent military force, only 18 percent felt that Western Europe ought to align itself with Washington.[47]

FIGURE 10.1

Military Hardware Given to Spain by the United States in Accordance with Articles 31 and 37 of the 1970 Agreement

Export-Import Credits

36 F-4c Phantom fighter bombers
2 KC-130 aircraft
4 SH-3D helicopters
4 Huey Cobra helicopters
6 C-130 aircraft

Congressional Funds

54 M-48 tanks
48 M-108 howitzers
18 M-109 howitzers
49 armored personnel carriers
4 mortar carriers
7 command post carriers
16 Huey UH-1H helicopters
12 175 mm guns

Loans

2 Guppy 1A and 11A submarines
5 destroyers
4 minesweepers
3 landing ships
2 auxiliary ships

Note: In addition to this hardware, the United States was committed to provide the necessary ground equipment for the aircraft, machine tools for manufacturing munitions, 70 percent of the cost of modernizing Spain's air warning system, and personnel training.

Source: Greece, Spain, and the Southern NATO Stragegy, Hearings before the Subcommittee on Europe of the House Committee on Foreign Affairs, 92nd cong., 1st sess., 12, 14, 19, 21 July; 3 August; 9, 15 September 1971 (Washington, D.C.: Government Printing Office, 1971), p. 258.

FIGURE 10.2

**Military Agreements Not Superseded by Article 40 of the 1970 Agreement
of Friendship and Cooperation**

Agreement	Date
Mutual defense assistance	September 26, 1953
Facilities assistance	April 9, 1954
	May 11, 1954
	May 19, 1954
Offshore procurement	July 30, 1954
MAP (Military Assistance Program) surplus disposal	November 27, 1956
Ship loans	March 9, 1957
	June 23, 1959
	September 30, 1960
	June 19, 1962
	January 11, 1965
	April 21, 1966
	June 20, 1969
	July 14, 1969
	August 4, 1969
Claims settlements of Spanish subcontractors	February 8, 1960
	February 13, 1960
Interchange of patent rights and technical information for defense purposes	July 13, 1960
	July 21, 1960
Cooperative logistics arrangements	June 23, 1965
Contract for U.S. assistance in construction in Spain	May 31, 1966
Water desalting plant	June 25, 1968
Naval crew training	January 9, 1969
Nautical chart reproduction	January 21 and March 13, 1969

Source: Greece, Spain, and the Southern NATO Strategy, Hearings before the Subcommittee on Europe of the Committee on Foreign Affairs, 92nd cong., 1st sess., July 12, 14, 19, 21; August 3; September 9, 15, 1971 (Washington, D.C.: Government Printing Office, 1971), pp. 230-31.

Bonn with Luebble and Erhard, had all in effect preceded the French government in a policy which obligated Spain as much as it did those who were
engaged in the rapprochement effort."[51]

Besides its timidity, the *rapprochement* was militarily inefficacious;
according to *Nation,* the idea of a Franco-Hispanic Mediterranean pact is the
product of "fantasy or of a frenzied imagination."[52] Despite these criticisms,
the government maintained that "the defensive system of Europe does not have
sufficient depth. It is time to permit Spain . . . to participate fully in the defense
of the continent."[53]

Similarly, the Spanish have emphasized their Euro-Mediterranean role,[54]
and the utility of Hispano-French military cooperation. Antonio Sánchez Gijón,
for instance, has written, "The Mediterranean and Atlantic coasts of Spain from
[sic]two distinct fronts that are more easily defended if they are thought of as
continuous lines. . . . Each country's defenses along the Mediterranean coast are
dangerously distant from its defense along the Atlantic; but joint defense of the
two lines would double the defensive capability of each country. . . . The strategic conceptions of France and Spain should be fitted into a regional policy with
its center of gravity in the straits of Gibraltar."[55]

The tangible results of Spain's military cooperation with the French have
included the purchase of hardware, including Mirage III-E fighters, Alouette helicopters, and AMS tanks, plus the following joint activities: (1) weapons production; (2) Chief of Staff meetings; (3) naval maneuvers; and (4) exchange of
facilities.[56]

In contrast with the cameraderie between Madrid and Paris, the Franco
regime's relations with London have vacillated, depending upon who was in
Whitehall. During the Conservative Party's tenure, British interests in Spain were
cultivated without regard to ideological considerations, but with the Labour
Party's political ascendancy the Franco government was once again ostracized.
Beyond this, Anglo-Spanish relations also face the problem of Gibraltar, an
enigma Franco himself describes as a shadow between Britain and Spain that
cannot be resolved by the mere possession of common allies.[57] Although Spain
has been pictured as "aggressive, proud, and determined" on the Gibraltar
issue,[58] López Bravo has quietly taken a few tentative steps toward shelving the
dispute by initiating discussions on the possibility of reestablishing defensive
cooperation between London and Madrid.[59]

Several other European states play noteworthy, albeit less extensive, roles
within the scope of Spain's national security policy. Both Portugal and West
Germany have championed Madrid's entry into NATO, but whereas Lisbon has
renewed the Iberian Pact of Friendship and Nonaggression, Bonn has merely
sought a "harmonization of policies."[60] Though the Federal Republic has
acknowledged Spain's strategic value,[61] it recognizes the controversy that was
aroused by the proposed Leopard tank sale of the Kraus-Maffel firm and the
earlier German desire to use Spanish military facilities.

By way of contrast, Italian policy has remained indifferent to Spain's military overtures,[62] while Denmark, Norway, Belgium, and the Netherlands have opposed Franco's admission to NATO. In the final analysis, then, Spanish bilateral military cooperation with the United States, France, and Portugal has made Spain a significant factor in the Western defense system despite the absence of Madrid from NATO. Now that we have discussed some of the stresses and strains within this bilateral network, it is possible to scrutinize the costs and benefits of Spanish membership in NATO.

THE LOGIC OF COLLECTIVE ACTION

According to William and Annette Fox, the NATO alliance can be viewed in several ways: "as an international institution which formulates a program to deal with threats emanating from outside the NATO area; as a forum for bargaining among its members; and as an instrument of member governments to implement their respective policies."[63] When viewed from this latter perspective, it is useful to examine the gains and liabilities intrinsic to NATO membership. Individual utility may be increased by collective performance in two distinct ways: (1) by reducing some of the costs resultant from insular behavior; and (2) by securing additional benefits that cannot be attained through purely private activity.[64] Furthermore, beyond the common advantages accruing to all alliance members, collaborative behavior may also provide certain private benefits.* Traditionally, alliances have performed three such functions: (1) supplementing national capability by providing an accretion of power; (2) adding a degree of precision to interstate relations by furnishing a mechanism for restraining allies and preempting adversaries; and (3) engendering either domestic or international stability.[66] With this conceptual framework as a backdrop, we will now turn to consider the costs and benefits of Spain's admission to NATO from the standpoint of Madrid and also of various NATO members.

On the surface, Spain's policy toward NATO is extremely perplexing. In the words of one observer, "Selected commentators are officially encouraged to point out the advantages of a neutralist (in effect, anti-American) Mediterranean pact; then the Spanish ambassador in Washington is authorized to call for Spain's admission to NATO; then a government-guided newspaper says Spain cannot consider joining NATO so long as Britain holds Gibraltar."[67] Much of this ostensibly desultory behavior is a consequence of pragmatic feelers emanating

---

*The distinction between the Bentleyan notion of common group interest and the purely individual benefits that various members may obtain by virtue of their participation in the collectivity is made by Mancur Olson, Jr.[65]

from the Prado insofar as Franco maintains, "In politics it is necessary to distinguish between what is possible and what is not possible and to know the exact moment in which to act. Every battle needs a plan and a strategy, and an elementary rule of the latter is to give battle only when victory is certain and not when there is a chance of defeat."[68]

Membership in NATO, once Spain's fervent desire, is presently less of an allurement.[69] Though as early as 1951 the Caudillo had declared that "a direct agreement with the United States would be less complicated than the inclusion of Spain in the Atlantic pact,"[70] admission to NATO would have afforded the heretofore blackballed leader the private benefit of international respectability and increased domestic prestige. As Miera asserts, "for Franco, such admission would have signified, in a certain sense, the beginning of the end of the isolation to which his regime was subjected and would have given the regime great prestige, a kind of tacit recognition abroad and increased popularity domestically."[71] The current military accords with the United States, however, now offer Madrid many of the common advantages received by Europe's NATO members.[72] The situation is curiously similar to that described by Henry Kissinger wherein "neutrals, or in this case, a non-NATO member with bilateral links to the United States, enjoy most of the protection of allies."[73] Hence, "a country gains little from being allied and risks little by being neutral."[74]

Since the renegotiation of the Bases Pact in 1963, the Spanish have taken the position that in the event of conflict, "NATO would find itself in the absolute necessity of utilizing Spanish territory in order to avoid being logistically strangled."[75] Spaniards now allege that the 1970 agreement with the United States has enhanced Madrid's peacetime relationship with NATO. Besides the interconnection between NATO's defenses and Spain's new air warning system, the Joint Committee on Matters of Defense with the United States gives Madrid a formal linkage to the Atlantic Alliance through the membership of the commander-in-chief of the U.S. European Command. Richard Mowrer has speculated that Spain's affiliation with NATO has been further strengthened by the holding of a 1971 plenary session of the Joint Committee at the general headquarters of the U.S. European Command in Stuttgart.[76]

In addition to establishing the bond with NATO provided by the SACEUR's (Supreme Allied Command Europe) dual role, the 1970 agreement states in Article 35 (emphasis added), "Both Governments consider it necessary and appropriate that *the cooperation for defense regulated by this Charter form a part of the security arrangements for the Atlantic and Mediterranean areas,* and to that end they will endeavor to work out by common accord the liaison deemed advisable *with the security arrangements for those areas.*"[77] Given these ties, plus the informal briefings Spain receives from Portugal regarding NATO Council meetings, it is not surprising that many believe "in certain determined circumstances Spain would be able to participate fully in the organization and structure of NATO, even without being a member."[78] Nevertheless various

TABLE 10.2

Military Expenditures as Percentage of Gross National Product

Year	Spain	European NATO Members (mean)	United States
1961	2.9	4.9	9.2
1962	3.3	5.1	9.3
1963	3.0	5.1	8.9
1964	2.9	5.0	8.1
1965	2.6	4.8	7.6
1966	3.1	4.6	8.5
1967	3.5	4.6	9.5
1968	3.6	4.2	9.3
1969	3.3	4.0	8.7
1970	3.6	3.7	8.0

Source: U.S. Arms Control and Disarmament Agency, Bureau of Economic Affairs, *World Military Expenditures, 1971* (Washington, D.C.: Government Printing Office, 1972), pp. 26-27.

Spanish army officers have expressed their preference for full NATO membership and, arguments of economic strain on the defense budget to the contrary (see Table 10.2), López Bravo has admitted: "Spain has never applied for admission to the Atlantic Organization, but that does not mean that if the organization were interested in a direct collaboration on the part of Spain, we should not give due study and attention to the subject."[79]

In contrast to Madrid's vacillating public pronouncements concerning entry into NATO, Washington has been a steadfast and vocal exponent of Spain's candidacy.[80] Moreover, irrespective of the strictures voiced by an occasional gadfly,[81] most observers have concluded that "whether by continuing bilateral agreements or by closer association with NATO, in the future Spain will become an increasingly valuable ally."[82] The crux of the reasoning underlying this outlook has been summarized by Hanson W. Baldwin:

[Spain] offers a geographic backdrop position and air dispersal area in the defense of Western Europe against massive Soviet ground attack through Germany. Its airfields are still useful to the bombers of the Strategic Air Command as postrecovery bases, and the U.S. Navy has no comparable alternative to Rota as a logistics and supply base. But its airfields today, in the age of missiles, are of primary importance as dispersal sites for Western Europe's tactical air power. If the whistle blew and Soviet tanks started across the North German plain, Spanish fields might well become the key to success or failure of Allied delaying tactics.[83]

Spain's prospective value to the defense of NATO's southern flank has also been stressed. Unlike defensive policies on the central front, those of the southern region emphasize a maritime approach to the security of noncontiguous countries. Sensitive to politicomilitary vulnerability in the Mediterranean, NATO has sought to remedy what Schratz calls its "strategic void."[84] Owing to the inability of NATO to augment the southern region in a crisis situation without reducing its defensive posture in Central Europe, special multinational units have been created to demonstrate NATO solidarity by assuring the immediate involvement of several alliance members. Among these internationally integrated groups are the Allied Command Europe Mobile Force (AMF); the Standing Naval Force, Atlantic (STANAVFORLANT); the On-Call Naval Force, Mediterranean (NAVOCFORMED); and the Maritime Air Force, Mediterranean (MARAIEMWS).[85]

Presumably the admission of Spain would help rectify these "deficiencies" in NATO's conventional defense and "anomalies" in NATO deployments.[86]

Not all NATO members agree with Washington's assessment of Spain's strategic value. The motive behind this intra-alliance disagreement can be discerned by juxtaposing the potential collective versus private costs and benefits that would be derived from Madrid's admission to NATO. Each state would conceivably share in the common advantages in the realm of logistics and rear-area training, such as at the Bardenas Reales gunnery range.[87] From the standpoint of private gains and losses, however, the incentives for backing Spain's entry would vary because of the suboptimal contribution of alliance members to the collective good (defense) and the absence of marginal cost-sharing in altering defense levels. For the United States, Spanish membership would afford the possibility of shifting the overhead ($96 million in fiscal year 1971[88]) on its bases. Conversely, other NATO states would be faced with the prospect of contributing to this expenditure, sharing in the outlays needed to update (see Table 10.3) and standardize the Spanish army, while not receiving any substantial increase in the protection given the present Hispano-U.S. ties.

Aside from this aspect of the debate, there is also disagreement pertaining to (1) the utility of the bases and (2) the actual combat potential of Franco's armed forces. First, noting the lentitudinous pace at which the bases were constructed, during a period when the American deterrent revolved around the B-47

TABLE 10.3

Total Number of Students Trained, 1964-71

Training Category	Total Number of Students
Flying	38
Operations	204
Communications	160
Maintenance	88
Logistics	23
Administration	19
Professional	258
Orientation	157
Missiles	1,402
Total number of students	2,349
Program value (in thousands of dollars)	5,685

Source: Greece, Spain, and the Southern NATO Strategy, Hearings before the Sub-committee on Europe of the House Committee on Foreign Affairs, 92nd cong., 1st sess., July 12, 14, 19, 21; August 3; September 9, 15, 1971 (Washington, D.C.: Government Printing Office, 1971), p. 160.

bombers, critics have begun to question whether they ever constituted an indispensable element in Atlantic security. Though the exigency for bombers has decreased, the facilities in Spain remain pivotal for contingency deployments in the Middle East or the North African littoral.[89] Secondly, because of past charges against the Spanish military* and the unsatisfactory result of the Barroso

---

*Eléna de la Souchère denounced the military in the following terms: "Ill paid, the officers cast about for other sources of revenue. The most influential hold desk jobs in over-crowded offices. Those with the best inside information plunge into an ingenious racket involving supplies and provisions. Others take up a second career on the outside. . . . Involved in plots, rackets, and gossip, the officers have little time left in which to instruct the recruits."[90] Similarly, the Spanish Communist Party has insisted that "as an instrument of national defense in the event of having to face a foreign aggression, these forces are unfortunately inadequate."[91]

FIGURE 10.3

Composition of the Spanish Military, 1971

Army: 220,000

     1 armored division*
     1 mechanized infantry division*
     1 motorized infantry division*
     2 mountain divisions*
     12 independent infantry brigades*
     1 armored cavalry brigade*
     1 high-mountain brigade
     1 air-portable brigade
     1 parachute brigade
     2 artillery brigades
     1 SAM battalion with HAWK missiles
     M-47 and M-48 medium tanks
     M-24 and M-41 lt tanks
     Greyhound armed cars
     M-113 APC
     105 mm and 155 mm SP guns
     105 mm, 155 mm, and 203 mm howitzers
     90 mm SP AT guns
     AML-60/90 and M-3 scout cars

Navy: 47,500 including 6,000 marines

     3 submarines
     1 helicopter carrier
     1 cruiser
     16 ASW (antisubmarine warfare) destroyers
     3 destroyers
     8 frigates
     6 frigate-minelayers
     6 corvettes
     1 ASW patrol vessel
     3 torpedo boats
     13 fleet minesweepers
     12 coastal minesweepers
     8 landing ships
     3 ASW helicopter squadrons
     1 light helicopter squadron

Air Force: 33,500; 221 combat aircraft

     12 Mirage-IIIE fighter-bombers
     50 F-5 fighter-bombers
     55 HA-200 fighter-bombers
     36 F-4C fighter-bombers
     21 F-104G interceptors
     48 F-86F interceptors
     25 T-6 armed trainers
     1 ASW squadron with 11 Hu-16B
     About 150 transport aircraft and helicopters, including C-47, C-54, 12
       Caribou and 20 Azor.

Paramilitary forces: 65,000 Guardia Civil

    *At about 70 percent of strength.
    Source: International Institute for Strategic Studies, *The Military Balance, 1971-72*
(London: the Institute, 1971), p. 24.

reforms in 1958,[92] observers have carefully scrutinized the armed forces' post-1966 buildup. (See Figure 10.3.) In sum, the question of Spain's role in Western defense cannot be answered simply by positing (a) if NATO is to be considered a military defense system against the Soviet bloc, then Spain would be admitted; or (b) if NATO is to stress protecting democracy and assuring the development of free institutions, then Madrid's admission ought to be denied.[93]

CONCLUSION

Two sentiments have prevailed among the numerous opinions concerning the strategic role of Spain in Western defense: one argues against complicating the present alliance machinery with the mere formality of admitting Spain to NATO, and the other affirms that the Atlantic Alliance can no longer overlook Madrid's strategic contributions.[94] From this vantage point, both positions neglect the critical issue of exchange outcomes. In view of the costs and benefits that would accrue to each state in the Spain-U.S.-NATO security triangle, General Norstad's wise council of 1961 still seems pertinent: there is no overriding urgency at the moment to press for Spain's immediate admission into NATO.[95]

The impending relationship between Madrid and the Atlantic Alliance is contingent upon two variable clusters. On the governmental level, Stanley G. Payne observes that "much will depend on the precise circumstances attending Franco's demise."[96] On the systemic level, the key factor will be the future configuration of western European security arrangements.

The strategic literature is replete with alternative futures. Alternative strategic systems have been designed for transatlantic,[97] intra-European,[98] and north-south[99] relations. Perhaps the most interesting possibility involves the "pretzelization" of Europe into a series of regionally specific (but overlapping) mutual defense agreements.[100] As Robert Hunter remarks, "The means (if not the ends) of changing the patterns of confrontation in Europe do not seem at all simple or straightforward."[101]

Predicting the future is indeed a risky undertaking. Nevertheless, one need not be a soothsayer to note that the solution to the enigmas presently confronting the Spain-U.S.-NATO tridad will be a significant part of the crucible in which a new European order is formed.

NOTES

1. Gregorio López Bravo, Spanish Foreign Minister, speech to the Cortéz Foreign Affairs Committee, May 16, 1973, as quoted by Pedro Gómez Aparicio in *Hoja de Lunes,* 21 May 1973.

2. William T. Salisbury, "The United States, Spain and the EEC: Two Special Relationships," paper delivered at the Fifth Bi-Annual Conference of the Atlantic Community, February 1973, Georgetown University.

3. Henry A. Kissinger, address to the Associated Press, reported in New York *Times*, April 24, 1973. For greater elaboration see Richard Nixon, *U.S. Foreign Policy for the 1970's, Shaping a Durable Peace* (Washington, D.C.: Government Printing Office, 1973).

4. Timothy W. Stanley and Darnell M. Whitt, *Detente Diplomacy: United States and European Security in the 1970's* (New York: Dunellen Publishing Co., 1970), p. 102.

5. David Calleo, *Atlantic Fantasy* (Baltimore: Johns Hopkins Press, 1970), p. 139.

6. Raymond Vernon, "Rogue Elephant in the Forest: An Appraisal of Transatlantic Relations," *Foreign Affairs* (April 1973): 585-86.

7. See, for example, Juan de la Cosa, *España ante el mundo* (Madrid: Publicaciónes Españoles, 1955), p. 231.

8. Cited in William T. Salisbury, "Spain and the Common Market: 1957-1967" (unpublished Ph.D. dissertation, Johns Hopkins University, 1972), p. 62.

9. Eduardo Adsouara, "Commercial Relations Between Spain and Ibero-America," *Spain Today* 3 (May 1970): 64.

10. See Eric N. Baklanoff, "Spain and the Atlantic Community: A Study of Incipient Integration and Economic Development," *Economic Development and Cultural Change* 16 (July 1968): 589; or Samuel Cohen, *Geography and Politics in a Divided World* (New York: Random House, 1963), pp. 128-31.

11. See Bruce M. Russet, *International Regions and the International System: A Study in Political Ecology* (Chicago: Rand McNally & Co., 1967); and Steven J. Brams, "Transaction Flows in the International System," *American Political Science Review* 60 (December 1966): 889.

12. For a discussion of Spain's African policy see Nuno Aguirre De Carcer and Gonzalo Fernandez de la Mora, "The Foreign Policy of Spain," in Joseph E. Black and Kenneth W. Thompson, eds., *Foreign Policies in a World of Change* (New York: Harper & Row, 1963), pp. 212-14.

13. Quoted in Salvador Paniker, *Conversaciones en Madrid* (Barcelona: Editorial Kairos, 1969), p. 306.

14. This analogy is made by Albert Martin-Artajo, "L'Espagne et ses Relations Internationales," *Synthèses* (December 1962): 165.

15. Arnold Wolfers, *Discord and Collaboration* (Baltimore: Johns Hopkins Press, 1962), p. 147.

16. Alan Lloyd, *Franco* (London: Longman, 1969), p. 209.

17. For a representative example of works employing an exchange paradigm, see Norman Froehlich and Joe A. Oppenheimer, "Entrepreneural Politics and Foreign Policy," in *Theory and Policy in International Relations,* ed. Raymond Tanter and Richard H. Ullman (Princeton: Princeton University Press,

1972), pp. 151-78; Mancur Olson, Jr., and Richard Zeckhauser, "An Economic Theory of Alliances," *Review of Economics and Statistics* 48 (August 1966): 266-79; and Sidney R. Waldman, "Exchange Theory and Political Analysis," in *Perspectives in Political Sociology,* ed. Andrew Effrat (Indianapolis: Bobbs-Merrill Co., 1972), pp. 101-128.

18. Carlton J. H. Hayes, *The United States and Spain: An Interpretation,* reprint ed. (Westport, Conn.: Greenwood Press, 1951).

19. *Arriba España* (Madrid) as quoted in Ovidio Gondi, "La Hispanidad in Hitler's Service," *Free World* 3 (June 1942): 63.

20. Eugene Hinterhoff, "Spain and NATO," *Military Review* 51 (March 1971): 41.

21. Max Gallo, *Historia de la España Franquista* (Verviers: Gerard & Co., 1969), p. 349.

22. Graham T. Allison, *The Essence of Decision* (Boston: Little, Brown and Co., 1971).

23. Theodore J. Lowi, "Bases in Spain," in *American Civil-Military Decisions,* ed. Harold Stein (Birmingham: University of Alabama Press, 1963), p. 678.

24. Robert O. Keohane, in "The Big Influence of Small Allies," *Foreign Policy* 2 (Spring 1971): 173-74.

25. Ibid., p. 166.

26. *Pueblo* (Madrid), 2 March 1948.

27. Arthur P. Whitaker, *Spain and Defense of the West* (New York: Frederick A. Praeger, 1961), p. 52.

28. Ray Alan, "Franco's Spain and the New Europe," *Commentary* 34 (September 1962): 234.

29. Franco as quoted in Brian Crozier, *Franco: A Biographical History* (London: Eyre & Spottiswoode, 1967), p. 480.

30. Bravo as quoted by Pedro Gomez Aparicio, op. cit.

31. "Between Past and Future," *The Economist,* February 19, 1972, p. 12.

32. Ibid.

33. E. Inman Fox, "Trends in Spanish Foreign Policy," *Naval War College Review* 23 (February 1971): 32.

34. Antonio Sánchez Gijón, "Acuerdos España-USA de 6 de Agosto de 1970," *España Perspectiva in 1971* (Madrid: Guardiana de Publicaciones, 1971), p. 250.

35. "That's better," *The Economist,* August 15, 1970, p. 31.

36. José Maria Gil Robles, "La política exterior de España in 1970," *España Perspectiva 1971* (Madrid: Guardiana de Publicaciones, 1971), p. 49.

37. *Greece, Spain, and the Southern NATO Strategy,* Hearings before the Subcommittee on Europe of the House Committee on Foreign Affairs, 92nd cong., 1st sess., July 12, 14, 19, 21; August 3; September 9, 15, 1971 (Washington, D.C.: Government Printing Office, 1971), p. 237.

38. Arthur P. Whitaker, "Spain and the Atlantic Alliance," *Orbis* (Spring 1966), p. 44.

39. ABC (Madrid), March 6, 1948.

40. "Washington's Policy of Isolating Castro," New York *Times.*

41. *Combat* (Paris), November 21, 1968.

42. New York *Times,* October 3, 1970.

43. U.S. Department of State, *United States Foreign Policy 1972,* General Foreign Policy Series 274 (Washington, D.C.: Government Printing Office, 1973), p. 306.

44. *Relazioni Internazionali* (Milan), April 4, 1970.

45. Robert P. Huff, "The Spanish Question Before the United Nations" (unpublished Ph.D. dissertation, Stanford University, 1966), p. 468; Albert J. Dorley, Jr., "The Role of Congress in the Establishment of Bases in Spain (unpublished Ph.D. dissertation, St. John's University, 1969), p. 196.

46. Werner J. Feld, "The Enlargement of the European Community and Atlantic Relations," *Atlantic Community Quarterly* 10 (Summer 1972): 219.

47. Ruben Caba, *389 Escritores Españoles opinan sobre candentes cuestiones de politica nacional e internacional* (Bilbao: Editorial La Gran Enciclopedia Vasca, 1971), pp. 89, 91, 117.

48. Whitaker, *Spain and Defense of the West,* op. cit., p. 301.

49. Cited in *Il Corriere della Sera* (Milan), June 2, 1964.

50. *Le Monde* (Paris), June 2, 1964.

51. *Le Figaro* (Paris), May 18, 1964, "On ne saurait prétendre, au surplus, que Paris ait fait preuve d'une particulière audace en l'occurrence, Washington avec Eisenhower et McNamara, Bonn avec Luebke et Erhard, nous ont, en effet, precédés sur une voit qui engage d'ailleurs autant l'Espagne que ceux qui s'en rapprochent."

52. *Nation* (Paris), May 29, 1964.

53. *Carrefour* (Paris), June 3, 1964.

54. Interview of Lopez Bravo in *Suddeutsche Zeitung* (Munich), April 22, 1970.

55. Quoted in "Between Past and Future," op. cit., p. 12.

56. "France, 1, America, 0," *The Economist,* June 27, 1970, pp. 35-36.

57. S. F. A. Coles, *Franco of Spain* (London: Neville Spearman Limited, 1955), p. 205; and George Hills, *Franco: The Man and His Nation* (New York: Macmillan, 1967), pp. 426-27.

58. John D. Stewart, *Gibraltar: The Keystone* (Boston: Houghton Mifflin Co., 1967), p. 199.

59. *The State* (Columbia, S.C.), May 6, 1973.

60. The term is used by the *Frankfurter Allgemeine* (Frankfurt), September 27, 1972.

61. See *Die Welt* (Hamburg), April 23, 1970; or *Stuttgarter Nachrichten* (Stuttgart), September 26, 1972.

62. For a critique of this position see Alredo Signoretti, "France and Spain Collaborate More Closely, And Italy?" *Roma* (Naples), February 1970.

63. William T. R. Fox and Annette Baker Fox, *NATO and the Range of American Choice* (New York: Columbia University Press, 1967), p. 7.

64. James Buchanan and Gordon Tullock, *The Calculus of Consent* (Ann Arbor: University of Michigan Press, 1962), pp. 43-46.

65. Mancur Olson, Jr., *The Logic of Collective Action* (New York: Schocken, 1965), p. 8.

66. For a discussion of these functions see Edwin H. Fedder, "The Concept of Alliance," *International Studies Quarterly* 12 (March 1968): 67; Robert E. Osgood, *Alliances and American Foreign Policy* (Baltimore: Johns Hopkins Press, 1968), p. 21; George Liska, *Nations in Alliance*, 2nd ed. (Baltimore: Johns Hopkins Press, 1968), p. 30; Hans J. Morgenthau, "Alliances in Theory and Practice," in *Alliance Policy in the Cold War*, ed. Arnold Wolfers (Baltimore: Johns Hopkins Press, 1959), pp. 184-212; and Henry A. Kissinger, *Problems of National Strategy* (New York: Frederick A. Praeger, 1965), p. 163.

67. "Europe of Bust," *The Economist*, August 21, 1971, p. 37.

68. Franco as cited in "Franco's Foreign Policy," *The World Today* 9 (1953): 512.

69. Rafael Calvo Serer, *Franco frente al Rey* (Paris: Ruedo Ibérico, 1972), p. 80.

70. Franco as cited in Gallo, op. cit., p. 219.

71. Felipe Miera, "La política exterior Franquista y sus relaciónes con los Estados Unidos de America," *Horizonte Español 1966* (Paris: Ruedo Ibérico, 1966), p. 189.

72. Mariano Aguilar Navarro, "España y la crisis de la sociedad internacional," *España Perspectiva 1972* (Madrid: Guardiana de Publicaciones, S.A. 1972), p. 74.

73. Henry A. Kissinger, *The Troubled Partnership: A Reappraisal of the Atlantic Alliance* (New York: McGraw-Hill, 1965), p. 16.

74. Ibid., p. 18.

75. *Ya* (Madrid), May 31, 1964.

76. Richard Mowrer, "U.S.-Spain Arms talks in Germany," *Christian Science Monitor*, October 23, 1971.

77. Reprinted in *Greece, Spain, and the Southern NATO Strategy*, op. cit., p. 266.

78. Sánches Gijón, op. cit., p. 275.

79. Quoted in *Journal de Genève* (Geneva), May 23, 1970.

80. For a concise discussion of this point see William Gerber,"Spain and the West," *Editorial Research Reports* 2 (September 1968): 681-700.

81. For example, Sam Pope Brewer, "Spain: How Good An Ally?" *Yale Review* 41 (March 1952): 348-59.

82. Edgar O'Ballance, "The Strength of Spain," *Military Review* 43 (July 1963): 44.